The Perennial Solution Center

The Perennial Solution Center

Conversations and Readings in Mysticism and the Psychology of Religion

Walter Horn

2003

The Perennial Solution Center

To Carol, Emma and Chloe, the three numinous sirens who make any desire of mine to transcend the everyday world seem almost too silly for words.

Introduction

Why would anyone pick up a book with the audacity to trumpet a claim to some kind of "perennial solution"? And, more fundamentally, the perennial solution to *what*? A good portion of what follows is devoted to answering those two questions, but I'm happy to provide a sneak preview here. I anticipate that most readers with even a passing interest in the pages that follow will be individuals who harbor the age-old suspicion that "there is something missing in their lives," a gap that resists being filled by cultural distractions, material wealth or accomplishments, sexual or other adventures, artistic/intellectual endeavors, or even romantic or familial love. They may suffer from a gnawing sense that life is, in some perhaps hard-to-explain way, entirely meaningless. Or, while not denying that their lives have a certain significance during the few short years allowed them by the unmerciful gods of biology, these individuals may nevertheless be haunted by recurring thoughts of their own mortality. It is often such qualms, with their implication of a final separation from all we know and love, that engender a turning from worldly pursuits to the quieter hunt for psychological, philosophical, or religious "solutions."

In his *Perennial Philosophy*, Aldous Huxley sought to alleviate worries about human transience by setting forth some of the more consoling common threads that run through many of the great world religions. Huxley noticed, for example, that both Christian and Eastern mystics have repeatedly claimed that each of us is in some sense identical to God. But these assertions, no doubt made sincerely by those favored with the requisite visions, can seem little more than half-mad rantings to the rest of us. A Vedantist conviction that the universe somehow flows from a common, impersonal *Self* found deep inside each of us doesn't seem like the sort of thing one can gain simply by being informed that innumerable others have shared this belief. After all, think of the many peculiar, but now provably *false* things people have believed during the past 3000 years. Isn't any supposed fact that there are mystical tenets that are common to a number of religious traditions just a bit of anthropological trivia we can use to impress people at cocktail parties? And isn't it just an inappropriate appeal to authority to point to these common threads in the context of a philosophical discussion about the meaning of life? I hope that what follows will provide an indication of how such appeals may be useful to spiritual seekers, but it's important to proceed with extreme caution here. The fact that a large number of otherwise intelligent individuals have insisted that we are in some sense part of an Eternal Absolute or something of that kind, doesn't by itself prove anything about our "real nature" other than that there seems to be a recurring tendency to embrace a specific set of religious viewpoints. The mere rattling off of the opinions of brilliant or saintly pundits is unlikely to satisfy anyone with a skeptical bent.

The Perennial Solution Center uses a different method to illuminate a—perhaps *the*—way to a particular kind of solace, and it is extremely important not to be distracted when carrying this lantern. We could, for example, get lost in discussions about whether any deity must be personal or impersonal, about what sort of "life" is possible after bodily death, about the nature of mind, or about countless other interesting and pertinent issues. We could also (if I were capable of it) spend chapter upon chapter discussing the nature of human knowledge and the types of evidence or warrant needed to obtain it. We cannot go far without touching on all these topics. But while there are arguments aplenty in what follows, we're not principally looking for philosophical information here. I want to emulate a certain Enlightened One of the distant past in focusing as exclusively as possible on *suffering and the end of suffering.* It is a *method* rather than a *philosophy* that will provide our "solution." I don't deny that there are important objections to this sort of approach, but it is better to attempt to answer those criticisms as we go along than to lose sight of the central issues this book is intended to address.

Though the title of the book does indeed trumpet loudly, I am acutely aware of how slight my own contributions are. I have done little more than riffle the contents of a particularly exotic intellectual treasure chest, holding first this and then that jewel aloft. No doubt I have left many of the most valuable gems at the bottom, and held others at angles that have kept their most beautiful facets hidden from view. When excerpting from Eastern and Western religious writings, I have often been mindful of the obnoxious Mr. Casaubon of Eliot's *Middlemarch*, the self-centered misanthrope who spent most of his life making revisions to his never-completed *Key to All Mythologies.* I make no claim whatever that the solution discussed in this book is to be found in *every* religion, or that there are no important differences in the dress it has received from those traditions where it *can* be found. I am no expert in comparative religion, and have no particular interest in anthropology. I do find it both interesting and comforting that solutions of the type I discuss have found their way into a number of widely different traditions (including entirely secular ones) and that they have re-emerged regularly throughout recorded history. But, unlike the dauntless Casaubon, I have neither the expertise nor the inclination to make the kind of study necessary to assert that solutions of this sort have shown up in every major religion from time immemorial. In fact, whatever the word "perennial" may suggest, I don't even claim that such answers have remained a constant feature in those belief systems in which they *have* turned up. My goal isn't anthropological at all: I simply want to provide a new description and defense of an ancient mode of thought and method of consolation.

Let me now say a few words about the dialogue format I have chosen, a conceit that will certainly seem odd or circuitous to many readers. The "fictionalizing" of philosophy and theology is nothing new. Using stories to make what would otherwise be dry argument entertaining is at least as old as Plato or the *Gita*. Surely *The Bible* would have had many fewer readers than it has actually enjoyed if it contained nothing but commandments, prophecies, and theological discussions. I knew I wanted to quote from a number of sources in describing the virtues of and arguments against mystical approaches to the world, but I wasn't sure how to do this without producing a textbook or a dusty (if meaty) anthology in the style of Huxley's *Perennial Philosophy*. I was then struck by the the idea of using a series of conversations that include brief quotations from a wide variety of works as a way of keeping the reader's interest. How better to get the full flavor of a flood of excerpts from religious, psychological and philosophical works, than to have these words play an essential role in the lives of characters who, over time, may become important to the reader? In keeping with this model, what follows are discussions that take place among a couple of modern day "aspirants" and the man to whom they have come with the hope that he can, like a Zen *sensei*, somehow free them from fear and invest their lives with meaning. The book can thus be seen as a kind of progress report on two seekers who spend three months in a Vermont retreat called, of course, "The Perennial Solution Center." Because of the dialogue format, what follows will look something like a play, but it would doubtless make for several very unusual evenings at the theatre.

I call the spiritual founder of this center "Rabi" both because it was the nickname of Rabindranath Tagore, a favorite writer of mine, and because it resembles "rabbi," which is Hebrew for "teacher." We will not be told much about Rabi's history besides what we can glean from his conversation, the books that comprise his library, and the rule of his center. He is a dark-complexioned man of Indian descent in his sixties who grew up and was educated in England and America. He has taught and written on spiritual matters, and has been able to attract a sufficient number of students to keep his center running for about ten years. He dresses something like a professor, in sports jacket and slacks through three seasons, but in golf shirt and khakis in Summer. There is no beard, turban, or any of the other occasional indicia of guruhood about Rabi.

I think it will be necessary to tell a bit more here about the two students whose discussions (both with Rabi and with each other) during their stays at The Perennial Solution Center will be set forth in these pages.

Gina (or "G") is a 32-year-old single woman, a graduate of a small private liberal arts college in upstate New York, where she majored in religion. She toyed with the idea of going to divinity school after college, but ended up taking an editorial job in Boston. She has never been married, but has had a couple of live-in boyfriends during the past decade: there's no one special right now, however. She was raised as an Episcopalian and has long enjoyed inspirational literature and attending various churches and temples. She believes in God and considers herself a Christian. She has remained close to her family, though she has an uneasy relationship with her sole sibling – a younger sister – for whom things have always seemed to come more easily. Although she is reluctant to talk about herself, G is outgoing and gregarious. At times, she's a bit too quick to laugh or get angry, making her seem nervous even to casual observers. In fact, she *is* anxious about things in general. In her late twenties she had several years of psychotherapy which she found somewhat helpful, but then she drifted away, largely because of the cost and inconvenience. She read a magazine article about The Perennial Solution Center and its founder, and decided to take three months off from work to attend the twelve-week summer session.

Paul is 40. He and his wife of nine years have been separated for eleven months. They have a seven-year-old daughter. He has always been witty, outgoing, and smart. He earned an undergraduate degree in psychology from one Ivy League school before receiving a masters degree in philosophy from another. He then moved to New York City to look for a job. While working as a technical writer for a brokerage house, he made enough money in investments to quit work completely after his daughter was born. He continues to enjoy reading and discussing philosophy and psychology, but he has always been skeptical about religion, considering it little more than an opiate. He's been so unhappy lately, though, that a dependable opiate doesn't seem like such a bad thing to him anymore. His wife sent him away when she discovered that he had engaged in a number of extra-marital affairs. Like G, Paul has had several years of psychotherapy. He began therapy while in college soon after his mother died, and continued it intermittently until getting married. Lately he has suffered frequently from insomnia and anxiety attacks, but he hasn't had much luck with prescription drugs, and he just hasn't felt like seeing any more shrinks. He came across a brochure for The Perennial Solution Center at an Indian restaurant. The idea of philosophical/psychological "treatment" in a naturalistic setting appealed to him.

The Center itself is little more than a big old Victorian house in the woodsy hills of central Vermont. It has a sizeable lawn and garden, with a few metal chairs and tables about, and the rolling green mountains and rippling rivers are close by. Whatever its original design, the house has been converted to something like a ten-bedroom inn. Instead of a great room, there is a high-ceilinged library, with rolling ladder-stools and a large marble fireplace. In addition to a couple of small library tables, the room is furnished with a number of comfortable leather chairs and side tables, as might be found in a Victorian men's club. There are also two sofas. The west-facing wall has a large picture window through which one can see several soft-peaked, pine-covered mountains. Rabi's individual "sessions" with his students are held in this room, but it is also available for browsing, chatting, and book-borrowing from 7-10 in the morning and 7-11 in the evening. As one would expect, the selection of books is heavy on philosophy, religion, and psychology, but there are a smattering of non-fiction books on other subjects as well as many novels and books of poetry. There are several copies of each title and visitors are encouraged to borrow books during their stay. One copy of each book is marked

"Not To Leave The Library": as we will see, this is because reading aloud from library books plays an important part in the sessions with Rabi.

There is a kitchen in the Center, but it is reserved for use by Rabi's family, and no common meals are provided. Each bedroom is equipped with a small refrigerator, a hot plate, a few dishes and kitchen utensils, and a sink. Each is also fitted with a private bathroom. Some visitors cook in their rooms, but many prefer to eat at one of the four or five restaurants in the town, about four miles down a dirt road.

Rabi gives no lectures, and there are no officially scheduled meetings among the guests, but the visitors often get together for informal chats in the library or the garden. They occasionally eat out together or make hiking, skiing, golfing (or supermarket) trips as well. There are few rules, but visitors are requested to return to their rooms each night by 11:30, and it is suggested that they not "enter into any new romantic relationships" while at the Center. Each bedroom contains a bed, a portrait of some inspirational figure (Spinoza, Jesus, Buddha, William James, etc.), a bookshelf, a writing table, a couple of chairs, a meditation mat on the floor, and a radio/alarm clock. There is also a small washer/drier for laundry. There are never more than eight individual visitors (no couples or groups) at one time. Visitors must send an application form describing themselves and what they hope to gain from their visits. Each visitor is scheduled for a session with Rabi three times per week—either on Mondays, Wednesdays, and Fridays or on Tuesdays, Thursdays, and Saturdays. Nothing is scheduled on Sundays, when the library is open to visitors all day. Sessions can last up to two hours, but they generally run a little over an hour. Visitors may also see Rabi at night if they feel they are having some sort of crisis and cannot wait until their next scheduled session. They do this by ringing him up on the house phone. Night sessions are generally briefer than regularly scheduled meetings.

Promotional materials for the Center stress that Rabi is not a licensed physician or psychotherapist: people who think they may need professional psychiatric care are encouraged to postpone their visits until they feel confident about their ability to handle the secluded life offered by the Center. The cost for a three-month stay, which does not include housekeeping, is significant, about what it would cost to stay in a mid-range hotel in rural New England for the same period of time. The tuition must be paid in advance. Rabi, his wife, Vera, and an old gardener/caretaker are the only permanent residents.

That's the set-up. Perhaps a gradual shift into a Stephen King-style rural horror fest or a D.H. Lawrence fantasy about what happens between the gardener and a few of the more lonely and uptight female visitors would make the following pages more traditionally dramatic. But such plot turns, even if I could navigate them, would not serve the function played by the fictional characters and backdrop here: the provision of an additional, non-distracting motive for readers to push on during abstract discussions of spiritual or philosophical matters. This device is why certain works of Plato and George Bernard Shaw are so much fun to read despite their weighty subject matter, and it's the quality that makes Saint Theresa's *Autobiography* so much more engaging than many straightforward discourses on mysticism. This tack has also been taken by many "novelists of ideas" in developing their pet theories. Perhaps, if my own history had been more dramatic, I could

xviii   The Perennial Solution Center

have dispensed with the dialogue format and seasoned the philosophy and psychology with riveting stories about my own spiritual development. But, alas, we must play with the cards we are dealt.

Thanks are due to Carol Calliotte, Burt Feinberg, Roger Hecht, Tracy Mayor, and Tom Schmidt for their encouragement and editorial acumen.

I.

Week One

Monday, 10 AM — The Library

Paul (entering, walks over to Rabi sitting at one of the chairs). Good morning.

Rabi (standing up). Good morning, Paul. (Shakes Paul's hand and motions for him to sit down). I hope you slept well?

Paul. Yes, thanks. I was very comfortable. (He sits down and there is an awkward pause). I guess I really don't know how to get this started.

Rabi. Well, why don't we start by discussing why you have come here. You know, what you think we may be able to do for you, what you hope to find here, that sort of thing. Of course, I've read your application, but perhaps you'd like to elaborate.

Paul. I guess there's a bunch of reasons. A lot of it was curiosity. I have a background in philosophy, and I was attracted by the philosophical approach you take here. Also, while I've always been kind of skeptical about religion, I've been pretty worried about dying lately, and I guess I figured a relaxing stay here couldn't do any harm... Plus, I...well, I was kind of interested in meeting a...I don't know....guru...a religious leader. Is that what you are? I'm not trying to be smart here, I really don't know.

Rabi (smiling). Maybe you wanted to see how similar I was to Chance the Gardener?

Paul (laughing). The guy from *Being There*? Yeah, maybe there was some of that too.

Rabi (portentously). In the Spring there will be growth.

Paul (laughing). You know, I feel better already. This place was really worth the money....But, really, *do* you consider yourself a guru?

Rabi. If you mean "teacher," yes, I do.

Paul. Well, what can you teach me?

Rabi. I want to teach you how to be happier. I may be able to help you understand a part of the world that has been eluding you. You said you have been worried about dying lately?

Paul. Yeah. It seems like I've been plagued by this terror of dying ever since I can remember. You know, ceasing to be, the end of everything. It just seems so horrible... Unutterably horrible.

Rabi. Do you mind if I get a book? I often like to use them as resources during these talks. And sometimes it's easier if I walk around and grab books rather than sit. I hope it won't disturb you.

Paul. Not at all. Go ahead.

Rabi (fetching a book). Thank you. (From this point on, he gets up frequently and sometimes paces as he talks, listens or reads aloud.) And please feel free to do the same, especially if you think what you are trying to say is expressed well in one of the books here—or another you have brought with you....Here it is. Tolstoy's *Death of Ivan Ilych*. Is this what you have in mind?

> Ivan Ilych saw that he was dying, and he was in continual despair.
> In the depth of his heart he knew he was dying, but not only was he not accustomed to the thought, he simply did not and could not grasp it.
> The syllogism he had learnt from Kiesewetter's Logic: 'Caius is a man, men are mortal, therefore Caius is mortal,'

had always seemed to him correct as applied to Caius, but certainly not as applied to himself. That Caius—man in the abstract—was mortal, was perfectly correct, but he was not Caius, not an abstract man, but a creature quite, quite separate from all others. He had been little Vanya, with a mamma and a papa, with Mitya and Volodya, with the toys, a coachman and a nurse, afterwards with Katenka and with all the joys, griefs, and delights of childhood, boyhood, and youth. What did Caius know of the smell of the striped leather ball Vanya had been so fond of? Had Caius kissed his mother's hand like that, and did the silk of her dress rustle so for Caius? Had he rioted like that at school when the pastry was bad? Had Caius been in love like that? Could Caius preside at a session as he did? Caius really was mortal, and it was right for him to die; but for me little Vanya, Ivan Ilych, with all my thoughts and emotions, it's altogether a different matter. It cannot be that I ought to die. That would be too terrible.[1]

And...what does it say...no matter how Judge Ilych tries to distract himself, to banish this thought of death, this *It*...

It would come and stand before him and look at him, and he would be petrified and the light would die out of his eyes, and he would again begin asking himself whether *It* alone was true. And his colleagues and subordinates would see with surprise and distress that he, the brilliant and subtle judge, was becoming confused and making mistakes. He would shake himself, try to pull himself together, manage somehow to bring the sitting to a close, and return home with the sorrowful consciousness that his judicial labours could not as formerly hide from him what he wanted them to hide, and could not deliver him from *It*. And what was worst of all was that *It* drew his attention to itself not in order to make him take some action but only that he should look at *It*, look it straight in the face: look at it and without doing anything, suffer inexpressibly.

Paul. Yeah, that pretty much sums it up. Doesn't Ilych

have some kind of revelation on his deathbed? He sees a bright light, understands everything and dies happily?

Rabi. Right.

Paul. Well I'd really prefer not to wait until my last breath to get past this *It* problem. I guess that's the main reason why I'm here.

Rabi. Even more important than meeting Chauncey Gardener?

Paul (laughing). Well, of course, that's pretty big too... So what "solution" do you have for this issue here at the Center?

Rabi. It's pretty simple, really. I talk to you. I advise you to spend a great deal of time praying, or, if you prefer, meditating—I use the two words interchangeably. I try to help you look at things a bit differently than you may have seen them in the past. And I try to do this in ways that I think will be beneficial to you.

Paul. With all due respect—and Joni Mitchell notwithstanding—the term "praying" suggests that there's someone or something out there that you're praying to.

Rabi. I didn't get the reference. You mean Joni Mitchell the folksinger?

Paul. Right. She has a song that has the line "So I sent up my prayer wondering who's there to hear."

Rabi. Interesting. I often quote her line, "Never mind the questions there's no answers to." But to get back to your point, as I said, if you prefer the term "meditate," that's fine, too.

Paul. So you're saying that we should meditate as a simple psychological palliative, whether or not there's any kind of God? That doesn't seem very religious.

Rabi. Well, to use a couple of clichés, we have to begin at the beginning and keep our eyes on the prize. You tell me you've come to the Center because of a psychological issue: you have this persistent anxiety about dying that you'd like to do something about. I suggest to you that a steady diet of meditation could help that problem. Let's not bother about whether this is a religious prescription or not at present. Let's see, (gets book) the American physician Dr. Herbert Benson wrote,.

> The altered state of consciousness associated with the Relaxation Response has been routinely experienced in Eastern and Western cultures throughout all ages. Subjectively, the feelings associated with this altered state of consciousness have been described as ecstatic, clairvoyant, beautiful, and totally relaxing. Others have felt ease with the world, peace of mind, and a sense of well-being akin to that feeling experienced after a period of exercise but without the fatigue.[2]

Paul. I suppose that's fine, but you might just as well prescribe Prozac or St. John's Wort or whatever is being used for anxiety these days. I mean, even if this...self-hypnosis...helps control my unpleasant symptoms, it's just kind of a trick really, isn't it? I mean, to have something called "The Perennial Solution Center" and have the solution just be the repetition of a nonsense syllable for a couple of hours straight. It's sort of unsatisfying. I don't know if that's because of its lack of any actual religious content, or because if you simply waved a pocket watch in front of me and convinced me that I was an untroubled duck swimming around a pond, we'd see it as a circus act rather than as a "solution" with a capital "S". Again, I'm sorry if this seems disrespectful, but since I don't have this fear of dying while I'm asleep, why not just give me a sleeping pill and put me to sleep: that would seem to me to be more honest than having me repeat some gibberish for long periods and calling it prayer. It would probably be more effective too, which is why Western medicine seems to prefer it to prescribing mantras and incense.

Rabi. Ah, you've made a number of complaints here, covering any number of important issues, and we probably won't be able to discuss all of them today, but they're sure to come up again, numerous times. For now, I'd just like to suggest that you seem to have come to me with something more ambitious than the simple desire to be released from your persistent fear of dying. You want a general contentment with life.

Paul. Right.

Rabi. And you want this contentment to be based on your beliefs, rather than just result from the operation of some psychotropic drug or the electronic stimulation of some part of your brain.

Paul. I guess so, yes.

Rabi. And there's more. You want these beliefs to be reasonable. You don't want to have come by them by being brainwashed at the hands of some...let's say "cult leader." You'd like to be convinced by the clear light of your reason that the world has a meaning, that death is not something to be feared.

Paul. Yes. I suppose that's all true. It does seem kind of a lot, but remember the capital "S" in the solution offered here.

Rabi. I don't mean to rule out anything; but I will point out you've invested a very great deal in a couple of capital letters. In any case, it's usually better to take one step at a time, isn't it? After all, I'm certainly no Buddha, and even the Enlightened One himself became impatient with those who wanted more than to understand the causes of their sufferings and the way out of them. When his disciples showered him with Byzantine metaphysical questions he responded,

> "Did you ever say to me, 'Reverend Sir, I will lead the religious life under The Blessed One, on condition that The Blessed One elucidate to me either that the world is eternal, or that the world is not eternal...or that the saint neither exists nor does not exist after death?'...So you acknowledge that I have not said to you, 'Come, lead the religious life under me and I will elucidate to you either that the world is eternal, or that the world is not eternal, or that the saint neither exists nor does not exist after death'....The religious life does not depend on the dogma that the world is eternal; nor does the religious life depend on the dogma that the world is not eternal. Whether the dogma obtain that the world is eternal, or that the world is not eternal, there still remain birth, old age, death, sorrow, lamentation, misery, grief, and despair, for the extinction of which in the present life I am prescribing. The religious life does not depend on the dogma that the world is finite. The religious life does not depend on the dogma that the soul and the body are identical. The religious life does not depend on the dogma that the saint both exists and does not exist after death; nor does the religious life depend on the dogma that the saint neither exists nor does not exist after death....And why have I not elucidated [these things]? Because this profits not, nor has to do with the fundamentals of religion nor tends to aversion, absence of passion, cessation, quiescence, the supernatural faculties, supreme wisdom, and Nirvana; therefore I have not elucidated it.
>
> And what have I elucidated? Misery have I elucidated; the origin of misery have I elucidated; the cessation of misery have I elucidated; and the path leading to the cessation of misery have I elucidated. And why have I elucidated this? Because, this does profit...[3]

Paul. I take your point, and I'm willing to slow down and discuss matters in the order you suggest. But I must say that if Buddha was nothing more than a psychotherapist, it's at least possible that therapeutic devices have improved a bit since his time. Today, at any rate, most of us in the West have gone beyond imparting what are really just psychological exercises with religious significance.

Rabi. Most people come to the Center knowing full well that there is a healthy measure of what you're calling "religion" in the solutions offered here. Like you, they don't just want to learn how to calm down. But they don't mind learning that as well: in fact, they demand it. I'm not entirely sure whether one *must* take meditation to be a form of religious practice, rather than, say, a mental exercise or a psychological game, but it may be a start toward such practice, an essential first step, as breathing is to growing. To me, the two approaches of psychology and religion seem complimentary rather than contrary. So, I do believe I'm offering something more than a relaxation technique here, but you must be the judge.

Paul. Well, I guess I can't really tell yet whether what you're offering is the sort of religion I'm searching for, or you're just profiting—forgive me, I don't mean to suggest you're doing anything unethical—from the fact that certain people have remained ignorant of the long-known fact that repeating a mantra can make one senseless. When I was in college, there was a young man known as "the 16-year-old-perfect-master"—or something like that—who made millions of dollars simply by waiting until his crowds of followers were mentally and physically exhausted and then whispering a secret mantra in their ears. He used to put out magazines of himself being driven around in expensive cars or luxuriating in lavish mansions. I think he may have ended up being involved in some scandal and falling out of favor.

Rabi. I think I remember the boy you're talking about.

Paul. Well, what's supposed to follow from the fact that

someone can be hypnotized or put himself to sleep by the repetition of a word one thousand times?

Rabi. The Benson book provides data seeming to show that the physiological effects of meditation are distinguishable from those associated with sleep or hypnosis. But, be that as it may, I think you are forgetting again why you have come here, and what you expect from me. You say you are sick and tired of your death anxiety. I want to help you with this, and I claim that meditation may be useful in this regard. You then balk, saying what amounts to 'Well, if all I wanted was to get over my anxieties, I could have gone to a psychoanalyst, or a hypnotist, or gotten an anti-depressant. What do I need your so-called "Perennial Solution" for?' Obviously, you are free to try any or all of those things, and I get the sense you may have tried some already. When you come to me, I try to help you according to my lights, just as other healers will try to help you according to theirs. If you try my solution diligently and fail, so be it. We will at least have tried. What's more (smiling), if you fail miserably, and I have been convinced of your diligence, maybe you will even be able to get me to drop "Perennial" in favor of "occasional" and eliminate the capital letters.

Paul (laughing). I could see you losing some clientele with that change, but what do I know about the ashram business?

Rabi (after a pause). You seem a bit distracted. Shall we call it a day?

Paul. I'm sorry, I was just thinking. Why not get me started on this path you recommend? What would you suggest I do for openers?

Rabi. Go to your room or another quiet place. Sit or lie down in a comfortable position. Breathe regularly. With each breath you exhale, alternate between whispering "flow down" and whispering "flow out." Do this softly, so even you can barely hear it, but don't just think these things, say them. When you whisper "flow down" try to feel any tension in your chest flowing down to your waist. When you say "flow out" try to feel this tightness flowing down from your waist through your legs, down to the tips of your toes and out of your body. Your feet may begin to tingle. Try not to think of anything else but this flowing of the nervousness from your body, but if you catch yourself being distracted from your relaxation exercise, don't chastise yourself: simply go back to the meditation. I think you will find this very calming. This practice may even help when you are having death anxieties, although it is hard to breathe calmly and concentrate only on flowing down and flowing out, when you are in the middle of being very scared. If you do perform this meditation while lying down, you may fall asleep. I take it you don't object to knowing a technique that may sometimes help you fall asleep. I suggest you try to do this exercise as much as you can during your stay here, but no less than an hour a day in total.

Paul. Anything else?

Rabi. If you haven't done so already, I suggest you take a look through the Benson book I read from. His approach doesn't seem so foreign to scientific westerners. And there are some nice selections from mystical literature in it.

Paul. OK, I can do that...

Rabi. But...Something is obviously bothering you about this. You seem distraught.

Paul. Oh, it's nothing really. Nothing important, anyway. It's just...this Benson book. I've seen it. It was a best seller, wasn't it? It seemed like pretty simplistic stuff to me.

Rabi (laughing). You mean for all the expense of staying here you should be getting something more obscure. Perhaps I have a copy in Bengali....Look, I suppose *The Relaxation Response* could be said to be simple. But so in some sense is eating or breathing or seeing. You'd prefer something more difficult or esoteric to read. But we don't want to miss out on something good just because it may be available to everyone, do we?

Paul. I think I remember seeing in an article of yours that you agree with Spinoza that "All things excellent are as difficult as they are rare."

Rabi. I do. I do indeed. I think that mastering the solution I recommend is terribly difficult. Only one in a million—perhaps fewer—can manage it. But the *description* of the solution, which is something else entirely, is quite simple. Even a child ought to be able to understand *that*. It's like running a two-and-a-half hour marathon. Almost anyone can understand what one is supposed to do, but the accomplishment is another matter altogether.

Paul. Well, I hope that I won't be graded on my credulity after one meeting: I have to admit, I'm still a bit skeptical.

Rabi (laughing). Perhaps I can manage a gentleman's C for you as long as you keep coming on time and hand in your homework.

Paul. Well, I'll try, but you see, I have this unruly dog. He's constantly chewing up things.

Rabi (stands up). Maybe some of his traits can also be helped by relaxation techniques.

Paul. Hmmm. I'm not sure whether that would be a good thing or not....Just how much homework do you assign? I'll discuss it with him, anyway. See you next time.

Rabi. Goodbye, Paul.

ॐ

Tuesday, 9:00 AM—The Garden

(G is sitting at a table with a paper coffee cup, reading a book when Paul approaches her table with his own book in hand.)

Paul. Hi. Mind if I join you?

G. Not at all. I think I saw you unpacking your car at the same time I did on Sunday. Are you here for the Summer session.

Paul. Yup. You too?

G. Uh-huh. I'm G.

Paul. Paul. (They shake hands.)

Paul. This your first time here too?

G. Yeah. I can't really believe it: it seems like such a strange thing to be doing, spending three months at a retreat!

Paul. I'm in the same boat. I've never done anything like this before. It's sort of scary: (laughing) I keep expecting the Maharishi Mahesh Yogi to show up with Mia Farrow on his arm. It *is* pretty around here, though. I've always liked Vermont. And the rooms aren't half bad.

G. Who'd you get?

Paul. What do you mean?

G. What portrait is hanging over your bed? Every room seems to have a different one.

Paul (laughing). Oh. William James. How 'bout you?

G. Some strange-looking guy named Fechner...if that's how you pronounce it. I've never heard of him.

Paul. He's a German psychologist, I think. I seem to remember having learned about a Fechner-Webber law back in college, but I couldn't tell you what it was about today.

G. I think I would have preferred a landscape or

something. The picture of this guy creeps me out. I'm not sure why.

Paul. I know what you mean. Even though I kind of like James, hero adoration isn't really my thing. I'm just glad I didn't get a crucifixion scene or a laughing Buddha.

G. So...have you met with him yet?

Paul. Rabi?—It seems so weird to be calling him that...It's like he was one of the boys on "My Three Sons," isn't it? Well, I guess that's what he likes—Yeah, I had one session with him yesterday morning. That's what they call them, "sessions", right?

G. I think so. I had my first one yesterday afternoon. What do you make of him?

Paul. I found the whole thing pretty strange. He seems so professorial, with all that pacing around and reading from books, that I felt like I was in school again. And all these old feelings of wanting to prove how smart I am and catch the teacher in a mistake came rushing back. I left feeling like I wanted to be more prepared next time. You know, have my own quotes ready, stump him with a tough question, stuff like that. How was your meeting?

G. You're right about the professor thing. I felt that too, but...well...it kind of seemed like a therapy session sometimes, too. There was all this delving into my motives in coming here. I mean, I was impressed with him: he's obviously smart and well-read, but the whole thing made me nervous....(Laughs.) And I have this distinct impression that the main point in coming here was to be *calmer*....Oh, well, I guess I shouldn't make too much of one session.

Paul. I found myself being impressed by him, too—at least occasionally. But I could feel myself resisting his attempts to be...I don't know...ingratiating or something. It was the whole student thing again, maybe. You know how certain teachers try to impress their students with their hipness, quoting from current movies or TV shows or by talking about drugs or whatever, and it just makes you feel more resistant to them?....I know a lot of it is just immaturity on my part, because we've spent all this money to come here and everything. But there were times that he seemed so smug and self-satisfied that I felt this desire to throw a pie in his face or something. (Laughs) You can see how mature I am. I know it's stupid and counterproductive, but he just...*irked* me.

G. Well, I guess I think it *does* makes sense to give him more of a chance than one session.

Paul. Absolutely. I'm sure I'll get over it. But the readings he focused on bothered me too.

G. Don't get me started on that! If he's trying to win us over, he's got an awfully strange way of going about it. I mean, look at this! (She shows him her book).

Paul (laughing). You can't really be reading Mencken at this place! I wouldn't think that would even be allowed, much less encouraged.

G. I know. It seems crazy to me too. I come here to, I don't know, solidify my faith or "center" myself, or something mystical like that, and the spiritual adviser here recommends that I do some reading in one of the most skeptical books I've ever come across.

Paul. Well, at least Mencken's clever and fun to read: I'd be willing to trade you in a second. Rabi's got me reading a best-selling self-help book. (He shows her his copy of the Benson book.)

G. Oh, I read that years ago. I don't remember thinking it was so bad. A lot of stuff about how meditation can lower your blood pressure, right? Anyhow, it's not an anti-religion polemic like this thing. Listen to this:

Man's natural instinct, in fact, is never toward what is sound and true; it is toward what is specious and false. Let any great nation of modern times be confronted by two conflicting propositions, the one grounded upon the utmost probability and reasonableness and the other upon the most glaring error, and it will almost invariably embrace the latter. It is so in politics, which consists wholly of a succession of unintelligent crazes, many of them so idiotic that they exist as battle-cries and shibboleths and are not reducible to logical statement at all. It is so in religion, which, like poetry, is simply a concerted effort to deny the most obvious realities....Of all the unsound ideas preached by great heroes and accepted by hundreds of millions of their eager dupes, probably the most patently unsound is the one that is most widely held, to wit, the idea that man has an immortal soul—that there is a part of him too ethereal and too exquisite to die. Absolutely the only evidence supporting this astounding notion lies in the hope that it is true—which is precisely the evidence underlying the late theory that the Great War would put an end to war, and bring in an era of democracy, freedom and peace. But even archbishops, of course, are too intelligent to be satisfied permanently by evidence so inescapably dubious; in consequence, there have been efforts in all ages to give it logical and evidential support. Well, all I ask is that you give some of that corroboration your careful scrutiny. Examine, for example, the proofs amassed by five typical witnesses in five widely separated ages: St. John, St. Augustine, Martin Luther, Emanuel Swedenborg and Sir Oliver Lodge. Approach these proofs prayerfully, and study them well. Weigh them in the light of the probabilities, the ordinary intellectual decencies. And then ask yourself if you could imagine a mud turtle accepting them gravely.[4]

Paul (laughing). That's great stuff. I love that kind of writing, but, as you say, this is an odd place to be pushing it.

G. Exactly. I really don't understand it. Mencken ends up by saying that the cosmos is a gigantic spinning fly wheel, and while people are really just sick flies taking a dizzy ride, religion is the absurd theory that the wheel was designed and set spinning just to give us this thrill. You know, when I read that, it seemed like Rabi was making fun of everyone who comes here.

Paul. That *does* seem like it might be a bit disconcerting right after you've plunked down all this money and cleared away all this time with the hope that life will have *more* meaning when you're finished, rather than less. Rabi is definitely an interesting bird. Do you know he actually quoted a line from a Joni Mitchell song to me? And he did an imitation of Chance the Gardener from *Being There?*

G. Did he really? There was some pop culture at my session too. I'm embarrassed to say that when he asked me my purpose in coming to the Center I actually quoted George Harrison's "I really want to know you" song. Can you believe that's the best I could come up with after thinking about coming here for so long?

Paul. What was his response?

G. Oh, it was awful. He wanted to know what sort of entity it was that I thought Harrison was appealing to by the word "Lord" in his song. I think I babbled some incoherent answer about Krishna....Oh God, I really don't want to have my entire Summer here designed on the basis of a line from a Beatles song! But I guess I have no one to blame but myself: I was the one who brought the foolish thing up. I just couldn't think of anything else to say at the time. Ugh.

Paul. Hmmm. So he knows the quiet Beatle as well as Joni?

G. Yup. And he was familiar with the movie "Home for the Holidays," too.

Paul. You're kidding.

G. Nope, we had an interesting talk about it.

Paul. What about?

G. It's hard to explain...I love that movie. Have you seen it?

Paul. I think so, yeah. Holly Hunter, right?

G. Right. Well, the moral of it is that each person's life is centered around a single 10-second epiphany, a brief moment that defines us, shows us our purpose. For the Holly Hunter character it was, you know, swimming with her teenage daughter among a bunch of angel fish. For her father it was watching how fearless and excited Holly was when a giant jet plane flew right down at her when she was a little girl. For her brother it was a moment during the day he got married to another man—his longtime lover—on a sandy beach with all their friends around. For their mother it happened during an impromptu dance with her future husband at a bowling alley. Anyhow, the theory is that everyone has one of these glorious moments and never forgets it as long as he or she lives. And that's the point to everything. In my session I suggested—after the George Harrison debacle was finally over—that maybe I came here because I figured I was still waiting for *my* moment. I have this sense that there's something preventing me from...I don't know...breaking through to it or something. I told him that maybe I thought my stay here could help remove this obstacle.

Paul. How'd he take it?

G. He was sympathetic, but he didn't buy the whole premise that the point of a life is a brief epiphany. He said he didn't think I should be too concerned about the absence of any experience whose main characteristic is a sort of poignancy, even sorrow. And I had to admit that there does tend to be something sad about all these kinds of epiphanies. I guess it's the realization that they're fleeting that gives these moments so much significance.

Paul. And what makes them so sad. Do you have any kids?

G. No, I'm not married.

Paul. Well, I have a seven-year-old daughter, and I can tell you that I've had lots of experiences with her that have been invested with that kind of warm glow, though I don't know if any one of them can be singled out as *the* killer experience of my life. These feelings have arisen quite regularly, beginning with the moment of her birth. You know, all the greeting card things: the first time she put an ornament on a Christmas tree, her first time splashing around in the ocean, the day she first marched into a kindergarten class with all the other trusting little sweethearts. All the familiar milestones. But no matter how wonderful they are, they all have this unbearable sadness connected with them. As you said, it's that we always know each phase is gone in a flash, never to return. The gradual progress of our babies from utter helplessness to autonomy. It's devastating. Put a good soundtrack to any of these moments, and maybe a touch of slow-motion photography, and every parent would be sobbing almost continuously. I know lots of people – even parents of older children – who can't get through baby books like *Runaway Bunny* or *"More More More" Said The Baby* without completely losing it. And there's nothing objectively sad about any of these books: they just beautifully remind us how much we love our children. That's all it takes, since lurking behind everything there's always this horrible recognition that it isn't forever. That song in *Toy Story 2*, "When Somebody Loved Me" is another great, tearjerking example: it isn't really about toys, it's about parents.

G. Well, Rabi seems to think that these moments, for all their loveliness and apparent significance, aren't all they're cracked up to be....Maybe that's a good thing from my point of view, since I don't think I've ever had a defining one.

Paul. It's odd. He almost seems to be trying to disabuse you of the notion that life has meaning at the same time he's trying to shake me out of my suspicions regarding total pointlessness. It's like he's doing all he can to agitate you at the same time he's working to calm me down—or even completely space me out. You know, he wants me to practice a kind of meditation I've always considered to be nothing more than self-hypnosis. It's like the stuff they hype on TV infomercials involving a 50-dollar cassette full of 100,000 subliminal messages like "You're great!" or "Fall asleep now!" or "Making money is wonderful!" mixed in with the sound of ocean waves. Relaxation techniques aren't the kind of secret you should have to pay big bucks for anymore. They've been practiced for centuries. I mean, just listen to this:

> The altered state of consciousness associated with the Relaxation Response has been routinely experienced in Eastern and Western cultures throughout all ages. Subjectively, the feelings associated with this altered state of consciousness have been described as ecstatic, clairvoyant, beautiful, and totally relaxing. Others have felt ease with the world, peace of mind, and a sense of well-being akin to that feeling experienced after a period of exercise but without the fatigue. Most describe their feelings as *pleasurable.* Despite the diversity of description, there appears to be a universal element of rising above the mundane senses, a feeling beyond that of common-day existence. Many authors have pointed out the similarities between Eastern and Western mysticism, and have emphasized a universality of certain impulses in the human mind. Indeed, the subjective accounts of practitioners of different meditative backgrounds

are similar to many experiences depicted in religious, historical, and philosophical writings. We will attempt to show that the Relaxation Response has been experienced throughout history. We will do so by extracting methods described in various literatures, primarily religious. Some of these methods are thousands of years old. Our chief purpose is to illustrate the age-old universality of this altered state of consciousness by citing certain elements that appear to be necessary to evoke this experience, or "response." No technique can claim uniqueness.

This approach is not to be interpreted as viewing religion or philosophy in a mechanistic fashion. The ultimate purpose of any exercise to attain transcendent experience corresponds to the philosophy or religion in which it is used.[5]

Paul (laughing). I just love that last bit, which is in italics for emphasis. It's like an advance response to the religious right or anybody else who complains, "Wait a minute there, Doctor! Who the hell are you to reduce my deeply held religious beliefs to a breathing exercise!" Benson wants to parry all those criticisms with a warning label. You know, "Nothing in this book should be taken as a criticism of any religious position whatsoever. Any dogma considered sacred by the reader shall remain entirely unscathed by anything in these pages whether that position is consistent with the scientific results set forth here or not." I mean, if Benson's experiments show that religious ecstasy through the ages has been nothing more than a function of people making themselves dizzy by repeating the same word over and over, why doesn't he just come out and say so? It seems so false and cowardly to throw in a "No Offense, Anybody" label, doesn't it? Was it really so important to sell his book to people of every single creed? Either this technique actually has some of the religious significance Benson suggests that it has by including all these excerpts from mystics, or it doesn't. If it does, it would seem to have to be inconsistent with, for example, any religion that denies the importance of these pseudo-transcendent experiences. And if it hasn't got any religious significance at all, but is just a way to relax after a hard day at the office, why quote mystics like Saint Theresa and Chuang Tzu?

G. Oh, I don't know. I guess I'm not as disdainful of anything that can give me a feeling of calmness and contentment as you seem to be. I just take that sort of thing for what it's worth. If it relaxes you, where's the harm? I've meditated for years—I find it helpful. You seem awfully feisty about this.

Paul. Sorry. I do seem a bit defensive, don't I? Maybe it's fear of being alone in this strange place for three months. I suppose it's also my way of whining about the cost and the time commitment. It might have been naïve, but I took seriously the religious connotations of the name "The Perennial Solution Center". If this solution is something I could have picked up on any self-help bookshelf, I wish Rabi would have just offered a one-hour seminar. He could have packed in a couple hundred people at once and made the same money.

G (laughing). Boy, you *are* tough. I hope you won't mind me saying this, but you don't seem like the type that would sign up for a place like this.

Paul. I know. I know. I guess what I'm really after is for someone to prove conclusively to me that I'm not going to die....Was it Woody Allen who said, "I want to achieve immortality by not dying"? I feel the same way. I can take a pill to relax, but I don't *want* to relax knowing that I won't be around in 50 years or so. I guess it bothers me to think that I've just come here to be given a technique that doesn't even claim – at least consistently claim – to have any religious significance at all. Listen to this passage from my book,

> ...meditative practices may be found outside of a religious or philosophical context, and a rich source of descriptions of transcendent experiences is secular literature.... Wordsworth believed that every man could attain the vision of joy and harmony of life in nature, which for him transformed the whole of existence....Wordsworth's description of the method of realizing this condition emphasizes the practice of a passive attitude. If freed from distracting objects, petty cares 'little enmities and low desires,' he could reach an equilibrium of 'wise 'passiveness' or a 'happy stillness of the mind.' A cessation of the intellect and desires and a relaxation of the will could be used deliberately to induce this condition. With habitual training one could experience the 'central peace subsisting for ever at the heart of endless agitation.'[6]

And if Wordsworth isn't enough, Tennyson makes an appearance here too:

> Tennyson had peculiar experiences of a vision of ecstasy which was the foundation of his deepest beliefs of the 'unity of all things, the reality of the unseen, and the persistence of life.' This condition came about often with the silent repetition of his own name! He wrote several accounts of this experience: '...till all at once, as it were, out of the intensity of the consciousness of individuality, the individuality itself seemed to resolve and fade away into boundless being, and this not a confused state, but the clearest of the clearest, the surest of the surest, utterly beyond words, where death was an almost laughable impossibility, the loss of personality (if so it were) seeming no extinction, but the only true life.'[7]

G. I have to say, those quotes seem beautiful to me. I only wish I could have those sorts of experiences...(laughing) and that I could get assignments involving Wordsworth and Tennyson instead of Mencken. You think Rabi would mind if we traded?

Paul. *I* certainly wouldn't mind. But it's not that I don't think those quotes are nice too. I really do. It's just that I'm not here for sedatives or poetry. (Laughing) To quote another one of your mop-haired lads from Liverpool, "All I want is some truth; Just give me some truth."

G (laughing). I take it you don't follow Keats in identifying truth with beauty, then.

Paul. Well, not yet anyway. But, give me a chance. After all, I've only been here a couple of days.

G. It's a deal. I'll check you after you've had a little more brainwashing, And I expect you to have a dazed smile on your face and be drooling excessively. If not, I'm going right to Rabi and report that you're not doing your exercises correctly....But in the meantime, I guess I'd better get to my readings in wise-guy agnosticism.

Paul. And I think I have some incense I should be inhaling. So nice meeting you. I do hope we can get together for another talk soon. I promise not to rant. (He walks off.)

Wednesday, 3:00 PM — The Library

G. Hi.

Rabi. How are you today, Gina?

G. Oh, please call me G. No one's ever called me Gina except my grandmother.

Rabi. All right then, G. How goes the battle?

G (sighing). Not so good, really. All this Voltaire and Mencken and Russell. It's gotten me down.

Rabi. You disagree with them, or you don't like to hear the truths they utter?

G. Oh, I don't know. I guess I'd prefer to have whatever

prejudices I have reinforced rather than shattered....Isn't that natural?

Rabi. Absolutely. But it's customary for deep-seated prejudices to resist being shattered by the arguments of a few clever men.

G. Well, I don't know how to respond to them, anyway. I think there's more to life than what can be proven conclusively to a professional philosopher, and I've tried to take comfort from what little religion I have. I suppose my faith is pretty simple and unanalyzed, but I'd rather have it bolstered than attacked. Anyway, even if I wanted to, I'm not really equipped to get into a philosophical argument with Bertrand Russell. Take this passage:

> It is true that intuition has a convincingness which is lacking to intellect: while it is present, it is almost impossible to doubt its truth. But if it should appear, on examination, to be at least as fallible as intellect, its greater subjective certainty becomes a demerit, making it only the more irresistibly deceptive. Apart from self-knowledge, one of the most notable examples of intuition is the knowledge people believe themselves to possess of those with whom they are in love: the wall between different personalities seems to become transparent, and people think they see into another soul as into their own. Yet deception in such cases is constantly practiced with success; and even where there is no intentional deception, experience gradually proves, as a rule, that the supposed insight was illusory, and that the slower, more groping methods of the intellect are in the long run more reliable.[8]

That kind of thing doesn't exactly inspire confidence in either religious experiences or intuitions about one's personal relationships. I mean, if those experiences that seem the most certain are the least reliable....well, it's all paradoxical to me.

Rabi. It may not inspire the confidence you're looking

for, but I think it has the ring of truth to it. Though people often fail to realize it, it's at least as important to be careful about religious commitments as one would be about, say choosing a job or an apartment. (Laughing) Anyhow, I'm a practicing mystic, and I'm not daunted by that passage. I take Russell's admonitions quite seriously.

G. I think I'd rather have more constructive advice on how to enhance what intuitions I have and fewer warnings about their untrustworthiness. As a non-scientist I don't have much else to go on, either in my religion or my relationships. And he also makes this complaint:

> [the] mystic insight begins with the sense of a mystery unveiled, of a hidden wisdom now suddenly become certain beyond the possibility of a doubt. The sense of certainty and revelation comes earlier than any definite belief. The definite beliefs at which mystics arrive are the results of reflection upon the inarticulate experience gained in the moment of insight. Often, beliefs which have no real connection with this moment become subsequently attracted into the central nucleus; thus, in addition to the convictions which all mystics share, we find, in many of them, other convictions of a more local and temporary character, which no doubt become amalgamated with what was essentially mystical in virtue of their subjective certainty.[9]

This makes everything even worse. He's already told us we shouldn't trust our feelings of certainty, and now he throws in that we can't really even identify what it is we think we're certain about, because all these other beliefs get mixed in by mistake. I hate this shifting sand stuff. Where's the solid ground? All this fussing about what constitutes sufficient evidence for this or good reason for doubting that just roils me up. Why can't Russell let me have my little religion? I certainly have no quarrel with him keeping his gigantic logic.

Rabi. He thinks his logic is inconsistent with various religions, and it no doubt is. I don't think we need to worry about that, though. You shouldn't have any trouble fitting what you call your little religion into the space carved out for it by Russell's gigantic logic.

G. But I don't want to argue about the logical merits of this or that belief system, or customize my religion so it's compatible with Russell's attacks; I just want to feel content with my life, centered, fulfilled.... Frankly, I'm not terribly interested in attending a philosophy seminar, and if that's what this is going to be, maybe I should re-think my summer plans.

Rabi. Of course you must do whatever you think best, but I wouldn't give up quite so easily. Sometimes, as with surgery, things must get worse before they can get better. And I assure you, I'm no philosophy professor. I'm a religious man, and I don't consider either my faith or my religion little. But I don't think it is cramped in the slightest by the constraints of Russell's logic. I think we can render unto Russell that which is Russell's without losing anything of importance to me. But let's look at *your* situation a little. You say you like your faith because it comforts you. Obviously, I don't know you well enough to be certain about this, but I must tell you that to me this faith of yours seems a fragile reed of support for you. It seems to have failed to give you any comfort whatsoever when confronted by a couple of books which you think contain dissenting views. Now if this faith is nevertheless enough for you, fine. Perhaps you will never come across a skeptic or a skeptical book again. Or, alternatively, perhaps you can find another place to visit, or church to attend that will, as you say, bolster this support in some manner. I have no wish to dissuade you from such a course. I do have a premonition that your unease with your life may linger if you merely try to barricade yourself against opposing views, but I could certainly be wrong about this. There are many many ways to be happy.

G. But couldn't I get the sort of support I'm looking for *here*? I mean, I've talked to a number of the other visitors at the center who aren't being asked to read Russell or Mencken. People are carrying around stuff like the *B'hagvad Gita* and the *Imitation of Christ* Why did I get singled out for the surgery treatment rather than the massage therapy?

Rabi (laughing). Are any of these others happier with my recommendations?

G (laughing). Now that you mention it, No. Still, I'd trade with almost any of them.

Rabi. And, no doubt, many of them would jump at the chance too. You know that you are free to read what you like here and to ignore my reading recommendations if you want to. But I'm not sure this would change things much in our sessions—at least I hope it wouldn't. My approach is what it is. I would push the same buttons with you (or at least try to) no matter what books we discuss in our session. I make no promise that having these buttons pushed will be pleasant. They generally are not. And I try to make recommendations of works that will move you along more quickly to the place you tell me you seek. You've said you want to experience a sort of mystical communion with God. You want *samadhi* or *satori* or some sort of religious ecstasy like those you've read about in books. I respect this desire completely, I'm even tempted to congratulate you on it—although that's probably just a clubby attitude on my part: obviously there's something silly about congratulating people on their goals or desires.

In any case, I take my task to be to help you to reach your promised land as fast as you can. I like to think that the use of different literary sources wouldn't materially alter my travel map for you, though it could make things a bit more circuitous for us both. For example, I understand your faith to be of the non-denominational Christian sort, correct?

G. Yes. I suppose so.

Rabi. Then let us put Russell down for a moment and pick up a little book by C.S. Lewis called *Mere Christianity*. Do you know it?

G. Yes. I had to read it in school.

Rabi. I believe it's a short defense of a generic Christian faith, meant to be simple enough to be broadcast on the radio.

G. That sounds right.

Rabi. But do you recall that this little book is absolutely overflowing with arguments, arguments, arguments? Let me paraphrase a few:

1. We find ourselves prodded by moral urgings or "oughts."

2. These proddings couldn't be what Lewis calls "herd instincts" like eating when hungry, because if they were, we couldn't believe what we often do believe, that we *ought* to succumb to one herd instinct rather than another. That is, since the moral worth of particular herd instincts are themselves judged by the standards that produce our moral promptings, these standards couldn't themselves just be another group of herd instincts.

3. These proddings aren't just societal conventions either, like using a red light rather than a purple one to signal cars to stop, since that would make it impossible for us to judge one group of societal conventions as morally

superior to another. But we in fact often *do* make such judgments, as when we say the Nazi worldview was morally bankrupt.

4. The moral proddings we feel are, therefore, outside us in the sense that we find ourselves under a moral law we clearly did not make.

I have neither the inclination nor the ability to determine whether all of the many arguments embedded here are sound, but anyone can tell that there are a lot of them. Lewis has barely gotten started in his quest to defend the Christian faith, and he's already almost buried us in a mountain of premises and conclusions.

G. You're right, I'm dizzy again.

Rabi. But there's so much more. Lewis says that almost since the beginning of history people have wanted to know whether the world is the way it is by accident or because of the design of some powerful controlling authority. Then he writes,

> If there was a controlling power outside the universe, it could not show itself to us as one of the facts inside the universe—no more than the architect of a house could actually be a wall or staircase or fireplace in that house. The only way in which we could expect it to show itself would be inside ourselves as an influence or a command trying to get us to behave in a certain way. And that is just what we do find inside ourselves. Surely this ought to arouse our suspicions? In the only case where you can expect to get an answer, the answer turns out to be Yes....I find that I do not exist on my own, that I am under a law; that somebody or something wants me to behave in a certain way....Do not think I am going faster than I really am. I am not yet within a hundred miles of the God of Christian theology. All I have got to is a Something which is directing the universe, and which appears in me as a law urging me to do right and making me feel responsible and uncomfortable when I do wrong. I think we have to assume it is more like a mind than it

is like anything else we know—because after all the only other thing we know is matter and you can hardly imagine a bit of matter giving instructions.[10]

G. Good heavens.

Rabi. Then in just a few short pages Lewis quickly flies the hundred miles necessary to prove that this thing that he says produces our moral promptings is none other than the Jesus Christ of the Gospels, who is engaged, according to Lewis, in a sort of civil war with a fallen angel for the soul of the world. Note that Lewis doesn't seem to be relying on revelation for any bit of this voyage. It's all argument after unconvincing argument. And he even goes so far as to deride any less specific theologies as "Christianity with water" or simply "soft soap." None of this New Agey stuff for Lewis. Our moral sense leads directly to the Virgin Mary, the Resurrection and the Devil, or to nothing at all. Now, that is a reading claiming to contain nothing more than support for a simple Christian faith. Is that what you're looking for? Does that sort of thing satisfy you?

G. Not really, no. It seems like he's basing the entire Christian dogma as he's come to understand it on a few feelings of guilt.

Rabi. Surely that's what Freud would say.

G. And what do *you* think about it?

Rabi. Well, I'm only an amateur philosopher, and I don't want to opine on the validity or invalidity of so many arguments. But, as I've said, I find them completely unconvincing. If I had nothing but this sort of thing as support for my religious views, I think I might have to give them all up. Obviously, other people would disagree. Arguments that move from the existence of morality to the existence of God—if not to any particular Bronze Age mythology—are not unusual. One example is Robert

Pirsig's book *Zen and the Art of Motorcycle Maintenance*,[11] a book that has had a large following: it makes a great deal of our feelings of *quality*. Persig is mysterious, but he hints that these feelings tell us something of the greatest importance about the nature of the universe. It's an interesting issue and a difficult one. Perhaps we will have time on another day to discuss my pet theory that there are two main positions one can take on the matter of moral promptings and guilt feelings—that of Freud and that of Emerson.

G. I hope so. It sounds fascinating, and I adore Emerson.

Rabi. But we've strayed a long way from Russell.

G (laughing). Oh, I haven't minded too terribly.

Rabi. Ah, Russell's a pussycat. Did you miss this passage in your readings?

> I yet believe that, by sufficient restraint, there is an element of wisdom to be learned from the mystical way of feeling, which does not seem to be attainable in any other manner. If this is the truth, mysticism is to be commended as an attitude towards life, not as a creed about the world. The metaphysical creed, I shall maintain is a mistaken outcome of the emotion, although this emotion, as coloring and informing all other thoughts and feelings, is the inspirer of whatever is best in Man. Even the cautious and patient investigation of truth by science, which seems the very antithesis of the mystic's swift certainty, may be fostered and nourished by that very spirit of reverence in which mysticism lives and moves.[12]

Don't you see that he's actually an ally, so long as we are careful not to overstep our bounds?

G. But what is the "sufficient restraint" he's talking about?

Rabi. Well, it's rendering unto Russell. It's engaging in

as little metaphysics as possible. (Laughing) You could even say it's obeying Joni Mitchell's instruction to "never mind the questions there's no answers to."

G. That sounds much more palatable to me than arguing.

Rabi. Actually, it's often difficult, but I think we can manage it...But there is bound to be some tough sledding at times. At such times, I hope you will try to meditate as I instructed you.

G. Flow down, flow out.

Rabi. Right. I think you'll find it can be quite an effective way to relax. And, let's switch gears and read about the life of Jesus for a week or so.

G. This sounds promising.

Rabi. Be warned. These two books, one by Samuel Butler, the other by George Moore, are both attacks on the notion of Jesus' literal resurrection—Moore by historical novel, Butler by satire.

G. I have no problem with that. I'm not a literalist about these things. As long as they don't suggest that it's pointless to believe in *anything*.

Rabi. No need to worry on that score. I can assure you, both Butler and Moore are quite religious after their own fashions.

G. And what about this Fechner character?

Rabi. Gustav Fechner?

G. Yes, he stares down at me every night in my room, and I don't think I can stand another minute of not knowing the first thing about him.

Rabi. Well, there's a nice biographical sketch at the beginning of *Religion of a Scientist*, a book of excerpts from his writings. Actually, that seems like a very good choice for you too right now. Keep in mind, though, that the

Moore book, called *The Brook Kerith*, is very long and a bit dull. George Bernard Shaw said after reading the first few pages of it that he didn't see why it couldn't go on in much the same manner for 50,000 or even 50 million pages. You might just skip the whole first section about the childhood of Joseph of Arimathea and start somewhere in the middle, after Jesus has made his appearance on the scene.

G. Ah, a novel. It sounds lovely! (She takes the three books Rabi hands her and shakes his hand.) Thanks.

Rabi. Remember, you may find these upsetting too. It's most important to meditate. See you next time.

II.
Week Two

Monday, 3:25 AM—The Library

(G is sitting in a chair in jeans and a T-shirt. Rabi enters hurriedly in a bathrobe and pajamas and sits down in a chair across from her.)

G. Thank-you for coming. I'm so sorry to have gotten you up like this.

Rabi. It's fine. Please don't worry about it. What's the trouble?

G. Oh, it all seems so silly now. I was having an anxiety attack, and I didn't know what else to do, but I think I'm all right here, with the lights on and another human being around.

Rabi. It's perfectly fine to wake me at such times. You mustn't think I mind in the least, but what do you think could have caused this episode?

G. I think it was...well, I was reading in the Fechner book, and I learned how he had blinded himself and how he became so helpless, unable to eat...and he kept writing all these conflicting things...and everything seemed so... (bursts into tears)...terribly confusing. I just couldn't figure out what was going on. I...I feel like I can't understand anything at all.

Rabi. Specifically what part of the book were you reading?

G. It was in the biographical sketch. First there was this stuff about how Fechner would write books satirizing, you know, things like that all angels have to be spherical, and then a couple of years later he'd write a serious book in which he'd defend precisely the same position. I didn't know how anyone was ever supposed to tell whether he was kidding or not. And then he got that awful sickness; you know, first going blind and then crazy for such a long time—three years I think. I don't know how anyone could stand it. Each time it seemed like he was getting better, he'd relapse into another bout of insanity. What seemed like improvements were just more misleading evidence, and I started imagining how horrible it must have been for him to be in complete darkness, never sure about anything. And then I started to think...maybe...(starts crying again)...the same thing was happening to me.

Rabi (He gets up to get a box of tissues and the Fechner book. He hands her both and sits back down.) Do you think you can find any of these particularly upsetting passages? It may help to read them aloud.

G. The worst part was the last thing I read:

> Fechner describes the ways he found for passing the time with mechanical occupations: he 'twisted twine, unraveled bits of cloth, cut cardboard, cut the pages of books, wound yarn, and helped in the kitchen by sorting lentils, breaking the sugar-loaf, crumbling dry rolls, cutting carrots and beets.'...
>
> No wonder he says: 'My lot was a very sad one. I thanked God when a day was over, and was just as glad when a night was past, in which commonly I had no sleep.' No wonder he wished for death and would have given himself release if he had dared to do so.
>
> He dwells especially upon one feature of his mental weakness. 'I was unable to control my thoughts, which revolved constantly about the same point, returned to it again and again, bored and burrowed as it were in my brain, which was deteriorating to such a degree that I had a definite feeling I should be lost irreparably if I did not resist with all my strength. This labor, which for nearly a year occupied the greater part of

each day, was after all a kind of diversion, but it was the most painful kind that can be thought of....My inner man was as it were divided into two parts: my ego and the thoughts. Both fought with one another: the thoughts sought to overpower my ego and go their way independently to the destruction of my health; my ego on the other hand exerted the whole power of its will to master the thoughts, so that when a thought would establish itself and spin itself out my ego would strive to dispel it and introduce a remoter thought in its place. Thus my mental occupation consisted, not in thinking, but in constantly checking and expelling thoughts. I sometimes conceived of myself as a rider who was striving to subdue a runaway horse, or as a monarch whose subjects had revolted and who gradually was collecting troops and forces to reconquer his kingdom.[13]

Just think how it would be to be blind and unable to control your thoughts, reduced from writing books on chemistry to twisting bits of twine and wishing you would die. And when I took off my glasses to go to sleep, I saw all these little squiggly things floating before my eyes—even when I closed them. I got so scared.

Rabi. What do you make of this? Why would this description of someone's ailments—admittedly horrific ailments—back in the 1840s upset you in this way today?

G. I think it's...Don't be angry....I think it's that I feel you trying to make the same thing happen to me. (She starts crying again) You keep giving me these horrible things to read, things that that will make me doubt everything. I don't think Butler's *Fair Haven* is either enlightening or funny. It's just a cruel joke: it's like he's laughing at everyone who believes in the Resurrection: he puts all the stupidest arguments in the mouths of the Christians. And Moore has an elderly Jesus trying to convince Saint Paul to forget about the whole messiah thing, as if it were just some mistake Jesus was sorry he ever started talking about. But of course Saint Paul is too devoted to his own fanaticism to listen to anything sensible: he thinks the real, alive Jesus is just a deluded old man. Moore makes Saint Paul crazy and he even makes Jesus believe that he too was crazy back when he thought he was the messiah. And, of course, now Saint Paul thinks Jesus is crazy.....I already told you that I hate all this shifting sand stuff. (sobbing) I want to know why you keep doing this to me. It seems so...cruel.

Rabi. The books just suggest the possibility of looking at the life of Jesus in another way. Many Christians do this comfortably. Think of all the relatively tranquil Unitarians in the world. I personally would be much more anxious and uncomfortable if the Butler/Moore vision were wrong and the Jesus myths were literally true—not because they're not lovely, but because they contradict so many other deeply held beliefs that few of us can live without in the present epoch. I don't want these conflicting worldviews both humming along within me as if they weren't at odds with each other.

G. But you've probably never been Christian. Many of us have been taught since we were little children a very different vision from that painted by Butler and Moore .

Rabi. And instructed regarding the horrible fate that awaits you if you don't accept it all, lock stock and barrel? Butler himself was so instructed. His father was a clergyman, I believe.

G. Oh, can't you and your Russells and Butlers just leave us alone?

Rabi. I'm happy to do so, if that's what you wish.

G. That's...what I wish.

Rabi. That's fine, but you have come to me with an application, a well-thought out application if I may say so, that says quite clearly that you are *not* happy with your "little faith." You've said that it is not enough for you. Perhaps such a faith may be fine for others, but you must admit that it has been insufficient to provide *you* with spiritual contentment. I have agreed to try to help you remedy this. If you have reconsidered and would like to just go on as you have before, I certainly will have no complaints. But you must understand that I cannot be constrained in my teachings and be expected to be of much assistance to you in your spiritual quest. It is my own view that enlightenment, at least enlightenment of the only kind *I* may be able to help you to achieve, is dependent on a non-magical, an *adult* approach to the world. If one's religion is inconsistent with everything else one ever encounters in life, it's not clear to me how this faith can maintain a central position for the believer. An important doctrine of this Center is that religion must have a principal place in one's world for it to provide the kind of solace you seek. You have asked for my help, and since you have found your little faith unable to provide much solace even in the short time you've been here in the sheltered world of the Center, it may well be that you *could* benefit from what I have to offer. A bigger belief, a certainty in fact, something that far outreaches the almost helpless word, "faith." But, at least on my view of the matter, this may require certain refinements in your worldview with which you are uncomfortable. Naturally, the choice of paths must be entirely your own.

G. I don't see why it has to be the way you say. Saint Theresa of Avila, Saint John of the Cross, Meister Eckhardt—weren't these all Christian mystics who loved Jesus and received their ecstasies without losing the comfort of their church?

Rabi. They had their deeply religious experiences no doubt. But I'm not sure how content they were, how integrated were their belief systems. Besides, they weren't exactly orthodox parishioners: I believe Eckhardt spent a good deal of his life in trouble with the Church powers. Finally, you must not forget we now live in a much more scientific age. It is considerably more difficult for any of us to believe in Virgin births and resurrections after Hume and Darwin, Newton and Einstein.

G. Isn't that just the point of faith, firm belief in spite of all the odds, everything telling you it's impossible?

Rabi. It may be the point of certain kinds of "faith," but those kinds are not what I hope that visitors will find or deepen here at the Center. This is an interesting, important issue, but it's not one I want to discuss now.

G. Why not?

Rabi. Because our time is short this evening and I don't think an elaboration of what I take to be the shortcomings of this or that sort of faith will help you get through the night or make you more comfortable with your life tomorrow.

G. And just what will do that?

Rabi. Meditating and determining the cause of your episode.

G. I've already told you the cause of my attack. And I don't see how I can meditate when I'm this upset. I can't breathe calmly enough and I can't control my thoughts any better than Fechner could.

Rabi. I believe you told me what you suspect were the *reasons* for your anxiety attack this evening. I think we should be searching for deeper, longer term causes and explanations. With all due respect, I don't think Fechner, Butler and Moore accomplished this feat of agitating you so greatly all by themselves. I mean, why should Fechner's problems in the 1840s trouble *you* today?

G. You want me to talk about my personal problems now...like you were my therapist or something?

Rabi. I only want you to feel better. That's why you came to the center. That's why you called me tonight, right? I think it might help if you thought about the unconscious causes of your anxiety.

G (angrily). Well, there's a lot going on in my life right now, OK? I don't really want to talk about it.

Rabi. That's fine. I understand completely. And there's no need whatever to talk to me about these things. But *you* must understand as many factors that are affecting your life as you can, and then you must think about how these factors can be defanged. That is one of the most difficult tasks for aspirants here.

G. Are you sure this is religion you're offering? It sounds more like pop psychology to me.

Rabi (laughing). You can call it "karma cleaning," if you want to preserve the religious façade of this portion of the work. But a number of religions contain features of this sort. Directed introspection can be helpful in much the same way confession is. I'm not sure there's much hope for any religion without something like it.

G. But what should I do if I'm uncomfortable talking about these things? I was never much one for confession either.

Rabi. You need neither talk nor confess to anyone other than yourself. You are familiar with free association?

G. Yes.

Rabi. Well, after you go back to your room, I want you to do something similar, but a little different. First, try to relax a bit with the "Flow down—Flow out" technique we've already discussed. When you feel at least a couple of degrees calmer, take out five sheets of paper and at the top of each one, write down one thing going on in your life that you think may be upsetting you. Now, I suggest you take each of these issues up, one at a time, giving no less than twenty minutes to each. There's a good description of the technique I have in mind, called "The Meditation of the Thousand Petaled Lotus" in a useful little book by Lawrence LeShan called *How to Meditate*:

> The symbol for the lotus with the thousand petals is widely used in Eastern mysticism. It is a symbolic rendition of the idea that everything is connected to everything else and that nothing is really separate and isolated from all the rest of the universe. The center of the lotus is any object or event you may choose. Each of the petals symbolizes the connection between the center and something else. The idea of a "thousand" petals is symbolic of an infinity of them: there is no limit to the number of petals in this concept.
>
> This is a structured meditation of the outer way. A word, idea, image is chosen by you to be the center of the lotus for this exercise....Once you have chosen the center word, get comfortable contemplate it and wait. Presently your first association comes to you. You look at the two words connected by the first "petal path" and regard them for three to four seconds. You either understand the reason for the association or you do not. In either case you do nothing more than regard the center, the path and the association for the tree to four seconds. Then you return to the center word and wait for the next association and repeat the procedure, and so forth. This is *not* free association; you always return to the word you have designated as the center of the lotus and proceed again from there.
>
> [Suppose] I choose the word "light" as the center. My first association is "sun." I regard the two, "light" and "sun" and the petal path between them for three to four seconds. I understand the connection. I return to "light."...The next association is "dark." I understand it and, after three to four seconds, return to "light."...The next association is "umbrella." I do not understand it and return after three to four seconds to "light" and so on.

Sometimes I may run into clusters of associations. For example, "red" could have been followed by "blue," then by "green," etc. If this happens, simply stay with the discipline even if it means going around the spectrum several times. Presently it will cease. If you run into a series of associations you do not understand, there is a very good chance that if you stay with it they will clear up.[14]

When you have finished with one of your meditations, write a few of the associations that seem most salient to you below the center word you have written down at the top of the page. If you'd care to bring these sheets to your next session, it might be helpful to talk about some of them, though, again, I entirely understand if you'd prefer to keep all these matters private. If you feel yourself getting anxious as you meditate, switch back to "Flow Down, Flow Out" until you feel comfortable with returning to the subject upon which you have chosen to meditate. Sometimes, your anxieties simply will not flow out: it's as if there were blockage in your legs somewhere. At other times, your chest may seem to be re-creating nervous feelings at least as fast as you are able to guide them out through your feet. At both such times, you should understand that there is something bothering you that you haven't fully comes to grips with. When things are going well and you have made an important self-discovery, you should feel nothing but a downward rushing of tension and a tingling in your feet. This mechanistic picture of anxiety moving through our bodies as if it were some sort of liquid may seem simplistic to you, even ridiculous, but we're interested in results here, and I think both of these techniques can be extremely helpful. (Smiling) Much more useful than, for example, thinking about how hard I seem to be trying to drive you insane.

G (laughing). And, coincidentally, much easier on you too!

Rabi. Yes, there is that as well.

G. But I couldn't possibly do five twenty-minute sessions tonight. I'm sure I'd fall asleep long before I'd finished.

Rabi. Well, why don't you try one or two tonight and see how it goes. I think I'm scheduled to see you this afternoon?

G. Right. At three.

Rabi. Do you feel calm enough to go back to your room now, and we can talk again then? I think there is some sherry around here someplace if you could use a glass.

G. That's okay, I'm sure I'll be all right. It must be almost morning, anyway. I...I'm sorry I was so angry and obnoxious. I really appreciate you taking the time to see me in the middle of the night.

Rabi. It's fine. It's all part of the process. Don't chastise yourself, just meditate diligently. As Laura Archera Huxley said over and over again in her self-help book.[15] "It works if you do."

G. Good night then.

Rabi. Good night.

❧

Monday, 3:00 PM—The Library

(G enters. Rabi, in his accustomed seat, rises briefly, motioning her to sit down.)

Rabi. How did you make out last night?

G. Oh, much better. I think the lotus thing helped some. Anyways, I was asleep within an hour.

Rabi. I'm glad to hear it. Did you get anything written down that you'd like to discuss now?

G. I think I'm still a bit uncomfortable with that idea. Also, I'm so tired that I'm not sure I have the energy to do much talking at all: I woke up at about seven and couldn't get back to sleep.

Rabi. Well, in that case, maybe I can use our time today to expound a bit on what I take to be the theory and purpose of the "karma cleaning" we talked about last night. I always think it's helpful to understand what we seek when we introspect and why we do so. This understanding can expedite the process and enhance the benefit. I think this is the reason that people like Spinoza spent so much time discussing psychology. I'm not a licensed psychologist, but it's an area that I'm quite interested in: I consider it a close cousin to the studies of religion and philosophy.

G. Sounds good to me. I'm actually kind of curious to know what you think the connections are between religious exercises and psychotherapy.

Rabi. There are a number of fascinating facets to this question—at least to me. Why should it matter what sort of mood one is in when one meditates? Can anxiety reduction be both a cause and an effect of spiritual wholeness, or what some might call "closeness to God"? How do we get so out of kilter in the first place? These are are difficult questions, but fortunately so many religious geniuses have, like Buddha, been very psychologically acute, and so many leading lights in psychology have been intensely interested in religion. In any case, even if we make little progress, there's the secondary benefit that some of this material is so abstract that it may be useful to you as a sleep aid, right here in the library.

G (laughing). All the better.

Rabi. All right. I will start by listing a few propositions of psychology that seem true to me and that can be loosely called "Freudian." This seems to me a sensible starting point because Freud's work was so fruitful. Like Copernicus, he turned turned an entire science upside down. And he was both so brilliant and so critical of any religious interpretations of the psychological phenomena he encountered, that it seems to me that religious thinkers who ignore him will seem cowed. So, to begin.

1. We have unconscious thoughts, feelings and desires. That is, there are in us occurrent mental events of which we are unaware. This was an important discovery, though perhaps one that antedated Freud's own work. The idea that an event can be mental at the same time that it is not consciously being experienced by anyone is counterintuitive but very fruitful. I won't go into any arguments for this theory now except to say that the analogies with mental events of which we *are* conscious are just too numerous and significant to be ignored. For details on this subject, I suggest Freud's *General Introduction* or Karen Horney's *New Ways in Psychoanalysis*.[16]

2. Some of these submerged mental events are unconscious because they are repressed by the individual in whose mind they are occurring. We keep them unconscious so we will not be disturbed or upset by them. According to the Freudians with whom I am familiar, repression is the most important mechanism by which neurotic symptoms are either created or maintained or both. As we will see, however, I think there can be other sources of neurosis as well.

3. The content of certain unconscious mental events can be discovered by the interpretation of dreams, by various kinds of so-called "Freudian slips," and by the psychoanalysis of individuals with neurotic symptoms. It turns out that the "choices" an individual makes regarding

particular dream imagery, mental lapses, substitutions and other errors, and neurotic symptoms can be clarified by analysis. The particular neurotic symptom chosen—an irrational fear of clocks for example—is analogous to an *expression* of the repressed material. That is, unconscious thoughts may be said to be expressed by particular symbols or symptoms. The "choices" of this imagery or behaviors, of course, are largely made on an unconscious level. Freud called the dream images chosen by a sleeper to express unconscious mental activity the "manifest" content of dreams. And he called the deeper, unconscious thoughts and feelings being expressed, the "latent" content of dreams. Freud himself believed that dreams are almost invariably the expression of unconscious *desires*, rather than other kinds of thoughts or feelings, but this position hasn't been universally accepted among Freudians, and it doesn't ring true for me. In any case, neurotic symptoms are thought to be analogous to dream images in being a sort of manifest expression of latent, repressed thoughts and feelings.

4. Interpretation and analysis of unconscious mental processes are facilitated by free association, the activity of attending to—and usually expressing, either verbally or in writing—every little thing that pops into one's mind. The goal in free association is to exercise as little conscious censorship as possible. This technique provides rich information regarding what is happening "below the surface" of our everyday awareness.

5. Anxiety—and I believe this includes episodes of the type you experienced last night—is a little different from neurotic symptoms of the kind that express latent thoughts, since it doesn't itself express anything. But these fearful feelings may nevertheless give us clues about

our unconscious activities. Early in his career, during his work with Breuer,[17] Freud noticed that the repression of certain kinds of thoughts is often accompanied by anxiety and that this seems to be so whether or not other, more expressive symptoms were chosen as symbols of those unconscious thoughts. Anxiety is thus more of a side effect than a particular symbolic symptom or image. It provides a certain level of information by flaring up at particular times and places, but because of its more generic nature, anxiety can't be "read" in the same way as, say, an obsessive behavior or a phobia.

6. Some Freudians have noted that we may find some degree of relief from anxiety simply by what we've called the "expression" of a latent thought in dreams or symptoms. That is, it is often somewhat calming just to contemplate or describe the manifest content of an upsetting dream, or to "act out" in some neurotic fashion. So dreams and other symbolic representations have at least one useful function in the neurotic's life: they give him partial relief from the anxiety caused by repression. But, on the Freud/Breuer view, there can be no complete relief from the tension produced by the repression of a troublesome thought without the latent content being discovered by the symbolizing individual. This fuller relief is, in the end, the most important test of the correctness of an analysis.

To step away from Freudianism for a moment, there seem to be other causes of anxiety, even apparently irrational anxiety—since of course it makes perfect sense without any deep psychological explanations for someone be anxious while driving on ice or being threatened by someone with a knife. But even if we stick to anxiety that seems to lack a reasonable cause, repression doesn't always seem to be a key factor. For example, it has long been recognized that people—or animals—given negative reinforcement upon the occasion of a pleasurable activity, say by regularly receiving painful electric shocks or angry words whenever they eat, will start to become anxious when the desire to engage in that pleasurable activity arises. Here the anxiety seems to result from conflicting desires—to have the pleasure and avoid the pain. This anxiety can continue long after the course of negative reinforcement has ceased—and can go on even after the subject has found out that there is no longer good reason for being afraid. In some sense of "learn" that involves more than simply knowing a fact, these individuals must *learn* not to expect the pain anymore.

Now, these two types of anxiety—that produced as a by-product of repression, and that which arises from contradictory desires—probably overlap to a great extent, and certainly have a number of things in common. For example, they may be indistinguishable in their "affect"— the way they make us feel, the sweaty palms and so on. And it may also be true of either sort that the sufferer has little idea of the cause or causes. We may even want to say of both forms that, generally, they seek to be protective: they attempt as it were to seal us off from some of the real or imagined dangers and conflicts that all human beings are faced with in this world.

The important thing to remember is that, for one main type of anxiety, that caused by the repression of latent thoughts, temporary relief is often achieved just by coming to realize what is being repressed and expressing that thought in a different way. The "strangulated affect" to use the Freud/Breuer term, will normally be released when the cause is understood—though there is no reason to believe that the dangerous thought will not soon be repressed again unless the sufferer achieves other, deeper personality changes. On the other hand, it's hard to imagine more than a few people whose anxiety is drug-induced or has been caused by habitual negative reinforcement at inappropriate times who would derive much benefit just from seeing a video tape of the drugging or the administering of the negative reinforcement.

The up-and-down history of Freud and Breuer's famous patient, "Anna O." shows that, even with respect to anxieties and other symptoms that seem to have been caused by repression, the uncovering of latent thoughts and desires, and the feelings of "catharsis" associated with this uncovering has been of limited success. While perhaps *necessary* to a complete cure – and often capable of providing an immediate symptomatic relief – insight and catharsis have generally not been *sufficient* to produce a total cure. In addition, the repetition of symptoms that should have been permanently eliminated by what Freud and Breuer called "abreaction and catharsis" shows that Breuer's views regarding the causes and importance of what he called "hypnoid states" were incorrect. Whether or not these half-awake states really exist, they fit better as an *effect* within Freud's defense theory than they do as a *cause* of neurotic symptoms.

G. Whatoid states? I'm sorry, you've really lost me here....and I *do* hope I'm not going to be tested on any of this.

Rabi. I know, I'm covering an awful lot of ground here. Let me try to make this clearer. Breuer had maintained that the cause of an hysterical symptom was that some event in a person's life that should have been accompanied by a "significant quota of affect," was instead experienced in the absence of deep, appropriate feelings—in what he called a "hypnoid state." He believed that if the affect could be once appropriately "discharged," the symptom would be forever banished. Unfortunately, this was not the typical case history for the hysterics treated by Freud and Breuer, any more than it seems to have been for our friend Fechner. Something else must be at work, something requiring that the same analytic ground be covered repeatedly. Freud's mechanism of defense would seem to handle this problem nicely: the *reason* for repressing a particular thought may continue to exist subsequent to the discovery of the latent thought by the thinker. So, even if Breuer's hypnoid state *had* invariably been present at the birth of an original repression, it was certainly not present on subsequent repressions of the same thoughts. That is, these states don't have any explanatory power as a continuing cause or condition of the symptoms. It was therefore possible to dispense with these states completely, and that's what Freud did.

G. I'm not sure this is relevant, but this hypnoid state thing reminds me of a book I once read on Scientology. The writer said that if we fall into some kind of stupor at times when we really should be having strong feelings, we produce these things in our minds called "engrams," which have to be unearthed for us to be made well. Or something like that.

Rabi. That's it exactly. Hubbard's *Dianetics*[18] is almost an exact duplication of the Breuer theory using different terminology, and it has the same limitations. Unfortunately, a neurotic's discovery of his "engrams," whether in a state of "reverie" or otherwise, is likely to provide little more than temporary relief to someone who has a settled habit of repressing troublesome thoughts. It's a start, but once we understand the value to the individual in using repression as a defense, a protective device, why wouldn't we expect it to be so used again?

G. But if discovering latent thoughts and expressing them in more appropriate ways isn't enough to cure anxiety neurosis, what is? I mean that part alone has always been pretty hard for me.

Rabi. Yes it is hard. Extremely hard. But it isn't enough. If we don't discover what we gain from the repressions and figure out how to re-design our interactions with the world in such a way that we can dispense with the need to hide these feelings or desires from ourselves, we are likely to continue to use this device to protect ourselves. And, as you rightly say, the analysis alone is so horrendously difficult. You know, I have sometimes wondered: why *must* an analysis be correct for relief to ensue? With physical pain, this is easy to see. If it's caused by a thorn in one's foot, it's not surprising that removing a splinter from one's finger won't do much good. But this sort of connection hasn't always seemed obvious in the world of psychotherapy. So, for example, we've seen the emergence of things like "Primal Scream" type therapies, where it's claimed that a good loud yell can be curative, no matter what the particular trouble. There is something of the same wishful thinking in the type of therapy that involves looking intently into a mirror and telling yourself that you're OK over and over. These are cases in which "holistic" just seems to mean "simplistic." A psychiatric patient may talk about his childhood endlessly without doing himself much good if he is on the wrong track. And a good cry—no matter how lengthy or how primal—will likely be helpful to a neurotic only if he can find the appropriate object for the sadness, anger or whatever, the real content of a formerly repressed thought. I find it strangely comforting, however, that it's generally *not* enough to treat any old psychic wound or to "discharge affect" by having a long cry. To me, there's something absolutely wonderful about this fact: it tells us that the discovery of and adjustment to the actual, latent contents of our minds can be just as important in the treatment of psychological problems as the discovery and adjustment to actual physical processes in our nervous systems. I believe that Spinoza had something like this in mind when he theorized that there are two completely separate but perfectly parallel causal chains that are active in the physical and mental worlds. Just as I said that we can render unto Russell without losing anything essential to the mystic, Spinoza argued that we can give the neurophysiologist both his causal laws and the entire physical mechanism of the brain without any loss to mental independence. But this could be so only so long as mental states can in some sense be completely explained without reference to a single physical phenomenon: nothing at all must be added by descriptions of brain states.

G. That's pretty hard to believe. I mean, one glass of wine and there are definitely changes in *my* mental states.

Rabi. Spinoza's position is certainly obscure and counterintuitive, but, fortunately, we need not follow him all the way to parallelism. It is enough for our purposes to agree with the anti-Freudian Adolf Grunbaum[19] that if there is a failure to decisively connect particular therapeutic results with the bringing forth of repressed thoughts or feelings that have intelligible connections to the malady in question, Freudianism must founder. For example, if a phobia of clocks isn't always materially affected by uncovering one or more formerly unconscious clock-related thoughts, psychoanalysis can offer little clinical support for its hypotheses. I don't see, however, that any such therapeutic successes must be permanent in order for them to count as evidence for a Freudian theory. As I've said before, once we know the protective tasks that repression is performing for the neurotic, there should be no expectation that bringing even the right latent thought to consciousness—either with or without catharsis—will permanently prevent relapses. Why would it?

G. This is sounding more and more hopeless. We find the hidden thought, we get out the repressed emotion, and the next night we're still scared stiff.

Rabi. Well, if we are to get beyond the repetitive repression of various thoughts and feelings, we must know their causes in the sense of their systematic uses in the neurotic's life. We know these thoughts are repressed because the thinker is unconsciously uncomfortable with their content. Perhaps they're felt to be immoral or liable to cause us physical harm if we act on them, or maybe they're just connected with things about ourselves or the world that we don't like to acknowledge, some perceived weakness, or the permanent absence of our parents. As Karen Horney has pointed out, we all find ourselves in a scary world, full of pitfalls and punishments, and we necessarily develop strategies of self-protection. The suppression of apparently dangerous thoughts and desires may just be a common accompaniment to many of these strategies. The consequences of allowing these outlaw feelings or memories into our consciousness seem dire, just as to the negatively reinforced eater, the consequences of eating a bowl of soup may feel dire. In each case we must learn and learn well that the alternative is worse. As we have seen, attempted strangulation of latent content when an external event that has "roiled up" our emotions—say our clock phobic's encountering Big Ben on a tour of London—often results in feelings of anxiety that can be dissipated either by "acting out" or by bringing the latent content to consciousness. To the neurotic, each type of response has its advantages. Symptoms may have other, thrilling benefits and may be a good deal easier and quicker to produce than the insights resulting from a thoroughgoing analysis. On the other hand, there are often terrible downsides to "acting out" and the experience of a psychoanalytic insight provides its own thrills and long term life improvements, including the possibility of spiritual enlightenment.

Now, suppose we choose the road of "making the unconscious conscious." If we are to avoid recurrences of our symptoms we must see clearly that the supposed dangers invested in the repressed thoughts are at least partly illusory. But it can't be denied that the bringing of this latent content to light will indeed often produce its own batch of unpleasant emotions, different from anxiety perhaps, but no less unpleasant for that fact. I'm thinking of emotions like sadness, feelings of inadequacy, recognition that certain sexual or romantic desires are unreasonable, and so on. We must always keep in mind that as hard as these feelings might be to deal with, they aren't generally accompanied by the hell of free-floating anxiety. At least these new feelings are more clearly focused. We understand their connections to the objects to which they attach, and that alone is a comfort. What's more, as we escape the bondage forged by our repressions, we may find we can engage in meditations of deeper and deeper kinds.

G. But what about the other kind of anxiety, the stuff that *isn't* a result of repression? How can we get at that?

Rabi. Well, while repression-induced anxiety can perhaps be subsumed under the behaviorist variety by declaring "fear of unpleasant consequences"—or something of that sort—to be the root of all anxiety, there is also a sense in which the ability of negative reinforcement to produce anxiety over long stretches of time depends on a rather Freudian concept of what might be called "the retention of unpleasant thoughts" somewhere in the psyche of the sufferer. That is, unless the scared eater's current fears when confronted by food are the result of a kind of magical, action-at-a-distance causality stemming from long past electrical shocks, there must currently exist in the eater a "pool" of painful reminiscences, perhaps correlated with some physical residue like changes in brain chemistry, that have resulted from the shocks. This "pool" may or may not be accessible to the eater's consciousness, but either way it must be addressed comprehensively, so I don't think the road to health is much different from the road away from repression-related anxiety. What causes a particular neurotic's emotional pain and the particular mechanisms he uses to defend himself—either the choice of a particular symptom/symbol for inappropriate "pseudo-expression" or the extent to which he creates a "new personality" in order to engage in pleasurable activities that aren't associated with negative reinforcement—is all tied up with his general personality structure. It's an unfortunate fact that each "successful" defense that results in one's pool of dangerous thoughts becoming bigger or more complicated makes a real cure more difficult. And each instance of acting out or of avoidance of an unreasonably feared activity may feel like a success if it reduces our anxiety. These strategies will therefore tend to encourage more such activity by fortifying our barricades against both the real world and our real thoughts, feelings and desires. There seems to be a sort of synergy within these murky pools: it's as if each sunken idea borrows a bit of associated pain from the others in the bundle, making each more frightening and more likely to resist the light of analysis.

G. The more we repress the worse we feel, and the worse we feel the more we repress. Terrific.

Rabi. Of course, the flip side of this is more encouraging—by the same kind of "leveraging," the power of each repressed thought and that of the entire bundle is reduced significantly each time a latent feeling is expressed. One insight shines light on the entire pool. But our whole personality has to be understood for a single one of our burdens to be completely lifted from us—destroyed once and for all. Let me quote Karen Horney on this:

> Since every neurosis—no matter how dramatic and seemingly impersonal the symptoms—is a character disorder, the task of therapy is to analyze the entire neurotic character structure. Hence the more clearly we can define this structure and its individual variations, the more precisely can we delineate the work to be done. If we conceive of neurosis as a protective edifice built around the basic conflict, the analytical work can roughly be divided into two parts. One part is to examine in detail all the unconscious attempts at solution that the particular patient has undertaken, together with their effect on his whole personality....
>
> The other part covers the work with the conflicts themselves. This would mean not only bringing the patient to an awareness of their general outline but helping him to see how they operate in detail—that is, how his incompatible drives and the attitudes that stem from them interfere with one another in specific instances....[20]

G. It all seems so daunting.

Rabi. It's hard, no doubt, but it's fulfilling as well. And, as Horney points out, there are other reasons for optimism:

Fortunately, analysis is not the only way to resolve inner conflicts. Life itself still remains a very effective therapist. Experience of any one of a number of kinds may be sufficiently telling to bring about personality changes. It may be the inspiring example of a truly great person; it may be a common tragedy which by bringing the neurotic in close touch with others takes him out of his egocentric isolation; it may be association with persons so congenial that manipulating or avoiding them appears less necessary. In other instances the consequences of neurotic behavior may be so drastic or of such frequent occurrence that they impress themselves on the neurotic's mind and make him less fearful and less rigid.[21]

G. That book sounds wonderful.

Rabi. I think it is. You might look at her *Self Analysis* too.

G. Absolutely.

Rabi. Anyhow, I'm quite sure I've given you more than enough to think about for one day.

G. I *am* a bit overwhelmed, but it was very interesting. Thank you. And thanks again for the impromptu session last night and for teaching me the lotus meditation. I think it will be very helpful.

Rabi. I hope so. See you next time.

Tuesday, 1:30 PM — Joan's Luncheonette

(G and Paul are sitting across from each other in a restaurant booth with sandwiches in front of them and their books next to them).

Paul. So, how has it been going? Do you think you're getting anything out of all this solitude—with the occasional rap session thrown in?

G. Actually, it's starting to grow on me. I wish you could have been there during my last talk with him. He was amazing: if you hadn't seen him, you would have thought he was reading from a psychology textbook or something. He constructed all these arguments on the fly, without even stopping to think. There was all this stuff about what was right and wrong with Freud and other psychologists. Of course, I didn't absorb much of it, so maybe it was all gibberish. But it was pretty impressive. I wish there could have been a stenographer there, so I could read it over slowly.

Paul. Man, it seems like I'm missing everything! I'd love to get him into something like that. I studied psychology in college before switching to philosophy. What did he say was wrong with Freud?

G. I think it was mostly that there are other causes of psychological problems than repression, but, to tell you the truth, I'm not really sure.

Paul. But you're liking him more?

G. Rabi? Yeah, I really am. Mostly it's that he's taught me a couple of meditative techniques that seem pretty effective, but also he seems so smart. And his confidence in himself is appealing to someone like me who's pretty unsure of everything. (Laughing) I don't know if it's a cult/guru syndrome or some kind of psychoanalytic transference, but I can't deny that he's won me over somehow.

Paul. Oh, I can understand what you mean perfectly. He *is* quick on his feet. I find his facility with all his books appealing too. But...well...I'm still pretty frustrated with him though.

G. What do you mean?

Paul. Well, you've seen *My Dinner With Andre*?

G. Yeah.

Paul. Well, I keep feeling myself being put in the position of Wally Shawn I'm even having trouble not rolling my eyes sometimes. Something about Rabi's mysticism must appeal to me or I guess I wouldn't have come here at all, but I keep expecting him to start pontificating about Finhorn and his talking trees or something. You know, birds flying out of his car's exhaust pipe and all that.

G. It seems so strange to me that you have that view of him, since he comes off so rational and scientific in my sessions. I'm almost afraid to tell him about any naïve beliefs that I have for fear he'll laugh at me. I mean, my last session could really have been a psych seminar. Very dry. No paranormal birds at all. Has he really said anything to you that suggests talking plant life?

Paul. Well...actually...no. But he seems so credulous and earnest. Maybe it's that I'm more comfortable trusting people who have a little healthy skepticism about them. I mean, look at this insipid little book he suggested I read, *The Optimystic's Handbook*[22] The chapter titles alone make me squirm. Just listen to some of them: "Awakening to Your Mystic Self"; "Sit Down, Shut Up, Open Up"; "Is There Life *Before* Death?"; "Spiritual Litter is Against the Natural Law"; and my favorite: "Let the Glad Games Begin!" And there are lots of excruciating sub-headings like "Are You Due for a Spiritual Oil Change?" too. What's more, I think one of the authors has actually written a couple of books about angels! It's hard for me to take this kind of stuff seriously. I'm afraid that before another two or three weeks has gone by he'll have me saying things like "Rabi, I've been trying to awaken my hidden godmother within, but I'm having trouble just Being with a capital B. Do you think I need to sprinkle my spiritual seedlings with more sauce of life, or is it that I'm not sharing enough of my psychic pudding at eternity's smorgasbord?"

G (laughing). Is the book itself bad, or is it just the chapter headings?

Paul. Oh, well, it's about what you'd expect. Not terrible exactly, but mostly nice sounding platitudes. No arguments are provided for anyone who might have any doubts at all about their Pollyanna picture of the world. For example, they want you to take this quiz to test your "optimystic quotient"—don't all these kinds of books have quizzes?—Here are some of the questions:

> When your soul tries to speak to you, do you:
> A. Turn up your Walkman extra loud?
> B. Tell yourself that you're just imagining things?
> C. Ask if it can call back later?
> D. Stop to listen?
> E. Invite it in for coffee?[23]

And it turns out that on this quiz E answers are always better than D answers, Ds are always better than Cs, and so on. And if you get too many As and Bs you risk getting the following assessment:

> Danger! Diminishing optimystic pulse! Call in the life support systems! But remember, it's never too late to let passion, enthusiasm, love, generosity, humor trust, peace, and joy into your life.

So if it turns out I need life support, it could just be because I didn't offer my soul any coffee! But I mean, maybe I make a crappy cup of coffee. Or maybe I was just out of coffee, when my soul dropped by unannounced. Come to think of it, I happen to know that my soul is strictly a tea drinker and gets a sour stomach whenever it touches coffee, so wouldn't it have been rude to offer it coffee in the first place? Here I am on life support, just because I was a little too worried about being rude to my soul. And as for asking my soul to call back later, wouldn't that be all right if I was in deep conversation with my inner Raggedy Ann at the time? After all, I might have had a long confab with my soul just the day before, and maybe I hadn't had a chance to get together with my inner Raggedy Ann for three or four months. It seems awfully harsh, even cosmically impolite, to just hang up on my inner Raggedy Ann in favor of my soul when I can, you know, *always* talk to my soul—except maybe on Wednesdays, when it has its regular appointments with an ethereal gastroenterologist about its acid stomach problems.

G (laughing). At least your soul tells you about its heath issues: mine is so closed-mouthed about those things.

Paul. Well, maybe that's because you keep turning up your Walkman when it's around. My own soul, being something of an audiophile, hates any kind of music heard through headphones. That's why I knew not to answer A to that question. To tell the truth, it isn't even enough to turn *down* my Walkman when my soul pays a surprise visit; I have to hide it completely. Can you believe that my soul has been known to fly into a terrible rage at the very *sight* of a Walkman?! Fortunately, I've found that hiding my Walkman in one of my clothes drawers works pretty well: for some reason my soul has never thought to rummage around in there.

G. Uh-oh, that could be bad. I mean maybe there's a quiz question on how much your soul knows about your wardrobe. You might do badly on that one.

Paul. Exactly. See my point? I mean who is this kind of crap written for anyway?

G. Well, I'm embarrassed to say I've read my share of it. I know it's just "feel good" stuff, but sometimes there's a useful nugget or two among all the clichés. Besides, I like to read things that try to convince me that, no matter how bad things may seem, the world is pretty much OK.

Paul. This book is for you, then. It says things like if you see somebody lying lifeless under a truck you should try to understand why, from an optimystic perspective, it's all for the best....Although I must say I was surprised to read this:

> Imagine that a majestic tree in your neighborhood is being cut down in front of your eyes to make room for a shopping mall. What would you do?
>
> A reverent person would feel pain at the sight of a beautiful tree being wantonly destroyed; an *actively* reverent person would try to stop the proceedings if they hadn't gone too far or would become involved in some sort of volunteer environmental protection work to guard against similar desecrations in the future.[24]

I guess you can never be too mystical to oppose the building of shopping malls, can you? At least where the construction "hasn't gone too far" and there's a "majestic" tree involved. I wonder what you'd do if you were a committed political conservative optimystic or a left-wing laborite optimystic? Your political views might not allow you to fight against a development that would create a bunch of new opportunities either for capitalists or workers just because of a pretty tree. On the other hand, a devotion to optimysticism seems to require you to get out there and defend every tree—or at least every tree that's sufficiently "majestic." So, maybe this would be the time to get your soul to intercede on behalf of the tree, leaving *you* free to be on the side of the developers. But, of course, that might require your soul to take up coffee drinking. Otherwise, how's it going to get through those early morning strategy sessions? Dear, dear, dear, whatever is a left-wing laborite optimysticist to do?

G. Maybe your guardian angel could help out here?

Paul. I guess so, but with all these things flying around, your guardian angel, God, you, your soul, your inner Raggedy Ann, your Walkman, your coffee pot, it might get pretty confusing....Oh, I know I'm being too harsh. It isn't really such a bad book if you can get past all the pabulum. There are some nice quotes in there from various Eastern, Dalai Lama types anyhow. And besides, the other book he suggested isn't half bad.

G. What's that?

Paul. It's a Huxley novel called *Eyeless in Gaza*. It may not be Faulkner or Joyce, but I'm really enjoying it. It's about an aloof, cynical intellectual....(with mock anger) Hey! you don't think Rabi could have been trying to say something about me, do you?

G. I can't see how.

Paul. But the protagonist seems to get his head together in the end—which you can tell before finishing the book, since it hops around in time a lot. And there's some touching stuff about the main character's difficulties with his parents that really resonates with me. It's quite lovely. But enough about me and my readings. I have this vague memory of having promised you that I wouldn't get into any more rants. Hmmm. I guess it's too late to keep that promise now, huh? But I *would* like to hear what's been going on with you.

G. Well, Rabi really *has* seemed to pick out the readings carefully in my case—even though I must say I haven't liked many of them. How can I put this?...I normally resist talking about my personal problems with people I don't know very well. I've had some unpleasantness in my life lately, and I don't really feel like getting into the details with anybody. But these Karen Horney books he recommended seem like they're going to be really helpful to me in working on these issues myself. She seems to have such a comprehensive grasp of what makes people tick. This book, *Our Inner Conflicts*, absolutely blows me away on almost every page. Listen to this:

> The most comprehensive formulation of therapeutic goals is the striving for *wholeheartedness*: to be without pretense, to be emotionally sincere, to be able to put the whole of oneself into one's feelings, one's work, one's beliefs. It can be approximated only to the extent that conflicts are resolved.
>
> These goals are not arbitrary, nor are they valid goals of therapy simply because they coincide with the ideals that wise persons of all times have followed. But the coincidence is not accidental, for these are the elements upon which psychic health rests. We are justified in postulating these goals because they follow logically from a knowledge of the pathogenic factors in neurosis.
>
> Our daring to name such high goals rests upon the belief that human personality can change. It is not only the young child who is pliable. All of us retain the capacity to change, even to change in fundamental ways, as long as we live. This belief is supported by experience.[25]

Paul. I remember liking her *New Ways in Psychoanalysis* in school. And you know what's strange? Our readings seem to be converging a bit. Amazingly, that quote could be in either of my books. And the common vision being expressed does seems true, doesn't it, I mean if you take out all the stuff about inner lube jobs that's in my optimysticism book.

G. It seems true to me, anyway. And I obviously can't speak about your books, but this one certainly isn't a book of platitudes. Horney diagrams all the various ways different personality types handle conflicts, and she discusses in gruesome detail all the consequences that can result from unresolved conflicts. Stuff like anxiety, hopelessness, ineffectuality, sadism. Reading her chapter on how we construct and hide behind idealized images of ourselves and the damage this can do to us is harrowing. At least to someone like me who is aware—vaguely anyway— of engaging in this kind of protective castle building. But I can tell it's not just painful to read; it's helpful too. I think it's a great, great book.

Paul. I'd like to read it sometime. I remember liking her the most of the neo-Freudians we had to read in college, maybe because she was so critical of Freud. But even *her* brand of Freudianism wasn't too popular at the time. We usually concentrated on more narrowly focused stuff. It all seems to me now to have been pretty boring material. How can it not be more important to find out about how we turn ourselves into nutcases and what we can do about reversing that tendency? I wonder how similar Horney's theory about idealized images is to this view put forward by the main character's guru in *Eyeless*:

> 'Really and by nature every man's a unity; but you've artificially transformed the unity into a trinity. One clever man and two idiots—that's what you've made yourself. An admirable manipulator of ideas, linked with a person who, so far as self-knowledge and feeling are concerned, is just a moron; and the pair of you associated with a half-witted body. A body that's hopelessly unaware of all it does and feels, that has no accomplishments, that doesn't know how to use itself or anything else. Two imbeciles and one intellectual. But man is a democracy, where the majority rules. You've got to do something about that majority."[26]

G. Hmmm. That does seem kind of similar to

Horney's view. Maybe our readings *have* moved out of the diametrically opposed stage. One less thing for us to whine about, I guess. Well, we probably should get back, no?

Paul. Right. (They pay and leave.)

III.
Week Three

Monday, 10:00 AM—The Library

Rabi (in his accustomed seat as Paul enters). Hello, Paul. Sit down. How have things been going?

Paul. Oh, up and down. Mostly down.

Rabi. Any sense of what the trouble is?

Paul. I don't know how to put it, exactly. I've read all the books you've recommended pretty closely, and I've tried to follow your meditation instructions. But it all seems wrong to me, somehow.

Rabi. What do you mean?

Paul. Well...I may have said this before, but there seem to be two sorts of results. Either meditating has no effect at all, which kind of bums me out, or I notice that I've begun to feel a bit calmer, which makes me angry.

Rabi. Why angry?

Paul. I have trouble putting this in words, but it just seems wrong. Inauthentic maybe. Isn't that what Camus or Sartre would say about this kind of thing? I mean, look, what if I *can* get myself into alpha state or endorphin country or whatever. I'm not sure I really want to be zoned out in that way. I mean, maybe I'm being more faithful to the actual human condition when I'm ready to bounce off the ceiling like somebody in Sartre's *Nausea*. "Truth is better than illusion." That's the existentialist credo, isn't it? If transience, sickness, old age, and death are the real story behind human existence, is it right for us to get into a state in which we either deny these facts or don't care about them at all? Why should I trust any psychological state that's produced by a mantra-fed abundance of endorphins, anyway? I mean, I wouldn't trust any attitude that sprang from a case of Heineken? What's the difference?

Rabi. If it's all right with you, I'd like to take up the last of your questions—the one about brain chemistry—first, and, if there's time, come back to what might be called your *ethical* questions. Those are the questions involving what we *ought* to believe; whether a placid state is "inauthentic," things of that sort.

Paul. That's fine.

Rabi. The brain chemistry issues are discussed in some detail in William James' wonderful book, *Varieties of Religious Experience*. He called the theory that we ought to be skeptical about this or that belief because of the particular organic state of the believer "medical materialism." And he responds to that theory quite eloquently I think:

> Perhaps the commonest expression of this assumption that spiritual value is undone if lowly origin be asserted is seen in those comments which unsentimental people so often pass on their more sentimental acquaintances. Alfred believes in immortality so strongly because his temperament is so emotional. Fanny's extraordinary conscientiousness is merely a matter of over-instigated nerves. William's melancholy about the universe is due to bad digestion—probably his liver is torpid. Eliza's delight in her church is a symptom of her hysterical constitution....The macerations of saints, and the devotion of missionaries, are only instances of the parental instinct of self-sacrifice gone astray. For the hysterical nun, starving for natural life, Christ is but an imaginary substitute for a more earthly object of affection....
>
> ...Medical materialism finishes up Saint Paul by calling his vision on the road to Damascus a discharging lesion of the occipital cortex, he being an epileptic. It snuffs out Saint Teresa as an hysteric, Saint Francis of Assisi as an hereditary

degenerate. George Fox's discontent with the shams of his age, and his pining for spiritual veracity, it treats as a symptom of a disordered colon....

And medical materialism then thinks that the spiritual authority of all such personages is successfully undermined.

...[But] there is not a single one of our states of mind, high or low, healthy or morbid, that has not some organic process as its condition. Scientific theories are organically conditioned just as much as religious emotions are; and if we only knew the facts intimately enough, we should doubtless see 'the liver' determining the dicta of the sturdy atheist as decisively as it does those of the Methodist under conviction anxious about his soul....

To plead the organic causation of a religious state of mind, then, in refutation of its claim to possess superior spiritual value, is quite illogical and arbitrary, unless one have already worked out in advance some psycho-physical theory connecting spiritual values in general with determinate sorts of physiological change. Otherwise none of our thoughts and feelings, not even our scientific doctrines, not even our *dis*-beliefs, could retain any value as revelations of the truth, for every one of them without exception flows from the state of their possessor's body at the time.

It is needless to say that medical materialism draws in point of fact no such sweeping skeptical conclusion. It is sure, just as every simple man is sure, that some states of mind are inwardly superior to others, and reveal to us more truth, and in this it simply makes use of ordinary spiritual judgments. It has no physiological theory of the production of these its favorite states, by which it may accredit them; and its attempt to discredit the states which it dislikes, by vaguely associating them with nerves and liver, and connecting them with names connoting bodily affliction, is altogether illogical and inconsistent....[27]

Paul. But when was that written, in about 1900?
Rabi. That's right.
Paul. I'm no expert in neurophysiology, but I'm sure we have a better sense today about the likelihood of sensible

beliefs emanating from a beer-soaked brain than they had back then. Hasn't the study of the connection between brain events and psychological states progressed quite a bit since James wrote that?

Rabi. Very possibly, but I don't think any such progress has much bearing on the point James was making. I believe we still don't seek confirmation or disconfirmation of any particular belief by an investigation of any part of the believer's body. I don't see how neurophysiology, even if it ever reached the point where it could somehow be said to map each psychological state to a particular brain state, can ever be expected to find some kind of "mark" within these physical processes, that decisively determines whether or not what is believed is true. I take it that those who administer lie detector tests believe that they can, with some degree of confidence, tell whether a person *believes* what he or she is saying is true by looking at certain physical signs. To my knowledge, however, no one has ever suggested that science will ever be able to tell whether a belief is *actually* true by investigating the believer's nervous system.

Paul. Maybe not. But maybe we can now or will someday be able to tell whether the believer's report is likely to be dependable based on the chemical state of his brain. If we know that psychotics' brains usually have too much...I don't know...say, iodine in them, and Jones' brain is just spilling over with iodine, won't we have reasonable doubts when Jones tells us he can walk through cement walls?

Rabi. I think anyone who has doubts about *anybody* who says he can walk through walls is being reasonable, without doing any testing for iodine. The proposition is unbelievable on its face. We don't need to do any brain investigations.

Paul. Well, not in that case, maybe. But suppose it wasn't an intrinsically crazy statement. Maybe Jones just says something like "I had a cocker spaniel fifty years ago." or "I talked to God yesterday." And there's no empirical way to determine whether these statements are true or not. Wouldn't it then make sense—again assuming that psychotics all have this over-abundance of iodine in their brains—to check Jones' iodine level?

Rabi. Well, here's what James says about that:

> In the natural sciences and industrial arts it never occurs to any one to try to refute opinions by showing up their author's neurotic constitution. Opinions here are invariably tested by logic and by experiment, no matter what may be their author's neurological type. It should be no otherwise with religious opinions. Their value can only be ascertained by spiritual judgments directly passed upon them, judgments based on our own immediate feeling primarily; and secondarily on what we can ascertain of their experiential relations to our moral needs and to the rest of what we hold as true.[28]

Paul. Well, courts of law and legislatures seem to care about these biological matters. They understand that, for example, people shouldn't drive when they're drunk, that they can't generally be trusted to act responsibly when they're high on heroin, and so on.

Rabi. Societies have a good deal of experience with this, don't they?

Paul. Of course.

Rabi. Is there any evidence, so far as you know, of meditators being particularly untrustworthy?

Paul. Only with respect to these mystical reports of being one with God and stuff like that.

Rabi. But I take it that it's not the meditating that makes you doubt the veracity of these claims, but what is being claimed? I mean, other than items about which we *can* have no normal, empirical knowledge, do you have evidence that the reports of meditators, or those in alpha state, or those with high endorphin levels, should be passed off as nonsense?

Paul. I suppose not. I guess it *is* what they're saying that is suspect rather than their state when saying it. If I didn't think these claims were so hard to believe on their face, I wouldn't have any grounds for feeling one way or the other about them. On the other hand, these mystical views don't exactly recommend themselves to common sense, and if they are always being shouted out by people with high levels of endorphins, maybe we eventually learn not to trust the endorphins. Especially if we have independent verification that high endorphin levels always accompany some kind of outward stupor. Let me give a related example. I have a friend who, because of an attack of Krohn's Disease, was forced to spend a couple of weeks in the hospital and was given very high doses of prednisone. At the time of this attack he also suffered from two unrelated abdominal ailments. Neither of those two problems were terminal, and my friend knew that his Krohn's was treatable. Nevertheless, between being very sick for a couple of months and being fed high doses of steroids, he began to be sure that he actually had cancer, but no one would tell him. This wasn't just a suspicion, mind you. He was completely convinced. He was *certain*. When the drugs were stopped, his delusion ended with it. Doesn't it make sense in these cases to say that his conviction was just a result of brain chemistry?

Rabi. Perhaps, but remember, in this case we have independent knowledge that your friend does *not* in fact have cancer. We must be extremely careful about doubting *all* beliefs associated with certain endorphin or steroid or whatever levels simply because of the content of *some* obviously unreasonable beliefs—or beliefs that we independently know to be false—that occur at the same time the levels of such chemicals are high. Remember, each instance in which a true belief occurs simultaneously with high endorphin levels will serve as a powerful counterexample to this theory, and there may turn out to be countless disconfirmations of this kind. In any case, your desire to convict beliefs of falsity based solely on the believer's brain chemistry seems to me to involve a highly convoluted approach to assessing beliefs. Isn't it much more elegant and practical to judge beliefs on their more intrinsic merits and demerits. I think James was right about these matters:

> *Immediate luminousness,* in short, *philosophical reasonableness,* and *moral helpfulness* are the only available criteria. Saint Teresa might have had the nervous system of the placidest cow, and it would not now save her theology, if the trial of the theology by these other tests should show it to be contemptible. And conversely if her theology can stand these other tests, it will make no difference how hysterical or nervously off her balance Saint Teresa may have been when she was with us here below....
>
> Dogmatic philosophies have sought for tests for truth which might dispense us from appealing to the future. Some direct mark, by noting which we can be protected immediately and absolutely, now and forever, against all mistake—such has been the darling dream of philosophic dogmatists. It is clear that the *origin* of the truth would be an admirable criterion of this sort, if only the various origins could be discriminated from one another from this point of view, and the history of dogmatic opinion shows that origin has always been a favorite test. Origin in immediate intuition; origin in pontifical authority; origin in supernatural revelation, as by vision, hearing or unaccountable impression; origin in direct possession by a higher spirit, expressing itself in prophecy and warning; origin in automatic

utterance generally,—these origins have been stock warrants for the truth of one opinion after another which we find represented in religious history. The medical materialists are therefore only so many belated dogmatists, neatly turning the tables on their predecessors by using the criterion of origin in a destructive instead of an accreditive way....[29]

Paul (laughing). Well, I certainly don't want to be classed with the dogmatists! So I guess we're left where we were, and I'm left where I was—stuck with my vague feelings of uneasiness about meditating. Maybe the tranquillity isn't *per se* suspect just because its accompanied by an upsurge in endorphins.

Rabi. If it *is*. We don't even know that yet, do we?

Paul. Well, no, not really. I still think there's a valid argument here, though. Suppose we know independently that people with high levels of some chemical X are more likely to utter falsehoods than people without these levels. Now, I learn people in mystic states also have high doses of X. It seems like even if I can't *convict* the mystical statements of error, I've got enough evidence to *indict*, don't I? Plus, as I said when I first came in, they mostly seem to me to be examples of wishful thinking. If the world is really little more than a horrible joke played on humankind, it's got to be immoral or at least cowardly to avoid facing this fact by lulling ourselves into a kind of half-sleep. At least it seems that way to me.

Rabi. I think I see what you mean, and it's an important point. But I note that if the claims of mystics are intrinsically outrageous or immoral, we're hard pressed to accept them, with or without the X. I'm not sure the chemical investigation really adds much to the critique. And if the tranquillity that—paradoxically—*upsets* you is akin to an inarticulate version of one of these crazy-sounding or unethical claims, it seems clear that you shouldn't accept it without further proof. You don't need any additional chemical analyses to be sensibly skeptical. As James says,

> ...[N]ot its origin, but *the way in which it works on the whole*, is [the] final test of a belief....and this criterion the stoutest insisters on supernatural origin have also been forced to use in the end. Among the visions and messages some have always been too patently silly, among the trances and convulsive seizures some have been too fruitless for conduct and character, to pass themselves off as significant, still less as divine. In the history of Christian mysticism the problem how to discriminate between such messages and experiences as were really divine miracles, and such others as the demon in his malice was able to counterfeit...has always been a difficult one to solve, needing all the sagacity and experience of the best directors of conscience. In the end it had to come to our empiricist criterion: By their fruits ye shall know them, not by their roots.[30]

Paul. I guess I can agree with that and leave my chemical speculations to one side for awhile. But what do I do with my discomfort with your meditation proposals? That's been the main fruit in my own case.

Rabi. I suggest that you continue to think about what you hope to find here at the Center. I suggest also that you reminisce about your happiest, most fulfilling experiences and ponder the question of whether these experiences would have been in some sense better if you had been anxious or, as you say, bouncing off the ceiling, as you had them.

Paul. It does sound kind of silly when you put it that way.

Rabi. Many people who come here tell me they want to learn to accept what they take to be the fact of their mortality with equanimity. I try to help them with this. But if you actually believe that it's preferable, more authentic or—again paradoxically—*less cowardly* to live in a state of fear, a horror movie or a scary book might be more up your alley. I think I have some Poe on the shelf behind you that might serve the purpose.

Paul (laughing). Well, I don't want to be afraid, exactly. It was a nagging fear that brought me here in the first place. But I don't want to be lulled to sleep either. I want to be wide awake and unafraid....at least if you can't prove to me that I'm immortal.

Rabi. I entirely concur with your desire to be wide awake and unafraid. It seems eminently reasonable. I think our main difference is that I don't associate calmness with stupor as you seem to do. As you know, there are many types of meditation, and I think it will do you good to take a look at some books on Zen.

Paul. Oh no. I won't have to describe the sound of one hand clapping, I hope.

Rabi (Laughing). In fact, one of the books I have in mind *is* a book on *koans*. But I think you should focus on the goals—stated or unstated—of the seekers and the descriptions given of their *satori* or enlightenment experiences rather than on the meaning of the koans. As you read, try to keep in mind what these aspirants were searching for as they underwent their years and years of study. And then try to assess what you think the successful monks got out of all this effort. If you can, compare their situations with your own. And maybe take a break from meditating for a few days.

Paul. Got it. I'll let you know how it goes. (Gets up to leave.)

Rabi. Good-bye. Be well.

❦

Monday, 3:00 PM—The Library

Rabi (on one of the book ladders as G enters). Hello, G. I'll be right down. Have a seat.

G. Looking for a book? What have *you* been reading, anyway?

Rabi. Oh, I thought I had something by Thoreau on the *B'havgad Gita*, and I wanted to have a look at it again before recommending it to someone. But now I can't seem to find it.

G. What about your own reading?

Rabi. Well, I love Trollope novels, and I just started *John Caldigate*, but I'm so busy in my work here, that I have little energy left even for recreational reading.

G. I can well imagine.

Rabi (sitting down). And what have you been up to?

G. Well, I'm enjoying the two Horney books very much. She seems very wise to me. I think there's a lot there that I can work on.

Rabi. I'm glad to hear it.

G. But I must say it seems so different from—even contrary to—what I've always thought of as the Eastern approach to the world?

Rabi. Really? How so? You know, Horney herself was quite interested in Buddhism.

G. I didn't know that. Well, my picture is probably all wrong. But isn't there this Hindu stereotype of bald people with little pony tails chanting "Hari Krishna" for hours in airports, trying to, you know, get past what most of us think of as real life. I assumed they believe that anything about their childhoods or their relationships with their parents or whatever was just transient baggage, and we have to somehow become engulfed in Being or Brahman or God or the universal consciousness or something where these mundane things don't matter at all. But Horney wants us to focus an awful lot of attention on stuff that's not, you know, eternal—at least I hope the issues I'm dealing with aren't. Anyhow, don't western psychologists like Horney encourage us to discuss our earthly problems and, if necessary, express our feelings about them in ways that will free us from their power over us? I guess my picture has Freud on one side telling us to uncover all our dirty laundry and a yogi on the other side advising us to let it be, or flow with the Tao or something.

Rabi. Yes, this is a prevalent picture, and I'm not sure it's completely mistaken. But I take a little different view than either of the protagonists in your picture. Suppose we believe the truth of the old saying "Blessed are the pure in heart, for they shall see God." We want to avoid a Catch-22 situation where in order to see God we must first be pure, but in order to become pure we must first see God. So I look for other methods of purification. That's what I take to be the importance of psychotherapy to mysticism. Huxley discusses this issue a bit in his anthology of mystical literature:

> The Perennial Philosophy is primarily concerned with the one, divine Reality substantial to the manifold world of things and lives and minds. But the nature of this one Reality is such that it cannot be directly and immediately apprehended except by those who have chosen to fulfill certain conditions, making themselves loving, pure in heart and poor in spirit. Why should this be so? We do not know. It is just one of those facts which we have to accept, whether we like them or not and however implausible and unlikely they may seem.[31]

Horney attempts to teach us precisely how we can overcome the obstacles to becoming more loving and so on. Without this often grueling initial work, it seems doubtful to me that, at least for most of us, our spiritual quest can get us very far.

G. Ah, another glum prospect to deal with. What a depressing place this can be!

Rabi. Do you think so?

G. So many obstacles, and so little magic! And, to be frank, I'm not really sure that the goal of all this trouble appeals to me that much. It seems so flat, so colorless. There's plenty of meditation and analysis and work, but where are the simple pleasures at the end of the road? Not enlightenment, mind you—I'm sure there's plenty of *that* around, but simple joy. There's a passage in a book by Chesterton I found here the other day that expresses what I mean. Do you mind?

Rabi. Not at all, I'd love to hear it.

G (after finding her book).

> In the round of our rational and mournful year one festival remains out of all those ancient gaieties that once covered the whole earth. Christmas remains to remind us of those ages, whether Pagan or Christian, when the many acted poetry instead of the few writing it. In all the winter in our woods there is no tree in glow but the holly....
>
> Take away the Nicene Creed and similar things, and you do some strange wrong to the sellers of sausages. Take away the strange beauty of the saints, and what has remained to us the far stranger ugliness of Wandsworth. Take away the supernatural, and what remains is the unnatural....
>
> ...let [the sophisticates] be very certain of this, that they are the kind of people who in the time of the maypole would have thought the maypole vulgar; who in the time of the Canterbury pilgrimage would have thought the Canterbury pilgrimage vulgar; who in the time of the Olympian games would have thought the Olympian games vulgar. Nor can there be any reasonable doubt that they were vulgar. Let no man deceive

himself; if by vulgarity we mean coarseness of speech, rowdiness of behaviour, gossip, horseplay, and some heavy drinking, vulgarity there always was wherever there was joy, wherever there was faith in the gods. Wherever you have belief you will have hilarity, wherever you have hilarity you will have some dangers. And as creed and mythology produce this gross and vigorous life, so in its turn this gross and vigorous life will always produce creed and mythology.[32]

Rabi. Well, he makes some interesting empirical claims, but I think at least a couple of them are false.

G. What are they?

Rabi. First, that there can be no joy without mythology. Second, that the common lot of mankind, what he calls the vulgar, are, generally, happy in their mythologies. I mean, they're no doubt happy *with* their myths, in the sense that they get a certain level of comfort from them and they have no wish to be disabused. But I don't think that these mythologies, whatever value they have, have ever been sufficient to make their adherents generally content with their lives. Perhaps in the world's history there have been such cultures. I haven't heard of them, but I'm not an anthropologist, and I haven't studied the matter. In any case, if Chesterton has actual examples, he hasn't given us any. He suggests that there was some idyllic period of paganism or early Christendom, but I'm not sure that the facts will bear him out on that. There has always been a good deal of misery in the world, so far as I know.

G. But what about the first claim, that there can be no real joy without the gods and the magic. That certainly rings true for me. Remove all the supernatural elements and the world just gets flatter, doesn't it?

Rabi. If that's *all* one does, perhaps. These myths must be replaced with *something*, without doubt. Didn't you once mention to me that Meister Eckhardt was the sort of Christian you thought you might learn to emulate here?

G. Uh-oh. I feel another refutation coming.

Rabi (laughing). Oh, I hope that's not what I spend my time doing here, trying to refute my visitors! What a rotten host you must think me! I just wanted to point out that there are a number of Christian mystics who feel that the deepest joy requires a moving beyond all the stories. Let me see if I can find a passage where Eckhardt says that. Here we go. First he says there is a power within us with which we can grasp things, reason and understand. Then he says:

> Whenever this power sees something which is an image, be it the image of an angel or the image of itself, then it does not yet see perfectly. Even if it sees God or how he is an image or a trinity, then it does not see perfectly. But when all images have departed from the soul and it sees single Unity, then the pure being of the soul, passive and resting within itself, encounters the pure formless being of Divine Unity, which is being beyond being. O wonder of wonders!
>
> It does not seek God in so far as he is the Holy Spirit, nor in so far as he is the Son: it flees the Son. Nor does it desire God in so far as he is God. Why? Because there he still has a name. And even if there were a thousand Gods, it would break through continuously, for it desires him where he has no name. It desires something better, something nobler than God, in so far as he has a name.[33]

G. And is there any actual joy for the person who achieves this, or just a feeling of accomplishment, like getting an A on an exam or something?

Rabi. Most mystics, Christian or otherwise. have thought that mystical union is the greatest joy that human beings can ever experience. I myself think so. No doubt

Eckhardt would agree. And certainly Saint Teresa goes into great detail on the subject:

> While seeking God in this way, the soul is conscious that it is fainting almost completely away in a kind of swoon, with a very great calm and joy. Its breath and all its bodily powers progressively fail it, so that it can hardly stir its hands without great effort. Its eyes close involuntarily, and if they remain open, they see almost nothing....The whole physical strength vanishes and the strength of the soul increases for the better enjoyment of its bliss. The outward joy that is now felt is great and most perceptible.
>
> However long this prayer lasts, it does no harm. At least it has never done me any; however ill I might have been when the Lord granted me this grace, I never remember an occasion when I experienced any bad effect from it. On the contrary I was left feeling much better. But what harm can so great a blessing possibly do? The outward results are so evident that there can be no doubt some great thing has taken place. Nothing else could have robbed us of our bodily strength, yet have given us so much joy that it is returned to us increased.[34]

And the Eastern mystics have been just as insistent on the bliss that accompanies their own religious observances. There's even an attempt to quantify it in the Upanishads.

> Of what nature is this joy? Consider the lot of a young man, noble, well-read, intelligent, strong, healthy, with all the wealth of the world at his command. Assume that he is happy, and measure his joy as one unit.
>
> One hundred times that joy is one unit of the joy of Gandharvas has the seer to whom the Self has been revealed, and who is without craving.
>
> One hundred times the joy of Gandharvas is one unit of the joy of celestial Gandharvas: but no less joy than celestial Gandharvas has the sage to whom the Self has been revealed, and who is without craving.
>
> One hundred times the joy of celestial Gandharvas is one unit of the joy of the Pitris in their paradise: but no less joy than the Pitris in their paradise has the sage to whom the Self has

been revealed, and who is without craving.

One hundred times the joy of the Pitris in their paradise is one unit of the joy of the Devas: but no less joy than the Devas has the sage to whom the Self has been revealed, and who is without craving.

One hundred times the joy of the Devas is one unit of the joy of the karma Devas: but no less joy than the karma Devas has the sage to whom the Self has been revealed and who is without craving....[35]

And this admittedly bizarre geometrical progression goes on through the Ruling Devas, Indra, Brihaspati, Prajapati, and Brahma.

G. I have no idea what most of those words mean, but it does seem like somebody's trying to describe a giant heap o' joy, doesn't it?

Rabi. It does. And without attempting to deride Chesterton's practices or beliefs in any way, I would stack such ecstasy against Chesterton's delight in the maypole or the *tennenbaum*—even if we throw in the naïve belief in a jolly, flying Santa Clause. William Penn once said, "There is something nearer to us than Scriptures, to wit, the Word in the heart from which all Scriptures come." He might have added that this Word is nearer to us than fairies too.

G. I just can't help feeling that I want both. The ecstasies and the myths; the tranquillity and the magic.

Rabi. I think, in the end, you will have to choose. But if you can just glimpse nirvana for the briefest moment, the choice will become easy to you. And I would add—though you have correctly pointed out that I've never been a Christian—that the historical Jesus provided by Moore's vision seems to me anything but flat, even without the miracles. Remember this passage where the elderly Jesus tells a dubious Saint Paul about his life during his long, isolated years as a shepherd, the years after he was taken down in a swoon from the Cross?

> For many years, Paul, there were no thoughts in my mind, or they were kept back, or I was without a belief; but thought returned to my desolate mind as the spring returns to these hills; and the next step in my advancement was when I began to understand that we may not think of God as a man who would punish men for doing things they have never promised not to do, or recompense them for denying themselves things they never promised to forgo. Soon after I began to comprehend that the beliefs of our forefathers must be abandoned, and that if we would arrive at any reasonable conception of God, we must not put a stint upon him. And as I wandered with my sheep he became in my senses not without but within the universe, part and parcel, not only of the stars and the earth, but of me, yea, even of my sheep on the hillside. All things are God, Paul: thou art God and I am God, but if I were to say thou art man and I am God, I should be the madman that thou believest me to be....The pursuit of an incorruptible crown leads us to sin as much as the pursuit of a corruptible crown. [36]

G. Well, let me think about—I guess I should say "meditate on"—all this and report back. As usual, you've left me with a lot to chew on.

Rabi. See you next time then.

Tuesday, 8:30 PM—The Library

G (entering, sees Paul reading intently at a table, quietly sneaks up and startles him by dropping her armful of books down next to him).

Paul. Aaah! You scared me!

G. Think of it as a Zen experience.

Paul. Shouldn't you yell "Wu!" at the same time, or whack me with a brick or something?

G. Wu!

Paul. That did it! I finally see it all! I understand!

G. Bah! If I had a brick I'd hit you with it now.

Paul (sheepishly). That's because you know that I really haven't seen the whole *it* and, in reality, I don't understand a single thing, right?

G. Exactly, and you have to spend at least 20 more years sitting cross-legged and concentrating on "Wu!" before I'll consider your enlightenment claims again. Plus you have to read one thousand self-help books.

Paul. I think I'd rather get hit by a brick.

G. Sorry, my mind's made up.

Paul. In that case, I think I should hear about your own spiritual development and come up with an equally horrific prescription for you.

G. Well, Rabi's one step ahead of you there: yesterday he told me I have to give up Santa Clause.

Paul. Really?

G. Yeah, he said it was up to me to choose, but that mysticism was better than any old flying fat man .

Paul. I pity you. I just went through this Santa thing with my daughter a couple of months ago, and it was awful—for me anyway.

G. What happened?

Paul. Well, Kelsey's seven, so most of her friends either have no doubts at all about Santa Clause or never express them, and it was the middle of Spring, so I don't know what made her think of it, but completely out of the blue she asked me if it wasn't really the parents that put all those toys in the stockings at Christmas.

G. Yikes. What did you say?

Paul. I was totally unprepared. The first thing I did was ask her why she thought that.

G. And?

Paul. She said that while some of her friends had said they heard Santa on Christmas Eve, it seemed like nobody had ever seen him. Then she reminded me that I'd promised to never lie to her, and she asked me point blank whether Laura and I had bought the new sled for her and the other stuff we'd said had been from Santa.

G. And you told her?

Paul. Yeah. I guess I panicked. I was heartbroken about it too. I figured she had at least another year or two to get excited about the reindeer and the cookies and milk and all that stuff. I just didn't know what else to say. I know Laura thinks I blew it, and I probably did.

G. Well, I suppose Kelsey had to find out eventually. Did she seem upset about it?

Paul. More confused, really. She's gotten so much conflicting information about Santa Claus from books and movies and things that people have said to her that she doesn't really know what to think about this anymore. It's just another growing up milestone, I suppose....I hate them all so much. I never want to lie to her about anything, but there's so much I don't want her to know about the world too. I just want to protect her from everything ugly. So I somehow manage to make a hash of everything....It's probably better for her that I'm not living with her very much anymore.

G. I can't believe that's true.

Paul. Well let me give you another example. Last year on Martin Luther King Day, the kids in her class heard about King's "I have a dream" speech and were asked what dream they have for the world. Kelsey said "I have a dream that everyone stays young." I know she's getting that kind of fear from me.

G. It doesn't sound like such a bad dream to me. Anyway, since you're the one who told her about Santa Claus you can't be accused of trying to keep her too sheltered from truths about the world. So many parents try to keep that going until their kids are in their teens.

Paul. I don't know. Maybe. But I have this sense that I'm inculcating in her the same kind of life-fears I have. Aging and separation already seem to be issues for her. She seems to want to hug her childhood fantasies so tight they can never get away from her....It's the same way I want to hug her.

G. That's not unusual, is it? Aren't most children her age afraid of being separated from their parents and other things that make them feel safe, like their stuffed animals or dolls? And it's not just kids. I mean, Rabi's been chastising me for wanting to hang onto what he thinks is the same sort of magical view of the world that you wanted to keep for Kelsey just for another year or two. I must say, though, that I'm not too comfortable with the idea of comparing The Resurrection with Rudolph's red nose. And I'm not sure it's a fair comparison either. Obviously, the Santa story is intended for children: it's a fairy tale. But Christianity has provided solace to millions of adults for centuries—some pretty smart adults too. There's magic and then there's magic.

Paul. So he's taken some shots at Jesus too?

G. Well, he's comfortable with some kind of Unitarianism, I think. I mean, Christianity is OK with him as long as there are no miracles involved. But to me, that kind of Christianity isn't really a religion, it's something else. A philosophy maybe, or a scientific theory.

Paul. Like utilitarianism. Or maybe like the code of conduct people pick up when they join the Marines.

G. Right. One of the books I've read since I came here—actually this is a book I'd read years ago too—is C.S. Lewis' *Mere Christianity*. Lewis says this about Rabi's position:

> I am trying here to prevent anyone saying the really foolish thing that people often say about [Jesus]: 'I'm ready to accept Jesus as a great moral teacher, but I don't accept His claim to be God.' That is the one thing we must not say. A man who was merely a man and said the sort of things Jesus said would not be a great moral teacher. He would either be a lunatic—on a level with the man who says he is a poached egg—or else he would be Devil of Hell. You must make your choice. Either this man was, and is, the Son of God: or else a madman or something worse. You can shut Him up for a fool, you can spit at Him and kill Him as a demon; or you can fall at His feet and call Him Lord and God. But let us not come with any patronising nonsense about His being a great human teacher. He has not left that open to us. He did not intend to.[37]

It's not that I'm some kind of Bible-belt literalist. I'm really not sure what I believe at all. It's just that I don't like being put in the position of being told that I have to be convinced that Jesus was completely nuts—and that many of my closest relatives and friends are too—or I'm doomed to a life of meaningless despair.

Paul: Well, if it's any consolation, he won't leave me alone with my skepticism either. It's his way or the highway. As you know, I'm pretty agnostic about almost everything, but I have to say that your traditional Christianity is more comprehensible to me than most of Rabi's mystical pronouncements: at least I can tell what's being asserted without having to figure out what the hell "Wu!" means. Zillions of people have agreed on the basic tenets of

Christianity. With a lot of this mystical stuff, you can never tell if any two adherents are saying the same things. So much of it seems like complete gibberish. He seems to think your religion contains too much hocus-pocus, but he ought to be able to understand your desire to have something to hold on to. I mean does he want you to pray to your breath?

G. You know, it isn't so much the non-Christian aspect of all this that bothers me: like I said, I'm not particularly orthodox. It's partly the...*peculiarity* of it...whether it's Christians doing it or not. I mean, did you ever read *Franny and Zooey*?

Paul. Sure. Didn't everybody?

G. Well, Rabi seems to be pushing the same type of religion that appealed to Franny. Wait a minute, I've got it here. Remember, she's talking to this preppy date of hers at dinner, and she's trying, in her earnest, but somehow still always condescending, all-knowing, Salingerian way, to explain mysticism:

'[T]he pilgrim—this simple peasant—started the whole pilgrimage to find out what it means in the Bible when it says you're supposed to pray without ceasing. And then he meets this starets—this very advanced religious person....Well, the starets tells him about the Jesus Prayer first of all. "Lord Jesus Christ, have mercy on me." I mean that's what it is. And he explains to him that those are the best words to use when you pray. Especially the word "mercy," because it's such a really enormous word and can mean so many things. I mean it doesn't just have to mean *mercy*....[T]he starets tells the pilgrim that if you keep saying that prayer over and over again—you only have to just do it with your *lips* at first—then eventually what happens, the prayer becomes self-active. Something *happens* after a while. I don't know what, but something happens, and the words get synchronized with the person's heartbeats, and then you're actually praying without ceasing. Which has a really tremendous, mystical effect on your whole outlook. I mean that's the whole *point* of it, more or less. I mean you do it to purify your whole outlook and get an absolutely new conception of what everything's about....

'But the marvelous thing is, when you first start doing it, you don't even have to have *faith* in what you're doing. I mean even if you're terribly embarrassed about the whole thing, it's perfectly all right. I mean you're not *insulting* anybody or anything. In other words, nobody asks you to believe a single thing when you first start out. You don't even have to think about what you're saying, the starets said. All you have to have in the beginning is quantity. Then later on, it becomes quality by itself. On its own power or something. He says that any name of God—any name at all—has this self-active power of its own, and it starts working after you've sort of started it up....

'As a matter of fact, that makes absolute sense...because in the Nembutsu sects of Buddhism, people keep saying "Namu Amida Butsu" over and over again—which means "Praises to the Buddha" or something like that—and the *same thing* happens.

'...The same thing happens in "The Cloud of Unknowing" too. Just with the word "God"....I mean the point is did you ever hear anything so fascinating in your *life*, in a way? I mean it's so hard to just say it's absolute coincidence and then just let it go at that—that's what's so fascinating to me.

'...Even in India. In India they tell you to meditate on the "Om," which means the same thing, really, and the exact same result is supposed to happen....

'You get to see God. Something happens in some absolutely nonphysical part of the heart—where the Hindus say that Atman resides, if you ever took any Religion—and you see God, that's all.'[38]

Paul. Are you telling me that Franny Glass is our guru's guru?

G. It sure seems like it to me. And the problem is, I don't really like Franny. I've never sympathized with her—in spite of her extremely obnoxious date that night. And I find her religion worse than magical. It's not only weird, it's weak somehow, needy.

Paul. Doesn't the story end up with her fainting in the middle of the restaurant or something?

G. Right. She comes off as nervous and sickly more than anything else—except maybe superior. I don't want to be like her. I'd rather believe in Santa like her supercilious boyfriend.

Paul. You mentioned Franny being needy. You know, Rabi told me that he thought my suggestion that mysticism was cowardly was paradoxical. When he accused me of preferring nervousness to tranquillity it seemed like it was his view that being fearless is always less cowardly than being afraid. I didn't think of it then, but Plato has this dialogue where he distinguishes the absence of fear from courage. In fact, Plato thought that in order to be really courageous, you *have* to be afraid.

G. Because complete lack of fear might just be stupid?

Paul. Right. It's just foolhardy to be unafraid of, say, military combat or an on-rushing bully, but brave, apprehensive people will fight anyway. Maybe I was trying to tell him that I'd rather learn to be brave than to be entirely free from fear.

G. I don't really know what I want. Sometimes, when Rabi is talking, I tune him out completely so his voice becomes a pretty background. Once, the hymn "Tis a Gift To Be Simple" popped into my mind, and I focused on the sound of his voice until it almost sounded as if he were singing it. I felt then that that kind of familiarity was what was missing. You know, the church dinners and common prayers and good deeds in the community. I've grown to respect Rabi, even like him, and I think I've learned some valuable things in just the two weeks we've been here. But, as you can tell, his anti-Christian bias is getting to me.

Especially if the alternative is endlessly mouthing "mercy" with Franny.

Paul (laughing)....while lying on the floor of a fancy restaurant. Look, I don't see why you shouldn't have your magic. The world is a tough—to me, horrifying—place. If you need a person to pray to, a person who can actually hear your prayers and who you believe has the power to cure the sick and raise the dead, I don't see the harm. It's beautiful, in fact.

G (annoyed). C'mon, Paul, what is this? How old do you think I am, anyway?

Paul. What do you mean? I'm just agreeing with you that there's an importance to our sense of wonder about things like Bible stories.

G. I...It's....Oh, shit.

Paul. What is it? What's wrong?

G. Look, I can see what's happening here. You're just using this as a chance to make up for how you think you failed with Kelsey on Santa Claus. Maybe if you can help little G keep some magic in her world—even if it involves stuff that you think any really intelligent grown-up would snicker at—you'll have made things even. Listen, I'm not seven, I'm big now. And I'm not interested in your helping me conserve what you think are my fantasies or in your trying to protect me from a world that obviously scares you to death. Maybe you should....Oh, never mind....I better just go now. See you.

(Paul stands up as G quickly leaves. Then he sits back down, but he closes the book he was reading when G arrived and stares out the window.)

IV.
Week Six

Wednesday, 10 AM—The Library

Rabi (in his accustomed chair as Paul enters). Ah, Paul! How are you this fine morning?

Paul. Pretty well, thanks.

Rabi. I see you've brought some books.

Paul. Yeah. I had a few questions about a couple of books I've been reading over the weekend. I was wondering if we could talk about them today.

Rabi. Of course. What are the books?

Paul. W.T. Stace's *Mysticism and Philosophy* and Sartre's *Nausea*. I've brought you extra copies of them. (He hands them over.) OK, why are you smiling?

Rabi. Oh, it's just that I haven't looked at the Stace in so many years, and he seems to have been such an odd duck. As I remember that book, Stace argues that the experiences reported by mystics provide some kind of proof—even for non-mystics—of a Hegelian Absolute. Identity-in-difference and all that sort of obscure stuff.

Paul. Well, I was drawn by the title, and I have to admit that I liked coming across a book that at least nods in the direction of philosophical rigor. I guess I came to expect that in graduate school. But I agree that the book has a lot of weaknesses.

Rabi. Arguments and proofs. Proofs and arguments and more proofs. To me it seems such a waste of time.

Paul. Come on, Rabi. In spite of your protestations to the contrary, you haven't seemed so averse to philosophical argument during my sessions.

Rabi. I don't deny that it's important to try to be clear regarding what one is talking about. Philosophy is certainly useful in helping us steer clear of muddles and contradictions. But philosophical proofs of God or immortality or dualism or whatever seem to me so....well, let's say the whole notion strikes me as extremely peculiar. But maybe this attitude just reflects an Eastern prejudice of mine.

Paul. Or a Wittgensteinian one!

Rabi. Maybe so. Maybe so. In any case, what did you want to talk about in the Stace?

Paul. There are a couple of things, actually. First, there's what he calls his "Principle of Causal Indifference." It's on page 29:

> The principle of causal indifference is this: If X has an alleged mystical experience P_1 and Y has an alleged mystical experience P_2, and if the the phenomenological characteristics of P_1 entirely resemble the phenomenological characteristics of P_2 so far as can be ascertained from the descriptions given by X and Y, then the two experiences cannot be regarded as being of two different kinds—for example, it cannot be said that one is a "genuine" mystical experience while the other is not—merely because they arise from dissimilar causal conditions.[39]

I was wondering first whether this principle seems true to you. And second, I was curious how it relates to the medical materialism stuff in William James we were talking about a couple of weeks ago.

Rabi. Well, based on what you've just read and assuming the ordinary, commonsense meaning of the word "genuine" it seems wrong to me. But maybe we should read on a bit to see if Stace clarifies what he's getting at:

> The principle seems logically self-evident....It is introduced

here because it is sometimes asserted that mystical experiences can be induced by drugs, such as mescalin, lysergic acid, etc. On the other hand, those who have achieved mystical states as a result of long and arduous spiritual exercises, fasting and prayer, or great moral efforts, possibly spread over many years, are inclined to deny that a drug can induce a "genuine" mystical experience, or at least to look askance at such practices and such a claim. Our principle says that *if* the phenomenological descriptions of the two experiences are indistinguishable, so far as can be ascertained, then it cannot be denied that if one is a genuine mystical experience the other is also. This will follow notwithstanding the lowly antecedents of one of them, and in spite of the understandable annoyance of an ascetic, a saint, or a spiritual hero, who is told that his careless and worldly neighbour, who never did anything to deserve it, has attained to mystical consciousness by swallowing a pill.[40]

I must say, I'm still confused by this. His principle seems to make sense only if we give an interpretation to the word "genuine" that's different from what most of us usually mean by it. If he's saying that the *intrinsic* merits of two subjectively identical mystical experience are the same no matter what their separate causes, I can find no fault with it. But any other sense of "genuine"—including the normal one—and his principle seems to me false. Surely there can be two intrinsically identical perceptual experiences—say, of apparently seeing a dog—but we later find out that only one of them was genuine or real or, as the philosophers say, *veridical*. And I think we might say of the veridical experience that it's "genuineness" was in fact a function of it in some sense being *caused* by light bouncing off an actual dog and hitting the perceiver's eyes. So, where Stace says that genuineness can't have anything at all to do with causal conditions, he must not be talking about genuineness in the sense of corresponding with the world outside the mystic's head: he must just mean it in the sense of having certain *intrinsic* merits—and not be talking about whether the experience is veridical or not. For example, your joy can be as deep or as great as my joy regardless of what caused either of our emotions: in that sense we might say they are equally genuine. Now, as to your question about the similarities of Stace's principle with James' critique of medical materialism, I think Stace intended to be making a statement of the same general kind, but he puts it so confusingly that it's hard to be sure. James was talking about what should count as evidence for or against the truth of some idea, its correspondence with the actual world. He argued that certain types of causal conditions, those he called "medical," shouldn't count as evidence one way or the other. I think James would agree with Stace that the "medical" or bodily background of the experiencer also doesn't influence the *genuineness* of the experience in the sense of its purely intrinsic merits, but James' contention is more interesting and more controversial. On the other hand, James' view seems to me to have the benefit of not being obviously false, as Stace's principle seems to be if we take "genuine" in the commonsense way of meaning "true". I mean it's very hard to believe that the investigation of *every* causal condition—not just the "medical" ones—is entirely irrelevent to the question of whether someone's experience corresponds with reality. It's customary, for example, to look for signs of a dog—say footprints—if there's a dispute regarding whether or not one's apparent perception of a dog was veridical....Does that answer your questions? I'm sorry if I'm being abstruse.

Paul. Not at all. I think you've answered my questions, yes. I couldn't make much sense of Stace's causal indifference principle. It seemed flat wrong. And it also seemed similar enough to what James was saying to make *that* seem wrong too. But I guess we *can* interpret "genuine" in the way you described and come up with something easier to defend.

Rabi. Exactly. The problem is, it's *too* easy to defend. It's trivial. I think it's hard to imagine anyone denying that, for example, two experiences that seem to be of bright lights could give equally "blinding" feelings of brightness whatever their disparate causes. It's just that most of us would say that any of these experiences that weren't somehow caused by actual lights don't deserve the title of "genuine," regardless of any intrinsic similarities they may have to the real thing.

Paul (laughing). Boy, it's a good thing you don't care for philosophy or these sessions could get pretty abstract!

Rabi (laughing). Well, let me plead in my defense that I think it's really the Staces of the world who make things so much more complicated than they need to be. In fact it seems to me that such people suffer from an almost desperate need for proofs. When I was at University I had a weakness for Spinoza. As you know, he was the king, one might say, the Imperial Emperor of proofs. Imagine, an entire universe described as if it were a geometry problem! No *maya* infects his crystalline world. The more closely I studied his *Ethics*, however, the greater the number of his arguments that I couldn't get to work: so many ended up seeming fallacious to me. At first, I was crestfallen, but I came to understand that it's possible to get beyond this need for logical certitude.

Paul. Well, I don't see the use of logic or math or other scientific tools as a sign of some kind of psychological deficiency, but I do think we've found *something* that you and I can agree completely on: Stace's proof of the truth of mysticism seems completely bogus to me too. I wanted to see if you agreed, and I'm kind of relieved that you do.

Rabi. Yes, I think we can agree on that. I'm fairly certain that I won't have much more use for it today than I did thirty years ago. But, out of curiosity, would you remind me of the rest of it? Can you paraphrase his argument or is there a simple statement of it somewhere in his book?

Paul. Well, first he spends a lot of time filtering out from all these reports he's read of mystical experiences throughout history those that he wants to count as authentic examples. He tosses out the others as untypical or lacking in something that he feels is important to honest-to-goodness mysticism. Then, he puts together a list of the essential qualities of what he considers *bona fide* mystical experiences, focusing on the quality of what he calls "undifferentiation" as the most important. So, for Stace, experiences in which everything kind of melts into everything else—where nothing is individually identifiable from anything else—are the real prizes of the mysticism storehouse. And I think he believes assertions of ineffability are also key. Then he tells us that the test of the objectivity of any experience is whether it displays "orderliness": you know, whether it's internally coherent and fits in nicely with other experiences that people have. With this ammunition in hand, he's off to the races. This is from page 144:

> Mystical experiences are of course parts of the natural order in the same sense in which dreams and hallucinations are so. They have their causes and effects, and it is an objective fact that this man at this time and at this place has a dream or an hallucination or a mystical experience. But to discover whether an experience of any kind is subjective in the sense in which a dream is subjective, or objective in the sense in which a veridical

sense perception is objective, we have to look at the internal content of the experience to see whether, either in itself or in its relations to what lies outside its boundaries, it is orderly or disorderly. Now if we apply this test to the...mystical experience we find that it cannot be subjective for precisely the same reason which shows that it cannot be objective. It cannot be disorderly within its own boundaries as would be a dream of a kettle of water freezing when put on the fire. For there are no distinguishable items within it to constitute sequences which are contrary to the constant conjunctions in the world order. For the same reason it cannot conflict with the natural order in its external relations, for this too requires that specifiable items within the experience should conflict with items outside it—as for instance being in London in my dream conflicts with being in bed in America without traversing the intevening distance. But there are no items within the [mystical] experience which could conflict with anything outside it. It follows from these considerations that it is not subjective.[41]

Rabi. Stace seems to absolutely relish in using terms differently from everybody else—or at least every non-philosopher. Suppose that instead of leaning on philosophy words like "subjective" he just used something like "possibly inaccurate or wrong." Wouldn't it seem exceedingly odd for someone to say something like "I have an idea of the world that can't possibly be wrong because in my idea everything is undifferentiated from everything else." Is Stace suggesting that this person's idea wouldn't be wrong even if we knew that in the actual world items *are* distinguishable from one another? So far, his argument seems completely puerile to me, but perhaps I'm missing something. Let's press on.

Paul. It only gets worse, I'm afraid. On page 150 he says this:

If we...abstract from bodily differences, it seems clear to

me that there is only one circumstance which distinguishes one mind from another, namely that each has a different stream of consciousness or, what amounts to the same thing, a different stream of experiences. Over any given period of time the sensations, images, emotions, and thoughts which constitute *A*'s inner biography will be different from those which constitute *B*'s inner biography....And this, so far as I can see, is the *only* thing which distinguishes any one mind from any other. In other words, minds are distinguished from one another by their empirical contents and by nothing else. It follows that if *A* and *B* have suppressed within themselves all empirical contents then there is left nothing whatever which can distinguish them and make them two; and if *A* and *B* have thereby reached the mystical consciousness of their pure egos, then there is nothing to distinguish them or make them two pure egos.

If we make use of the philosopher's distinction between the pure ego and the empirical ego, then what follows from this argument is that there exists a multiplicity of empirical egos in the universe, but that there can be only one pure ego. Hence the mystic who has reached what seems at first to be his own private pure ego has in fact reached the pure ego of the universe, the pure cosmic ego.

There *is* therefore a universal cosmic self with which the mystic makes contact and with which he becomes identified....[T]he fact that self-transcendence is a part of the experience itself is the reason why the mystic is absolutely certain of its truth beyond all possibility of arguing him out of it. An interpretation of any experience can be doubted, but the experience itself is indubitable. This is not only the psychological explanation of the mystic's feeling of certainty, it is also a logical justification of it. [42]

Rabi. I'm afraid I don't know where to begin. I agree with his psychological claims regarding the mystic's feelings of certainty, and I also agree with his belief that these feelings are important, that they ought not to be ignored any more than our certainty with respect to the existence of durable physical objects or other minds ought to be ignored. But his "proof" seems to me to be little more than sophistry. I can't believe that anyone could ever be convinced by this sort of thing, and I find it difficult to imagine Stace himself believing that he might gain a single convert in this fashion. Wouldn't you think providing as solid a footing for mysticism as we have in our everyday beliefs in ordinary physical objects or in other sentient individuals would be enough for a philosopher? But no, Stace obviously feels the need to concoct a position according to which some kind of monistic mysticism isn't just true, it's logically necessary!

Paul. But his argument isn't only misguided in its aim, is it? It's also just wrong. Fallacious. I mean, it seems to me to depend on the theory—it's called "the identity of indiscernibles"—that where you might at first think you have two separate objects, where "they" have every single one of their properties in common, you must really have only *one* object: the *they* is really a single *it*. That's the theory, and it's wrong. I mean, I think it's just false that two separate objects can't have all their properties in common without being identical. I don't see why the experiences of mystic *A* and mystic *B* couldn't have all their properties in common without still being two separate experiences.

Rabi. You may well be right about that. I don't know whether or not indiscernible objects must be identical. But there isn't any relevant sense in which these two experiences have all their properties in common anyway. Let's take a concrete example. Suppose you and I both have what we think is the experience of seeing a Scottish Terrier and that there's nothing intrinsic to these experiences to distinguish them on that basis. It could still be the case that your experience was brought about by the presence of a particular dog, while mine resulted from eating too much curry. Furthermore, your experience has the property of being part of *your* life in New York and my experience has the somewhat different property of being part of *my* life here in Vermont. The *content* of these perceptual experiences might be the same, but that isn't sufficient for us to claim that the experiences themselves—these two events occurring at separate places and times—are identical. Remember, one has a real dog as its object, the other doesn't, and one intimately involves *you*, the other *me*. These are real differences. There are mental events; there are the *contents* of those events and, sometimes, there are *objects* of those events. Stace concentrates on what he takes to be identity of experiential *content* and tries to derive the identity not only of the objects of these experiences but also, ultimately, the identity of the experiencers. I would hate to be dependent on such insubstantial bubbles of argument for my feelings of well-being. I admit, however, that in the mystical literature both of the East and the West, there is is a widespread tendency to confuse mental acts with their contents or their objects or both. This goes back at least as far as the *Upanishads* discourses regarding *OM* not just perfectly symbolizing a mysterious presence but also *being it*. It also shows up in the Western *Testaments*, for example in the pronouncement that the Word *is* God. There's been a tremendous amount of literature, both Eastern and Western, on how the *logos* can be thought of as being not only God and the world, but also the idea of these apparently disparate things. One only needs to have some kind of Hegelian or otherwise idealist picture of reality. But I wonder to what extent that entire edifice has simply grown out of a confusion of mental acts, their contents and their objects. In any case, Stace seems not to have been immune from this equivocation as late as 1960.

Paul. I agree completely. It's all rubbish. But I'd go one step further.

Rabi. Please.

Paul. Well, the group of experiences that Stace chooses as what he calls the "universal core" of mysticism—it's just artificial. He simply picks those experiences that support the conclusions he's interested in reaching and discards all the others, or those aspects of the others that don't support those conclusions. I want to contrast one of the reports of mystical experiences he relies on with examples from another tradition of mystical reports. We could call it the "fear and trembling" tradition if you want to. I think it's nearly as rich a literary tradition, and it seems to me to support a wildly different vision of the universe. Here's the Stace example. It's from an essay by a woman called Margaret Prescott Montague who wrote it while convalescing after surgery.

> Entirely unexpectedly (for I had never dreamed of such a thing) my eyes were opened and for the first time in my life I caught a glimpse of the ecstatic beauty of reality...its unspeakable joy, beauty, and importance....I saw no new thing but I saw all the usual things in a miraculous new light—in what I believe is their true light....I saw...how wildly beautiful and joyous, beyond any words of mine to describe, is the whole of life. Every human being moving across that porch, every sparrow that flew, every branch tossing in the wind was caught in and was part of the whole mad ecstasy of loveliness, of joy, of importance, of intoxication of life....I *saw* the actual loveliness which was always there....My heart melted out of me in a rapture of love and delight.... Once out of all the grey days of my life I have looked into the heart of reality; I have witnessed the truth.[43]

Rabi. That's lovely, isn't it?

Paul. I suppose so, but I've read so much stuff like that

over the last month that it's kind of blending together into a mystical undifferentiated blob.

Rabi (laughing). And you'd like to contrast this manifestation of the blob with a different version?

Paul. Right. That's where Sartre's *Nausea* comes in. Listen to these entries from the narrator's diary:

> Objects should not *touch* because they are not alive. You use them, put them back in place, you live among them: they are useful, nothing more. But they touch me, it is unbearable. I am afraid of being in contact with them as though they were living beasts. Now I see: I recall better what I felt the other day at the seashore when I held the pebble. It was a sort of sweetish sickness. How unpleasant it was! It came from the stone, I'm sure of it, it passed from the stone to my hand. Yes, that's it, that's just it—a sort of nausea in the hands.
>
> When I was little, my Aunt Bigeois told me 'If you look at yourself too long in the mirror, you'll see a monkey.' I must have looked at myself even longer than that: what I see is well below the monkey, on the fringe of the vegetable world, at the level of jellyfish. It is alive, I can't say it isn't...I see a slight tremor, I see the insipid flesh blossoming and palpitating with abandon. The eyes especially are horrible seen so close. They are glassy, soft, blind, red-rimmed, they look like fish scales.
>
> Then the Nausea seized me, I dropped to a seat, I no longer knew where I was; I saw the colours spin slowly around me, I wanted to vomit. And since that time, the Nausea has not left me, it holds me.[44]

See? The emotional residue can stick with you just like the life-changing experiences of the religious converts James talks about. But there's more:

> The Nausea is not inside me: I feel it *out there* in the wall, in the suspenders, everywhere around me. It makes itself one with the café, I am the one who is with *it*.

Rabi. Ah, there's what some people call the *noetic* aspect of mystical experience—the certainty that it's capturing something about the world and not just something about the mystic.

Paul. Exactly! And there are a couple of other excerpts I want to read:

> ...[W]ithout formulating anything clearly, I understood that I had found the key to Existence, the key to my Nauseas, to my own life. In fact, all that I could grasp beyond that returns to this fundamental absurdity. Absurdity: another word; I struggle against words; down there I touched the thing. But I wanted to fix the absolute character of this absurdity here. A movement, an event in the tiny coloured world of men is only relatively absurd: by relation to the accompanying circumstances. A madman's ravings, for example, are absurd in relation to the situation in which he finds himself, but not in relation to his delirium. But...[t]his root—there was nothing in relation to which it was absurd. Oh, how can I put it in words? Absurd: in relation to the stones, the tufts of yellow grass, the dry mud, the tree, the sky, the green benches. Absurd, irreducible; nothing—not even a profound secret upheaval of nature—could explain it.
>
> This moment was extraordinary. I was there, motionless and icy, plunged in a horrible ecstasy. But something fresh had just appeared in the very heart of this ecstasy; I understood the Nausea, I possessed it....The essential thing is contingency. I mean that one cannot define existence as necessity. To exist is simply *to be there*; those who exist let themselves be encountered, but you can never deduce anything from them. I believe there are people who have understood this. Only they tried to overcome this contingency by inventing a necessary, causal being. But no necessary being can explain existence: contingency is not a delusion, a probability which can be dissipated; it is the absolute, consequently, the perfect free gift.[45]

Rabi. Sartre certainly is the anti-Stace, isn't he? You've done an excellent job highlighting their differences.

Paul. But I don't see this as just a problem for Stace. Sartre makes a claim for these experiences as part of the mysticism's "universal core." Other than landing on Absurdity rather than the Absolute or God or *Brahman*, I don't see what can be the basis for excluding these as authentic representatives of mystical experience. But let me just get in a couple of more diary entries.

Rabi. Please.

> The trees floated. Gushing towards the sky? Or rather a collapse; at any instant I expected to see the tree-trunks shrivel like weary wands, crumple up, fall on the ground in a soft, folded, black heap. *They did not want* to exist, only they could not help themselves. So they quietly minded their own business; the sap rose up slowly through the structure, half reluctant, and the roots sank slowly into the earth. But at each instant they seemed on the verge of leaving everything there and obliterating themselves. Tired and old, they kept on existing, against the grain, simply because they were too weak to die, because death could only come to them from the outside....Every existing thing is born without reason, prolongs itself out of weakness and dies by chance.
>
> ...[T]he World was everywhere, in front, behind. There had been nothing *before* it. Nothing. There had never been a moment in which it could not have existed. That was what worried me: of course there was no *reason* for this flowing lava to exist. *But it was impossible* for it not to exist. It was unthinkable: to imagine nothingness you had to be there already, in the midst of the World, eyes wide open and alive; nothingness was only an idea in my head, an existing idea floating in this immensity: this nothingess had not come *before* existence, it was an existence like any other and appeared after many others.[46]

Rabi. Thank you for that. I'd forgotten how beautifully written that book is. I note, though, that in one of the quotes he focuses on the contingency of everything, while in this last one, he seems to be saying that it would have been impossible for anything that exists not to have existed.

Paul. Yeah. I noticed that too. I was wondering if he was talking about the contingency of the actual thing in the first quote and just the impossibility of *knowing* that it didn't exist in the second quote. You know, the thing wouldn't have been around for anyone to know *anything* about it if it didn't exist, so it's weird to talk about the possibility of *it* not existing. Anyhow, it seems like Sartre might have been involved in some kind of confusion between ontology and epistemology or something like that with those two quotes.

Rabi. Perhaps. Maybe one has to get through *Being And Nothingness* to understand what's going on there.

Paul. Ah, yes: Sartre's widely unread classic about the being of nothingness and the nothingness of being nothingness's being. Or is it the nothingness of being being? I've looked at a few pages of that book, and I think I'll pass....But, leaving his apparent contradiction about contingency aside, aren't you concerned about the consequences of Sartre's whole negative approach to mystical experience? Do you deny that it blows up the whole notion that there's something not only knowledge-giving, but *wonderful* about mystical experience?

Rabi. Yes. I deny it.

Paul. But I don't see how it's possible. What makes Saint Teresa's experience believable and Sartre's unbelievable.

Rabi. They're both believable, though I admit that they can't both be true if they're inconsistent.

Paul. Then why believe one rather than the other?

Rabi. Well, since these sorts of experiences generally seem infused with a kind of indubitability, I suppose one will believe whichever experience one has.

Paul. But don't you see that this equality of footing between the "fear-and-trembling" tradition and that of the Eastern and other mystics means the end of mysticism as an exclusively religious tradition? To me, it seems like the whole thing just comes tumbling down.

Rabi. I'm sorry. I don't see that at all. Different people have always believed different things and no doubt always will.

Paul. But the special authority some people...well, *you* for example...grant to mystical experiences....If equally authoritative experiences have exactly opposite conclusions, doesn't the whole mystical enterprise descend into uselessness? I mean, once you can just flip a coin between two interpretations of legitimately authoritative experiences shouldn't we just admit that we're not getting any real evidence of anything at all and stop the whole charade?

Rabi. Oh, you're going much too fast for me here, Paul. I don't see how this follows at all. For example, I haven't seen yet that the experiences actually *are* inconsistent: maybe just the descriptions of them are.

Paul. Well, I think I need to write some of this down. I mean in some kind of argument form. I think I'm right about this, but maybe it would help me to clarify my thinking if I could reduce my thoughts about this to writing and bring it back next time.

Rabi. That's fine with me, if that's what you'd like to do.

Paul. Well, I'm a bit out of practice at writing philosophy papers, but I think I can manage a page or two on why I think Sartre's *Nausea* shows that there's an important defect in the whole mystical approach. An essential defect.

Rabi. I'd love to read that, or have you read it aloud during our next session—whatever you'd prefer.

Paul (laughing). Even if it means removing the capital "S" in "Solution" again?

Rabi. Of course! Your argument sounds fascinating, and, frankly, I'm a bit tired of all these big letters anyway. They do seem a bit pompous, don't they? Like the utterances of our friend Chauncey Gardner.

Paul. Well, I'll start working on it today then. I'm kind of excited about it. Of course, I'll probably find out I was completely confused and come back with a crumpled up piece of paper with "God" scrawled on it in blood.

Rabi (laughing). Then we could talk about that instead! See you then.

Wednesday, 3 PM—The Library

G (walks in smiling broadly). Hi!

Rabi. Hello, G. You're beaming this afternoon. How are you?

G. Great actually. I feel like I've begun to put some sort of picture together—you know, a conception of religion—that I'm comfortable with, but that's more thought through. More grown up, you might say.

Rabi. Really? Tell me about it.

G. Well, I can see now that my idea of God really was pretty vague until I came here. But I think I've been able to narrow down what I'm...(starts laughing)...well, what I'm looking for in a God....Sheesh! This sounds like a product endorsement!

Rabi. Well, it should be as important to know what you want in religion as it is to know what you want in a shampoo or a car.

G. Anyhow, you know how I've said that any religion without someone or something I can make petitionary prayers to and give thanks to seems almost barren to me? That it isn't rich enough somehow?

Rabi. Yes.

G. Well, thanks in large part to my silent roomate—the mysterious Herr Fechner—I've noticed that over the last couple of weeks I seem to be constructing a picture of a God where this *does* make sense. I really feel I'm ready to give up my magic-spell-type God, so long as I can retain some of His important features. It's dawned on me that if God isn't really outside us, but we're inside Him, we can do without the magic. I mean if not only we, but everything is inside God, it seems like there might be a more sensible path from my prayer for help to the help received.

Rabi. Doesn't the amount of magic necessary depend on the type of help sought? I mean, it doesn't seem very magical in today's world of hospital-led meditation, imaging and biofeedback, that the concept of prayer as self-help is very effective. We've probably all had experiences involving asking for help during a dark night of the soul. On many of these occasions, even though no external change to our situation has occurred, we feel better. The power of prayer to work internal wonders—and not just on our minds, but on our bodies—isn't really much in dispute anymore, is it? I think it's almost commonplace now that physical ailments as different from each other as migraine headaches and warts can be helped—even completely cured—by psychological methods. And these methods could be considered a kind of prayer. When a baseball player crosses himself before taking his turn at bat, he's asking to be helped to do his best, to remember his form, to focus on his tasks. I have no doubt that this sort of prayer is efficacious. It probably improves his chances of a successful turn at bat. All the various methods of preparing for performances—meditating, deep breathing, fussing with rosary beads, even getting into a sensory deprivation box as the Julliard Quartet used to do before a concert—all these seem to me a kind of prayer that is commonly answered without the intervention of magic spells. There's probably a huge industry operating somewhere today that is devoted to creating efficient ways to harness this effect: they aren't telling their investors that their product is magical!

G. Yeah, you're right. All that kind of stuff is pretty mundane nowadays. It's terrific that you can better yourself in that way, but it's not entirely satisfying from a religious point of view. Sure, prayers to improve our health or focus or to resist temptation or relax can work, but that's because they aren't really what I'd call religious prayers at all. At least they don't need religion to explain them. But I'm talking about the big ticket petitionary prayers, like for *someone else* to be cured of a disease. At first I thought that either they were useless or God had to magically answer them, but now think there's a third possibility. I think that given a certain picture of the universe, the effectiveness of prayers for things outside us to happen make perfect sense.

Rabi. I remember some years ago hearing about a televangelist—Pat Robertson maybe—who enlisted all his viewers one afternoon to pray with all their might to steer a hurricane heading for North Carolina out to sea. When the hurricane actually *did* change course, the minister took credit for months. One wonders, of course, why they don't do this with *every* hurricane.

G. That reminds me of something. One Sunday when

I was about ten I remember having a particular dread about going to school the next day. It being winter in the Northeast United States, a major snowstorm didn't seem out of the question, so I prayed really hard. I remember standing outside, lifting both of my hands straight up over my head and just saying "Snow." over and over. I felt a kind of connection with the universe as I looked up into the admittedly grey, threatening clouds, and then I shut my eyes as tightly as I could and begged whoever was listening for snow with my desperate whisper. Within a few hours it was snowing hard, and there was no school for two days. That experience may have been what hooked me on this whole petitionary prayer thing. I just chalked up future disappointments to failures to make the same sort of connection. I figured I wasn't getting myself into the right frame of mind or praying hard enough or something. I know this must sound just like the magic you've been telling me I need to get over to get more solace from my faith, but what I picked up from Fechner yesterday is that there's another way that prayers can work outside us, a way that doesn't involve supernatural intervention. This is from his book *The Daylight View*:

> What is the use of prayer, if everything takes place in the world in accordance with laws which determine it by necessity? It can take its place among the grounds of necessity. Something, certainly, it does effect; first of all in man himself, and subsequently beyond him. For nothing operates in man which does not have effects, direct or indirect, visible or invisible, upon the world with which we are in contact, even though we are unable to trace such effects. When I see that a petition addressed by one man to another can essentially affect his decision to grant something which without the petition he would not have granted, I see in this an instance of a universal law, and hold it possible that a prayer addressed to God who

represents the universe in its totality has a like effect. The only difference is that to other men I make the petition outwardly, because they are outside me, whereas in the case of God this is not necessary because I am within Him. That makes our faith in prayer all the easier.[47]

You see, don't you? For the pantheist, prayer can have the power both to improve the petitioner and to change the outside world, without any hocus-pocus. Because while what we call the external world is outside us, it isn't outside the all-inclusive God in which we also live and move and have our being. We're parts of the same whole.

Rabi. I think I understand this theory. Spinoza once compared a human being to what he called "a worm in the blood." What he meant was, we go about our merry ways without usually being cognizant of the fact that we're integral parts of a larger organism. A more modern way of putting this is to consider that our relationship to some bigger thing, the Earth perhaps, might be quite similar to that of our own cells to us. As I understand it, according to this theory when a cell or a group of cells needs something – maybe a vitamin of some kind – we will suddenly crave a kind of food that has it. These subliminal urges, one might almost call them cellular petitionary prayers, are somehow communicated to us and a hankering for an orange or a slice of ham occurs—as if out of nowhere. We often grant our cells their "wishes" by ingesting just what they "ask" for. These petitioners within us don't always get what they want: our higher consciousness often knowingly or unconsciously turns them down in the interest of some higher good—sobriety maybe, or faithfulness. But in a great many cases, perhaps most of them, the primordial "prayers" made by our constituents are granted without us even knowing it. Fechner, like the modern *gaia* theorists, felt that the Earth was the organism in which *we* directly participate, in the same way that our cells participate in us. In fact, he thought that all the stars and planets participate in galaxies much as we participate in our planet. All this incessant praying may go on subconsciously in Fechner's view, but it does go on.

G. That's it precisely. If cells, simply by their pre-conscious desires, can make plants bend toward the sun and people drool over Burger King ads, why can't the completely conscious wishes of full-fledged human beings make things happen to the world *they* inhabit?

Rabi. Well, we know so little about how the cells in our brains and sinews conspire to enable us to perform even such simple activities as raising our arms, maybe we shouldn't be too skeptical about the powers of higher organisms to alter their environments through similar, hard-to-describe means. To me, this picture seems comparable to some of the suggestions made by the late physician Lewis Thomas.

> A good case can be made for our nonexistence as entities. We are not made up, as we had always supposed, of successively enriched packets of our own parts. We are shared, rented occupied. At the interior of our cells, driving them, providing the oxidative energy that sends us out for the improvement of each shining day, are the mitochondria, and in a strict sense they are not ours. They turn out to be little separate creatures, the colonial posterity of migrant prokaryocytes, probably primitive bacteria that swam into ancestral precursors of our eukaryotic cells and stayed there. Ever since, they have maintained themselves and their ways, replicating in their own fashion, privately, with their own DNA and RNA quite different from ours....Without them, we would not move a muscle, drum a finger, think a thought.
>
> Mitochondria are stable and responsible lodgers, and I choose to trust them. But what of the other little animals,

similarly established in my cells, sorting and balancing me, clustering me together? My centrioles, basal bodies, and probably a good many other more obscure tiny beings at work inside my cells, each with its own special genome, are as foreign, and as essential, as aphids in anthills. My cells are no longer the pure line entities I was raised with; they are ecosystems more complex than Jamaica Bay.

I like to think that they work in my interest, that each breath they draw for me, but perhaps it is they who walk through the local park in the early morning, sensing my senses, listening to my music, thinking my thoughts.[48]

And, like Fechner, Thomas feels that the earth is analogous to the entities of which it's composed:

> I have been trying to think of the earth as a kind of organism, but it is no go....It is too big, too complex, with too many working parts lacking visible connections....If not like an organism, what is it like, what is it most like? Then, satisfactorily for that moment, it came to me: it is *most* like a single cell.[49]

G. Ah, the backing of a respected scientist! What more could I ask for? Why can't it be that every hope is a prayer and every prayer has at least some power to bring us what we ask for? We don't need to know any magic rituals or Latin phrases to have at least some power to change the world. But it's not magic. The universe is looking out for us when it looks out for itself. If we just maintain a certain kind of connection with God, we may really be able to make it snow.

Rabi. I wonder how this sort of picture could affect one's daily life. Some people have mentioned to me that they feel guilty if a selfish desire slips through when they blow out their birthday candles or say a silent prayer in church. It's as if they think they're only entitled to a limited number of granted wishes in their lives and that they shouldn't squander them on something for themselves. Do you think, on this pantheistic view, that we are entitled to more consideration if we reserve our prayers for special occasions or for selfless causes? When a loved one is sick, ought we to feel guilty for not praying correctly or enough?

G. I'm not sure why there should be any limitations. Our cells don't seem to have them. But I was thinking about a lonely character in the Dorothy Parker story who's waiting desparately for a phone call. She promises God that she won't ask for a single other thing as long as she lives if the phone will just ring now. And there's also this kid's movie — I think it's one of the *Neverending Story* series — where each time the protagonist has a wish granted he loses a valuable part of himself, a memory. The more he wishes, the more he disappears.

Rabi. There's also the fairy tale of the fisherman and his wife. The flounder gets so annoyed at being asked for more and more things, he finally takes everything away. It seems a basic part of our psyche that while we want to get our heart's desires just by wishing, we somehow know that it isn't the right way to get them.

G. Are you saying that if my cells need vitamin C, and I later pick up an orange the cells should feel guilty?

Rabi. I guess I'd say that prayers of that sort may be the cells' way of working for their vitamins. It's a bit different from trying to change the weather or a loved one's diagnosis by hoping. And, of course, one wonders why, if praying could really change things like earthquakes, they wouldn't have disappeared from the face of the Earth by now. Is it perhaps the Devil's wishes that are undoing all the wishes of ordinary people for health and good crops? In any case, the main issue is really more fundamental. If those sorts of prayers could be granted, everything would be so much more unpredictable and disordered than we could handle. The world would be uninhabitable. Tagore has something on this....Let's see if I can find it....Ah, here it is:

> A student of mine once related to me his adventure in a storm, and complained that all the time he was troubled with the feeling that this great commotion in nature behaved to him as if he were no more than a mere handful of dust. That he was a distinct personality with a will of his own had not the least influence upon what was happening.
>
> I said, 'If consideration for our individuality could sway nature from her path, then it would be the individuals who would suffer most.'
>
> ...[I]f it is a truth that the yearning of our nature is for reality, and that our personality cannot be happy with a fantastic universe of its own creation, then it is clearly best for it that our will can only deal with things by following their law, and cannot do with them just as it pleases. This unyielding sureness of reality sometimes crosses our will, and very often leads us to disaster, just as the firmness of the earth invariably hurts the falling child who is learning to walk. Nevertheless it is the same firmness that hurts him which makes his walking possible. Once, while passing under a bridge, the mast of my boat got stuck in one of its girders. If only for a moment the mast would have bent an inch or two, or the bridge raised its back like a yawning cat, or the river given in, it would have been all right with me. But they took no notice of my helplessness. That is the very reason why I could make use of the river, and sail upon it with the help of the mast, and that is why, when its current was inconvenient, I could rely upon the bridge. Things are what they are, and we have to know them if we would deal with them, and knowledge of them is possible because our wish is not their law. This knowledge is a joy to us, for the knowledge is one of the channels of our relation with the things outside us; it is making them our own, and thus widening the limit of our self.[50]

G. Well, I'm not so sure that Tagore was up on current

theories involving mitochondria. Maybe there's more science behind petitionary prayer than he could realize.

Rabi. Perhaps.

G. It doesn't seem like you're very sympathetic to my vision. Still not adult enough, I suppose.

Rabi. On the contrary, I think pantheism is an absolutely beautiful vision, and one which I believe to contain a great deal of truth. But I'm not sure we ought to use it as a means for making us content in our dreaming. If our religion becomes an inducement to the increase rather than the diminution of our desires, I'm afraid it may not serve us very well. But getting back to the merits of the pantheistic view, I believe that there's a profound truth in there somewhere about the difficulty of consistently distinguishing self from not-self. There's a chapter in Butler's *Luck or Cunning* that I'd like to recommend on that subject...if you think you can tolerate any more Butler after your experience with *The Fair Haven*. I promise you that there's nothing satirical or ironic in *Luck or Cunning*.

G. I suppose I might give it a try...but...that's it? There's nothing else about this sort of religious view that appeals to you? Just the fuzziness about the self and not-self?...I don't know, I thought you'd be pleased or proud of me or something.

Rabi. I hope you won't misunderstand me. As I've said, I think pantheism is a beautiful, a magnificent vision, and one that I am personally quite attached to. If I weren't, I wouldn't have picures of Fechner and Spinoza scattered throughout the Center. It's a philosophy that is very appealing to me, just as it is to you. For example, the work these men have done on such issues as the compounding of individual thought into larger and larger consciousnesses seems to me very interesting and profound. William James has written compellingly about Fechner's contributions in this area in a wonderful chapter of his *Pluralistic Universe*. You might enjoy that as well.

G. Books! Books! Books! What you're actually saying is that in spite of all this beauty, you don't have much use for this vision as a basis for a religious faith.

Rabi. What you take to be my indifference may be rather a combination of two things: my concern that your version of pantheism will be used to increase your inclination to make wishes rather than to meditate and act in ways that will certainly improve your life, and my recognition of my incompetence to tell whether or not every detail of the *gaia* theory actually corresponds with reality.

G (sarcastically). Your mystical experiences shed no light on that?

Rabi. Sadly, not on any particular propositions of science, metaphysics or ontology. If they did, mystical experiences alone could make someone a great philosopher or scientist. I certainly make no such claim for myself.

G. Then what exactly *do* these experiences teach you?

Rabi. They show me what it is that I am part of, and what it is that I am. For me, this is enough. *Ist habe genug.*

G. So, tell us. Just what is it that you are part of?

Rabi. That, I'm afraid, I can't put in words. Besides, aren't you more interested in what it is that *you* are a part of?

G (angrily). And, like Dorothy in Oz, that's something I have to figure out for myself, right?

Rabi. Not "figure out"—*see.*

G. OK. (Gets up.) Look, I'm leaving now. Maybe I'll pick up the books you were talking about later. (mumbles) Maybe not.

Rabi (stands). Goodbye, G. Perhaps we can discuss your concerns further next time.

ॐ

Friday, 10 AM — The Library

Rabi. Ah, Paul! Come in. Sit down.

Paul. Hi.

Rabi. So, have you brought your essay?

Paul. I have. I'm not sure it makes too much sense, but I did get something down on paper....Should I read it?

Rabi. Of course. I've been looking forward to it.

Paul (unfolding some hand written sheets). Not with too high expectations, I hope. It's pretty rudimentary. But I guess I think it's right. Anyway, here it is:

"We're presented with a situation in which two propositions that are apparently contradictory both seem indubitably true to their believers. Let's call these propositions 'The world is really X' and 'The world is really Y'—where 'X' represents some sort of happy religious picture, like 'identical with the World Spirit,' and 'Y' represents the 'fear and trembling' picture, maybe something like 'a quivering mass of absurdity and nothingness.' Now, as neutral observers, what should we think when we hear both of these two deeply held propositions being uttered? I can think of a number of possible answers.

1. We can say that the two propositions really are inconsistent and claim that the apparent indubitability of each of them isn't evidence of anything at all; or

2. We can say that the two propositions really are inconsistent but decide that their indubitability somehow remains evidence of the truth of both propositions; or

3. We can say that the two propositions really are inconsistent and conclude that the indubitability is evidence of the truth of one picture but not the other; or

4. We can *deny* that the two propositions are really

inconsistent but nevertheless claim that the indubitability of each of them (if there really are two) isn't evidence of anything at all; or

5. We can deny that the two propositions are really inconsistent and claim that their indubitability provides evidence of the truth of both propositions; or, finally,

6. We can deny that the two propositions are really inconsistent but nevertheless claim that only the indubitability of one of them provides any evidence for its truth.

"So, which one of these approaches is the right one to take? Careful analysis suggests that the first approach must be correct. Let's split it into it's two parts. First, does the sentence 'The world is really X' in fact contradict the sentence 'The world is really Y'? I think the answer to this question must be *Yes*. As I have described X and Y, nothing can be both X and Y. That is, X includes the feature of being something benign and Y is intended to explicitly exclude any such feature. Sartre's picture isn't just not benign, it's actively malign. So if the world is really X it can't be Y and *vice versa*: the propositions really do contradict one another. Now, take the second part of the first approach. Since we can have no logical, or scientific, or any other empirical basis for believing one rather than the other, there can never be any grounds for choosing one feeling of indubitability over another. But, as I've shown, the two claims are contradictory, so they can't both be right. Therefore, a neutral observer ought never rely on either of these feelings.

"I infer from this that since (i) we can never have any basis for preferring one brand of mysticism—either the typical religious sort or the "fear and trembling" sort—over the other; and (ii) there can never be any other basis for believing what the mystic believes besides the existence of these allegedly special experiences; therefore, (iii) the neutral observer can have no basis whatever for believing in any sort of mysticism at all."

That's all I wrote. I was thinking of putting a "QED" at the end like Spinoza does, but I have to admit that I couldn't remember what it stands for.

Rabi. I can see you've thought a lot about this issue and put a good deal of work into it.

Paul. What do you think about my results?

Rabi. Well, I generally agree with your conclusion, that the non-mystic can have but little reason to adopt any of the conclusions of the mystic, though as James points out, there may be something about the changed behavior of the religious convert—a new ease with life, for example—that may convince us of the truth of what he says, at least if those behavioral changes aren't fleeting.

Paul. But remember, Sartre's narrator underwent a long-term change too.

Rabi. True, but not in a manner that would encourage a third party to agree with him. When a surgeon smooths down a bone so that it will function better within someone's shoulder, the change may be either for the better or for the worse. We will decide this by observing the patient's interactions with his environment. If they become effortless and pain-free we'll likely come to believe that the joint has been corrected. If they continue to be as halting, weak and painful, or if they get even more difficult than they were with no signs of improvement, we will likely come to consider the surgery a failure. The many stories of converts recounted in the works of James and Suzuki are accounts of people who emerged from their religious experiences with new-found strength, confidence and ease. In contrast, Sartre's narrator seems to have become an angst-ridden mess. I think it must only be existentialists who see that sort of alienation and nausea as a good thing.

Paul. I still think my argument is valid.

Rabi. Perhaps the conclusion follows from its premises. I don't know, I'd have to study it further. But I can think of several other approaches one can take to the apparent disagreement between the two skeptics besides those you mentioned.

Paul. I'd like to hear them.

Rabi. Well, think of it. Two people, call them Margaret and Jean-Paul, have experiences that are striking and unusual for them. One emerges elated, the other is filled with dread. "All is *Brahman*," says Margaret. "All is absurdity," counters Jean-Paul. Now you argue that these sentences are contradictory. Perhaps they are. But is it actually the propositions expressed by these sentences that the mystics find they are unable to doubt? I don't believe so. I mean, the concepts of *Brahman* and *absurdity* are so complex to begin with that it's hard to imagine one being completely certain of much of anything involving those terms.

Paul. Then is nothing they can communicate to us really indubitable? In spite of the insistent claims of these two?

Rabi. I do think they're right that *something* is indubitable, but I don't believe that what it is can be expressed in words. Let me give a related example. In his *Problems of Philosophy*, Bertrand Russell talks about what can't be doubted. He discusses Descartes' search for something that couldn't just be a dream or the trick of an evil genius, and Descartes' famous conclusion. But Russell demurs. It's his view that

'I think therefore I am' says rather more than is strictly certain. It might seem as though we were quite sure of being the same person to-day as we were yesterday, and this is no doubt true in some sense. But the real Self is as hard to arrive at as the real table, and does not seem to have that absolute, convincing certainty that belongs to particular experiences. When I look at my table and see a certain brown colour, what is quite certain at once is not '*I* am seeing a brown colour,' but rather, 'a brown colour is being seen.' This of course involves something (or somebody) which (or who) sees the brown colour; but it does not of itself involve that more or less permanent person whom we call 'I.'[51]

But why stop there? Can we be perfectly sure that what we're seeing is indeed brown? Couldn't we have developed some sort of color-blindness in the last minute, so that what we're seeing is actually green and only *appears* brown. And is what we're seeing actually a color? That is, is there any such thing as color that can be seen independently of colored things? When we say "A brown color is being seen" aren't we suggesting some kind of independent existence for this entity *color?* Perhaps we should say "Something that seems brown is being seen." But, while we're at it, how do we know for certain that there's any *seeing* going on at all? As Descartes pointed out, we might be dreaming, in which case there'd be no real seeing, just a dream of it. So maybe we'd be safer with "Something that seems brown is apparently being seen."

Paul. I remember there being some 20th Century philosopher—Roderick Chisholm I think it was—who tried to avoid any implication that there must be something that has the property of being green by saying that what's really indubitable is that *I am appeared to brownly.*[52]

Rabi. Interesting. But how do we put this if we are

concerned about not suggesting that there is a relatively permanent self that is being "appeared to"? Do we have to construct something as nonsensical as "There is a being appeared to brownly going on"?

Paul. Maybe we just blurt out "Being appeared to brownly" and leave it at that.

Rabi. But is there a coherent proposition being expressed here? And, in the end, why does it matter? As I've said, I don't want to deny that *something* is indubitable. But saying what it is may be impossible and the quest to do so just a waste of time. Even if something like "Being appeared to brownly" does express something of which we can be completely certain, surely such stuff as this must be useless as building blocks from which we can construct our everyday world. Can we start only with whatever might be connoted by these sorts of jerry-rigged adverbs and produce something as substantial as a single Vermont maple? I, at least, am perfectly content to give up the entire Cartesian enterprise and go on without any absolutely certain expressible beliefs at all. You know, if that's that's all that Sartre meant by "absurdity," then I think I agree with him!

Paul. Where does this leave my argument about the two mystics?

Rabi. I'm not sure. I suppose I'd say that "The world is X." and "The world is Y." probably *are* inconsistent, but that neither of them was ever really indubitable to anybody anyways. It may well be that what has led Margaret and Jean-Paul to their opinions were experiences the content of which they they were unable to doubt. But I can't tell whether the contents of those experiences imply anything inconsistent with each other because I don't think either Margaret or Jean-Paul—regardless of their considerable writing skills—is competent to express these experiences in words. No one could do it.

Paul. Well, if what's disclosed by mysticism is as obscure as all that, I can't see what use it can possibly have.

Rabi. For myself, I can say that I wish to know what it is that I am part of, and what it is that I am. I think the answers to those questions have been revealed to me whether or not I can express them in a manner anyone else can understand.

Paul. But both Margaret and Jean-Paul think *they* know what it is that *they* are part of too, but this so-called knowledge fills one with bliss and the other with dread. So how can what Margaret thinks she knows indubitably possibly be identical with what Jean-Paul is talking about?

Rabi. Well perhaps they aren't, but I don't see why they couldn't be. After all, even their descriptions are similar in certain respects. For example, they each talk about seeing the world in a strange, new light.

Paul. But Margaret no longer fears death, and Jean-Paul is seized with anxiety and despair.

Rabi. That's quite true, but I don't think it creates any problems either for them or for us. Saint Teresa, who was as interested in making careful classifications as a 19th Century botanist, might have attributed this difference to the fact that one of the two mystics had "reached a higher level" and so, as she put it, experienced a different "water."

Paul. But which one is "higher"? Aren't we just back to my original claim about the impossibility of judging between X and Y?

Rabi. More or less, yes. As I've said, I generally agree with your conclusion, at least as it applies to people who have not achieved *samadhi* or *satori* themselves. Although, again, there are certain behavioral activities that may make such observers tend to take one opinion over the other. If we wanted, like a scientist, to devise a test for people who claim to have suddenly come to understand the nature of reality, might we not try to predict how the behaviors of such a person would change? And what would we look for? Isn't it likely that we would say that the person who understood the world would get along well in it? That, at least, is what we do with claims to knowledge in the areas of, say, carpentry or boating: we see if they can navigate smoothly through the materials of which they claim to have an intimate understanding. But, be that as it may, such behavioral changes don't seem a strong enough base to support one's entire spiritual life. I, at any rate would need more.

Paul. Much more. Frankly, if this is all you have to offer, it seems pretty obscurantist to me.

Rabi. And to me it all seems so simple and clear, though of course it is quite difficult in practice to achieve the actual knowledge we seek. Listen, Paul. Listen. Listen. People that live well and meditate correctly and regularly often come to have very strong convictions regarding what it is that they are part of and what it is that they are. Such people also tend to lose all fear of dying and become happy, integrated individuals. They become more comfortable, better coordinated with their environments, like the repaired shoulder joint I spoke of earlier.

Paul. That's it?

Rabi. Yes. That's it. Will you practice and learn and be happy?

Paul. You know, I'm not sure whether you're saying anything at all sometimes. I'm not trying to be contrary or hostile when I say this: I honestly can't tell. (Gets up and

goes to a bookcase). Let me find Wittgenstein's *Tractatus*...
Yeah, here it is:

> For an answer which cannot be expressed the question too
> cannot be expressed. *The riddle* does not exist. If a question can
> be put at all then it *can* also be answered...For doubt can only
> exist where there is a question; a question only where there is an
> answer, and this only where something can be *said*.[53]

Now, if you'll forgive me, it seems to me that this means
that where you provide nothing more than an unutterable
grunt as an answer, there can't have been any real question.
I mean, it just seems like you're not really prepared to
answer any question that has genuine significance in the
English language. I, on the other hand, have a perfectly
comprehensible question that I think I can put quite
clearly. But I doubt that you can or will give any answer
to *it*. It is a simple question, and one that I would guess
most of the people who pay to come to your center would
also like to hear you answer. It is just this: "Will I die?"
Now when I use the word *I* here, I don't mean my body,
or at least I don't mean my body unless it turns out that I
am identical with my body. Of course, I understand that
something of *this* (he hits his chest with both hands) will
disintegrate into dust at some point. But I'm talking about
me — whatever that should happen to be, whether ego, or
physical body, or collection of experiences. Will *I*, with
all these memories and attachments, cease to exist some
day — go out like a candle? Can you answer this simple,
straightforward question?

Rabi. Only *you* can answer that question. And I've told
you what I believe you must do to learn the answer.

Paul. Oh Yes. You say, "Do this breathing exercise, and
you'll no longer fear death." But as I've told you many

times, I don't *want* to do this exercise if it's just a way of deluding myself, anymore than I'd want to take some drug that would have the same effect. I only want not to fear death if there *is* no death.

Rabi. But whether I told you that there was no death or that there was utter annihilation—even if I made these pronouncements with a look of profound seriousness on my face—would you believe me?

Paul. Well, I'd want to know why you believed it.

Rabi. And I would tell you that they stem from experiences that I have had. Experiences that I trust with the same sort of certitude that you trust in the reality of these chairs. But if you don't have such experiences yourself, why would you, why *should* you believe me?

Paul. Around and around we go. A straightforward question, and a riddle for an answer.

Rabi. Listen, Norman Hanson, a highly regarded philosopher of science once wrote,

> Nijinsky understood the dance. But, apparently, he could not explain it to others. He was inarticulate about it; others could not understand *from what he said* what the dance was! Similarly, the Wright brothers understood flight; but they were largely inarticulate with respect to it. Others could hardly gather, from their words, what flight was. The brothers were powerless to make them see. Our midwife, electrician, and fisherman *could not explain* (to others) childbirth, circuitry, and seasonal spawning. The *sentiment of comprehension* should therefore never be confused with the *structure of explanation*. *Feeling* and *logic* are as different as *brain* and *mind*. *Knowing how* and *knowing that* are as unlike as *retinal reaction* and *observing*. The distinction between understanding in the sense of intuitive familiarity and understanding in the sense of rationally comprehending the 'go' of things must never be collapsed.[54]

When, in Plato's myth, the first man walked out of

the cave and saw three-dimensional people instead of the two-dimensional shadows that had always been the sole perceptual objects of the cave's inhabitants, he could neither describe his new knowledge in any way his brethren could understand, nor convince them of it. All he could do was try to use this deeper understanding to make more subtle predictions of how the shadows might behave while at the same time helping his fellows to break out of their bonds as well.

Paul. Well, before I take your hand and let you lead me out of my darkness, tell me this. Forget about me and what I mean by *me*. Are you at least willing to divulge whether you believe that *you* will die? I mean, I understand that I might not believe you and all that: I just want to know what you think.

Rabi. If you mean in the sense that one ordinarily uses the word—for example when we say that Aldous Huxley died on the same day as John F. Kennedy—of course I will die. Why wouldn't I? There's nothing about me that exempts me from the common lot of all human beings.

Paul. C'mon, Rabi, you know perfectly well what I mean. What's the passage from The Bible? "In the sight of the unwise they seemed to die, and their departure is taken for misery, and their going from us to be utter destruction. But they are in peace. For though they be punished in the sight of men, yet is their hope full of immortality." I'm not saying I believe any of that stuff, but at least I know what it means. And now, I'd like to hear *your* view. Is there any sense in which you believe some inner *you* will survive your bodily death?

Rabi. Well, yes, I think there are such senses, though we may need to ignore your word "inner." However, I have no idea whatever whether these are types of survival that you'd find comforting. For instance, many people want to be remembered after they die, and—Woody Allen's joke about that sort of immortality notwithstanding—these people consider that a type of survival worth seeking. And, depending on the essence of self and the nature of memory, being remembered may well be a significant type of personal survival. To take another sense, presumably one's works, such as books or architecture or even in a sense one's children, survive one's bodily death. This too is often considered a type of immortality, but, again, we must understand the nature of self and the desires of the dying man to know its value for him. Exactly what is our relationship to our works? Are we truly separate from them? We must understand what we are and what we are part of to know the answer to your question.

Paul (muttering). Christ....And, we might not want to answer the question even if we think we do know these things. (Louder) Well, I guess I've taken up enough of your time for one day. (Gets up) Remind me to ask you some time why you felt it necessary to ignore my word "inner" in my question about the inner you—it changed the meaning a lot, if you ask me....Oh, and I'm already in the middle of a bunch of books, so I won't be needing any recommendations today, thanks.

Rabi. Would you care to leave me your essay on the two types of mysticism? It was quite interesting, and I'd like to read it more carefully.

Paul. Naw, I suppose it isn't much good. See you around.

Rabi. Goodbye then, Paul.

V.
Week Seven

Sunday 10:15 AM—The Garden

(Paul is at a table reading when he hears a car door and sees G getting out of her car. He stands up and calls to her and she walks over to his table.)

Paul. Out for breakfast?

G. Yeah, I can't seem to get enough of Joan's pancakes—even though they're turning this into a weight-gaining summer.

Paul. They really *are* good, aren't they? What kind did you get?

G. Cranberry nut. Outrageous....Listen, do you have a minute? I want to talk to you about something.

Paul. Sure, what's up?

G. Well, I'm so annoyed with Rabi I could scream.

Paul. You too? Actually, I'm pretty pissed off myself.

G. Yeah, but you know how *I* can be when I'm mad. I stormed out of my session after about ten minutes Friday.

Paul. Well, I guess there must have been something in the air that day because I did pretty much the same thing. His humble pie, "I-don't-know-anything-myself-but-at-least-I'm-not-a-complete-idiot-like-you-are" shtick really got to me. I always thought that Socrates was a big pain in the ass, and Rabi has a lot of his worst qualities. I wrote up this argument on why mystical reports can't really tell us anything at all about the world, and he pretty much just shot it down.

G. Of course. He found it threatening. Without these

mysterious experiences of his, what's he really got to offer? So if they're basically meaningless, this whole place is a sham. My Wednesday session was amazingly similar. I went in wanting to tell him about what I felt was a breakthrough for me. And it wasn't anything so foreign to his whole mystical thing that he couldn't fathom what I was talking about. In fact, I pushed a kind of scientific pantheism I put together from books *he* recommended, especially one by Fechner.

Paul. Your room fairy?

G. Right.

Paul. And he torched you?

G. Yup.

Paul. That doesn't seem very compassionate of him, does it?

G. Um, no. But that's what I wanted to talk to you about. I'd like to have you help me sink him with his own weapons.

Paul. Uh-oh. I've been on the business end of your temper and it's no fun at all. Just what do you have in mind for our dear old guruji?

G. Well, it's not like I want to poison his tea or anything. After all, I absolutely *love* Vera, and she might be a bit miffed finding a dead hubby in the library....though I must say I have absolutely no idea what she gets out of their relationship. She's so vital, and he's so....so cold.

Paul. Well, maybe he uses his infallible intuitions to correct her grocery list or pooh-pooh her gardening ideas. She may just be the type that likes having a know-it-all in the immediate family.

G. I can't see it. And they've got kids too. Can you imagine what it must have been like having him as a father?

Paul. Well, at least he knows more about Joni Mitchell and George Harrison than my folks did...if that's a good thing....And there's some other singer or group too, but I can't seem to place who it is. Has he given you that business about "what is it that we are part of and what is it that we are?"

G. Oh yeah. Over and over.

Paul. Don't you think there's something odd about that way of putting it? I mean, he could just say "what we are and what we're part of." But instead, he always uses this strangely formal, almost archaic way of expressing it.

G. It *is* kind of uncharacteristic of him. Usually he tries to be so *today*.

Paul. Yeah, I'm almost positive that line comes from some old rock song. I just can't put my finger on it. It's been driving me crazy. If I had my record collection here, I'm pretty sure I could find it. Oh well, it'll probably just come to me one night while I'm trying to concentrate on the tingling in my feet. But the point is, how weird is it to always be quoting from pop songs? I mean I love a lot of that stuff too, but let's face it, most of it was written for teenagers. Stoned ones, at that.

G. First, Franny Glass and now this! It's too much.

Paul. You're right, captain: he's got to be stopped before he kills again. But what's your plan?

G. Well, I found this philosophy book that has some dynamite arguments against mysticism that I want to throw in his face.

Paul. Or somewhere like that.

G (laughing). Right. But some of it's pretty technical, and I thought you might be willing to help me with it.

Paul. Absolutely. I could read it, and then we can get together and talk about it before your next session. I can think of some other stuff you might want to use as ammo too.

G. Well, the thing is...I don't want to have this fight alone. He's just too quick on his feet for me. I was kind of hoping we could meet with him together.

Paul. To be honest, I'm not sure I'm the guy for this job. I haven't exactly left him all helpless and suicidal myself. He's pretty clever.

G. I know. That's why I figured it might take both of us. You know, we could kind of gang up on him.

Paul. I gotta admit, it does sound more fun than meditating on lotus petals. When did you have in mind?

G. Well, my next session is tomorrow afternoon. Would you be free then?

Paul. Well, everyone's free pretty much *all* the time here, aren't we? But are you sure you want to use up one of your sessions for this? They're pretty expensive, you know. Plus, we don't even know if he'll allow two people in during one of his sessions, do we?

G. Oh, forget about the cost: it would be the best spent money since I came here if we could knock him off his high horse. And I don't think he'll mind having both of us show up. Someone else here—you know Gene?—well he told me that he and a friend of his went together once to talk about something they were both working on. He said Rabi didn't mind.

Paul. Hmmm. Well I've got him tomorrow morning at ten, and I don't think I could have a normal discussion with him while we were planning our frontal assault. Maybe we should start on him then and finish off what's left of his bleeding hulk in the afternoon during your time.

G. That's fine with me. Are you sure you don't mind, though? You know there's a chance we'll alienate him so much that any more sessions with him will be impossible.

Paul. To tell you the truth, I'm pretty alienated myself right now. After Friday, I was actually thinking I might bag the rest of the summer and go somewhere else a bit more vacationy. Or maybe just head back home and catch some decent movies: the pickings around here are pretty slim. But if I'm gonna end it anyway, this sounds like a lot more fun way of doing it. (Laughing) I've got this vision of a huge blaze in the library: I just can't tell if it's a blaze of glory or the room is on fire.

G. And is it our glory or his that's blazing?....Either way, I've got to do *something* with all this resentment I have for him right now. I don't know if he'd ever admit that he was wrong about any of this stuff or he'd just be a weasel about it. His whole career and personality seem completely wrapped up in his infallibility thing. Anyhow, it'll be enough for me if it's obvious to *us* that we've totally destroyed his claims to superiority, however *he* acts about it. If that's it for my sessions, so be it.

Paul. Yeah, I suppose *our* knowing we pounded him is all we can legitimately hope for....OK, I'm in. It's a pact. Either we we blow him out of the water and dump pigs' blood —or at least really ugly shoe polish—on his sign on the way out, or he convinces us he's on to something that we think might actually be useful, and I give up on decent movies for the rest of the summer.

G (Shaking hands with him). All for one and one for all!

Paul. So what's this book you've got? I better start studying fast. We've only got one day.

G. It's called *The Philosophical Basis of Theism* by someone named Gilbert Dawes Hicks. It's from the early 1930s. This guy seems like a really good philosopher. And he answers a bunch of the arguments I've heard Rabi use in support of mysticism.

Paul. Never heard of him. What's his angle?

G. Well, he spends a lot of time attacking the idea that we can have experiences that are completely trustworthy because they're somehow "unmediated" by our intellectual background. He says that, like it or not, we're all stuck with the usual avenues of knowledge. I can't wait to read some of these passages to Rabi. Listen to this:

> Even in soliloquizing with himself [the mystic] is construing his experiences intellectually. For instance, in his states of ecstasy he is assured that he is directly confronted with the ultimate Reality, that he is grasped by a higher power, that he has an immediate intuition of God. But that which he accepts on the ground of what he takes to be immediate intuition is clearly an interpretation....Whether true or false this interpretation implies that, prior to the experience in question, the mystic has acquired his religious beliefs precisely as his non-mystical neighbour acquires his, namely, through instruction and tradition, through habitual ways of thinking, and through rational reflexion. In other words, he brings his theological convictions to the mystical experience; he does not derive them from it. The seeming 'immediacy' of the experience need imply no more than that, at the moment, he is unaware of the fact that his mind is saturated with ideas previously entertained, ideas of previous suppositions and their inferred consequents.[55]

Paul. You're right, that's great stuff. I don't see how Rabi can deny any of it, and it seems like the death-blow to mysticism.

G. And get this:

> Take, for instance, the 'numinous' features suggested to the primitive mind by an oddly shaped stone. Would any theist in a cultured community admit for a moment that the 'uncannyness' which the primitive mind discerns therein is a veritable revelation to that mind of the supernatural? Is there any ground for assuming that the appearance of 'uncannyness" is other

than a natural delusion incited in a way which is psychologically explicable, or that it differs in any essential respect from the child's dread of being left alone in the dark?[56]

Paul. That's perfect. And, if I can give myself a shameless pat on the back for a second, it's not that different from what I was trying to say when I wrote that argument up for my session. Of course this guy puts it a lot better than I did.

G. Well, however it's put, I think it's devastating to the whole "Perennial Solution" thing, so I can see why Rabi was forced to downplay its importance in your session. It's about time somebody deflated *him* for a change. And with you there to help me prevent him from twisting these arguments inside out, I think he'll have a pretty tough time—which, of course, is now my main, if extremely babyish, goal in life.

Paul. Cool. I don't like being the only immature person around all the zombies here. But, just in case he tries to stagger to his feet like some Bengali cross between Glenn Close and Arnold Schwarzenegger, I've got some insurance. First, there's this great critique of Zen by Koestler that I've been waiting to ask him about. Koestler pretty much concludes that the whole tradition is cant and that the spontaneity everyone gets so excited about is just a reaction to the formality of Confucianism. He even makes a point of telling us that the so-called Zen archery masters have never been world class archers. It's always been ninety-five percent mystique. In fact, Koestler's got this whole section in his book on what he calls "the stink of Zen."

G. *Wu!* That's good, because Rabi seems very into the whole Zen thing.

Paul. But wait! Don't answer yet! There's so much more! (He shows her the book he was reading.) There's also some good stuff in this book by Alan Watts—*Psychotherapy East and West*. He argues that the entire guru business is basically trickery and that any spiritual healer worth his salt—including psychoanalysts—knows damn well that the whole thing is a sham.

G. Hunh. I thought Watts was into this stuff.

Paul. He is. He's totally Zenned out. But he's figured out how and why it actually manages to help anyone. I mean, it *is* hard to deny that there are people around whose lives have improved while they've stayed at places like this. The thing is, you don't have to deny that a Zen master can help a poor suffering soul. He can do it precisely because what he's mastered is the art of fooling his students. Check this out:

[T]rickery is basic to medicine and psychotherapy alike. It has been said that the good doctor is one who keeps the patient amused while nature works the cure. This is not always true, but it is a sound general principle. It is easier to wait for a natural change when one is given the impression that something is being done to bring it about. What is being done is the trick; the relaxed and rested waiting is the actual cure, but the anxiety which attends a disease makes direct and deliberate relaxation almost impossible. Patients lose confidence in their doctors to the extent that the trickery is exposed, and therefore the art of medicine progresses by the invention of new and ever more impenetrable tricks.

...The healer must then appear to be a magician, a master of the physical world. He must do whatever is necessary to convince the sufferer that he can solve what seems to the latter to be a physical problem, for there is no other way of convincing him to do what is necessary for acting consistently upon his false assumption. He must above all convince the sufferer that he, the *guru,* has mastered the imaginary problem, that *his* ego is not disturbed by pain or death or worldly passions....

Admittedly there may be many *gurus* who do not fully realize that this is what they are doing, just as there are many physicians who do not realize that some of their medications are placebos....Yet there is good reason to believe that some teachers of the ways of liberation know perfectly well what they are doing, that they are fully aware of their merciful trickery and also of the fact that the release attained is not from physical reincarnation but from confused thinking and feeling.[57]

G. Oh man, are we gonna be ready or what! But we've got to exchange these books so we'll each know what the other person is talking about.

Paul. Check. Do you want to try to get together again tonight after we've had a chance to do some reading?

G. How about tomorrow before your session: that'll give us more time for reading first. It's at ten, isn't it?

Paul. Double check.

G. Is nine tomorrow too early.

Paul. Naw, I'm usually up way before that.

G. Great. Let's get together for breakfast at about 8:30 then.

Paul. OK, but you drive. I'm gonna be too busy checking the muskets, powder, and shot to concentrate at deer crossings.

G. Deal. Should we pick up extra copies of these books in the library right now, and point each other to the important passages?

Paul. Why not?...Oops, I mean, "Triple check." (They get up and start walking toward the house.)....Hey, I just got it!

G. What?

Paul. Who did the song with "What is it that we are

part of?"in it! It was a group called The Incredible String Band. A guy named Robin Williamson wrote it.

G. The band's name sounds vaguely familiar, but I'm not sure if I've heard them.

Paul. Well, I'm pretty sure Rabi has. The Incredible String Band. Unbelievable. What's next, Teenage Mutant Ninja Turtles? (They disappear into the house.)

***

Monday, 10:00 AM—The Library

(Paul and G are sitting at a table when Rabi enters.)

Rabi. Good morning to you both. Paul, I believe it's time for your session.

Paul. Hello, Rabi. Yes, it is, but I was wondering if you'd mind if G joined us this morning. We discovered that we've been thinking about some of the same issues, and we thought it might be helpful if we could have a three-way discussion.

G. I hope you don't mind. Then, if it's OK, we could do the same thing this afternoon during my time. That way it will be fair to both of us.

Rabi. It's fine with me. One-on-one sessions tend to be a bit more instructive, perhaps because visitors are usually more forthcoming about their difficulties and less inhibited about asking questions when I'm the only other person present, but sometimes bigger groups can be fruitful too. Should I sit here at the table with you? (They assent to this, and he joins them.) What did you want to talk about?

Paul. There are a few things. But first, I've just got to ask you: are you familiar with the musical group The Incredible String Band?

Rabi. Yes, I'm quite fond of them. Why do you ask?

Paul. It's that expression you're always using: "What is it that we are part of?"

Rabi. Ah, of course. (He sings in a breathy, faltering tenor) *O it's the half-remarkable question. What is it that we are part of? And what is it that we are?*[58] It's a beautiful song, isn't it?

Paul. Robin Williamson, right?

Rabi. I believe so, yes.

Paul. It seems a bit strange having a pop song lyric function so centrally in your religion. But I thought it must have come from that song. I mean, it's such an odd, old-fashioned expression.

Rabi. Perhaps, but it's beautiful, and it describes precisely what I gain from my meditations. Often poetry can do that so much better than...

G (interrupting him). You mean what you *think* you gain from your meditations. It's not clear to me that those experiences deserve any more respect than we would give to any other basis of religious beliefs. Maybe less.

Rabi (laughing). My two wranglers. You'll make me feel like a bank robber with a bag of stolen money trying to escape The Lone Ranger and Tonto.

Paul (laughing). I like to think of myself as more the Cisco Kid type.

G. I don't know if it's exactly on the level of bank robbery, but, to be perfectly honest, I *do* think there's been some slight of hand going on here...and...I think Paul agrees with me about this.

Paul. Absolutely. And I'm sure it's no surprise to Rabi to hear this. I practically threaten to call the cops on him every week.

Rabi. He does indeed. I sometimes think we waste too much time with all these never-ending arguments about evidence, ineffability, the nature of religious solutions and the like, but at other times I realize that this struggle is often an important, inescapable part of the process of enlightenment.

G. But don't you see, it's just that attitude that's so maddening. It's parental and patronizing. You seem to be saying—in a sighing, long-suffering way— "Give me patience, Lord. If I just bear with these children a little longer perhaps they'll see the light." But maybe it's really *us* having to put up with *your* repetitive errors and unwillingness to face the truth that's the real problem here.

Rabi. How do we know there's any problem here at all?

Paul. Well, my test is that I generally leave sessions feeling worse about myself than when I went in.

G. Me too. Plus, there's this suspiciousness about you and your mystical experiences that, for me at least, is growing rather than receding. Without trust, how can there be any spiritual progress?

Paul. I agree with that. Look, I know that trust comes hard for me, generally. But when you throw in stuff like the "Perennial Solution" name, a substantial fee, a—I hope you'll forgive me—somewhat mysterious guru who quotes Joni Mitchell and Robin Williamson, and a bunch of portraits of religious icons, my antennae start quivering violently. If I want to determine in some kind of objective manner whether my lingering doubts are unfair to you, all I can really do is compare how I'm feeling today with the day before I came. To be blunt, I feel worse. And reading Alan Watts on how the whole guru/seeker relationship is based on conscious or unconscious trickery just confirms my worst suspicions. There's nothing I hate more than feeling like a rube at a carnival or a latecomer to a pyramid scheme.

Rabi. I'm sorry that you've both been so unhappy here. Naturally, I want you to be more comfortable with your lives rather than less. It may help you to know that I've seen many, many individuals have these sorts of crises during their stays and later find that their visits have been valuable for them. Obviously, you're free to leave whenever you like, but, as you've already cleared out your calendars and paid your fees, if you can stand to stick it out, it might turn out to be worth the pain.

Paul. If you don't mind me asking, just what happened to these people to make them come around? Did you manage to convince them of the rightness of your approach? Did they give up the fight from being beaten down by the regular repetition of your claims? Succumb to the self-hypnosis? Or what, exactly?

Rabi (laughing). It's simple. I slipped something into their drinking water.

G. It's a serious question, Rabi. Do the people here always come around to your way of thinking? Don't you ever come around to theirs? Or do you just rely on having sheep here?

Rabi. I'm sorry. I didn't mean to make light of Paul's question. I believe these visitors grew during their stays here. And I always try to learn something from each of my guests. You must know I have no aversion to skepticism: that's why I recommend readings like Voltaire and Mencken. I'm not interested in sheep.

G. It seems you have a limit to your tolerance for dissent, though. Personal deities are treated with scorn, for example.

Paul. Existentialism doesn't fare too well either.

Rabi. I try to remember the goals of my visitors. I have

no objection to any of their worldviews as long as they seem to me to be consistent with the ultimate goals they have expressed to me. For example, if a visitor comes to my Center because he is tired of being anxious about the inevitability of his death, but while he is here he tries to convince me of the value of a philosophy of life based on the horror of transience, I may try to dissuade him. Of course, he may prefer to discard his prior goal and embrace anxiety. In that case, he'll likely leave early. That's his choice.

G. But you could be wrong about what worldviews are consistent with a visitor's ultimate goals, couldn't you? You don't claim any infallibility about these kind of predictions, do you?

Rabi. Certainly not. I have only my limited experience to go by. But it is usually not too difficult to reach reasonable conclusions on such matters if one can look at them from the outside as I can. I mean, I'm obviously not tied up with the particular goals and solutions chosen in the same way as the visitors. Let me give another example. Suppose someone comes here with a terminal illness. Now, most of us realize—at least most of the time—that we can't get rid of cancer by wishing, even with some special kind of gemstone in our hands. But although this woman says she wants to learn to accept her fate, I see her start to drift into a search for magical, healing talismans. I would try to nudge this woman in a different direction. It's possible, of course, that I won't succeed, and her next stop will be a gem store or a witches' coven.

G. Or, maybe you *will* succeed and she'll have nothing whatever to lean on. Maybe her hope for a cure was all she had to keep her going.

Rabi. It's *my* goal to provide her with more than that. But of course you're right. Sometimes I fail and visitors leave more unhappy than they were when they arrived. Perhaps there are also instances when I have been wrong with my prescriptions and the visitor has later discovered exactly what she has always sought at a herbalist shop in New Hampshire. My point was that, at least in the vast majority of cases, it's not at all difficult to see a mismatch between a particular goal and a particular solution—if one has the right vantage point.

Paul. Can I interrupt here to say that everything I've heard for the last few minutes sounds to me like nothing more than introductory psychology. Obviously, when goals and solutions collide, people are likely to be unhappy. You can get that from any third rate therapist or self-help book. Where's the religion or spirituality in any of that?

Rabi. As you know, while I think the line between psychology and religion is dim and shifting, I do think there is a line. When the Zen aspirant has had his *satori* and for him, once again, a river is just a river and a mountain simply a mountain, there is a new significance to everything in his world. He knows now what he is part of and what he is. I don't think a purely therapeutic technique either promises or delivers that sort of understanding.

Paul. Do you mind if I quote something here from Koestler about these *satori* experiences?

Rabi. Please.

Paul. It's from *The Lotus and the Robot*. Here it is:

> The whole teaching of Zen seems to be directed against the inhibitions and restraints imposed by the Japanese code of behaviour. Against the Spartan self-discipline demanded by the code, stands Po-chang's famous definition of Zen: 'When hungry, eat, when tired, sleep.' The traditional dread of unforeseen situations is neutralized by springing surprises and shocks on the disciple and encouraging him to reciprocate in an equally eccentric fashion: the koan technique is designed to bring out

just that side of a person which the social code condemns: 'the unexpected man.' In the social code, 'self-respect' is practically synonymous with cautious and circumspect behaviour, designed to avoid adverse comment; Zen bullies the pupil into throwing caution to the wind, and teaches him to respond spontaneously, 'without even the thickness of a hair between impulse and act'....

Satori is a wonderfully rubbery concept. There are small satoris and big satoris. They occur when one solves a koan, or in meditation, but also through looking at a peach-blossom or watching a pebble hit a bamboo. The mondos, in which the disciple who asked a too rational question is whacked on the head, usually end with the line: 'at that moment he had his satori.'[59]

And Koestler also talks about the lengthy training in archery or flower arrangement or whatever, where the student attempts to remove all ego from his activity. That process—stripped of all the mumbo-jumbo—is just a matter of a complicated task becoming automatic over time. He says that the training could be shortened considerably if it were drained of all the superfluous metaphysics. And he tells us that the so-called "masters" aren't really world class archers anyway, at least not by any objective standards.

Rabi. I must say his criticism seems to me to be too harsh and to miss much that is valuable in Zen. But I do think there is truth in parts of Koestler's critique as well. I think there are important facets of Buddhism and older Vedantic thought that are left out of certain manifestations of Zen. For example, I don't think one can attain much in the way of the answers we three seek simply by sitting in meditation on one or more koans year after year. To use the terms of the earlier, Small Raft Buddhism, there are other paths that must be taken: those of right conduct and right speech, to mention just two. And the Zen approach seems to me overly simplistic at times, like an Eastern version of the song "All You've Got To Do Is Act Naturally." For if everything is already *Tao*, the real key must be to learn to forget about all this spirituality, which must just be superfluous nonsense. This desire for a perfect simplicity often reflects itself in a fondness for paradox that sometimes infects the Zen approach. To take one example, Ma-tsu, an early practitioner of Zen, has said,

> The Tao has nothing to do with discipline. If you say that it is attained by discipline, when the discipline is perfected it can again be lost (or, finishing the discipline turns out to be losing the Tao)...If you say that there is no discipline, this is to be the same as ordinary people.[60]

This seems a false dilemma to me. I *do* think enlightenment can be attained only through a rigorous discipline—what I call "The Perennial Solution"—but I'm willing to accept the fact that even perfect discipline can deteriorate or be lost. Why shouldn't a lasting *sadhana* require a vigilance that can never be completely relaxed? The fact that some formerly difficult task has gotten easier with practice doesn't imply that it can never become arduous again. Your friend Mr. Watts seems to relish the many puzzling stories strewn throughout the Zen literature, but he doesn't always take the trouble to determine whether the paradoxes they express are genuine or only apparent.

Paul. Do you consider yourself more of an old-school, *Hinayana* Buddhist, then?

Rabi. Well, I agree with the Four Noble Truths: that a certain type of suffering or frustration is nearly ubiquitous in our lives, that there is a common cause to much of this unpleasantness, that the solution to this problem involves letting go of certain types of attachments, and that there are methods available to effect this improvement in our own lives. Gautama's elucidation of these truths seems to me apt and informative:

> This, O monks, is the Ariyan Truth of Suffering: Birth is suffering, old age is suffering, sickness is suffering, death is suffering, to be united with the unloved is suffering, to be separated from the loved is suffering, not to obtain what one desires is suffering....
>
> This, O monks, is the Ariyan Truth of the Origin of Suffering: It is the will to life which leads from birth to birth, together with lust and desire, which finds gratification here and there; the thirst for pleasures, the thirst for being, the thirst for power.
>
> This, O monks, is the Ariyan Truth of the Extinction of Suffering: The extinction of this thirst by complete annihilation of desire, letting it go, expelling it, separating oneself from it, giving it no room.
>
> This, O monks, is the Ariyan Truth of the Path which leads to the Extinction of Suffering: It is this sacred Eightfold Path, to-wit: Right Belief, Right Aspiration, Right Speech, Right Conduct, Right Living, Right Effort, Right Recollectedness, Right Rapture.[61]

I also believe Gautama hit upon something extremely important with his doctrine of the middle way—his advice to eschew both hedonism and asceticism. It's only where the various individual Paths get fleshed out that I can't follow completely. I can't seem to digest quite all of the Buddha's extremely subtle arguments about the non-existence of the ego, and I do agree with the Zen tradition that my intellectual shortcomings here may not be so important, since philosophical argument is over-emphasized by the *Hinayana* school. At some point, each of us has to just *see*.

Paul. Watts seems to think that our notion of ego is actually based on a logical error. We don't really experience it: we just fallaciously infer its existence from what we actually *do* experience.

Rabi. Yes, there are similar arguments to be found in the earliest Buddhist scriptures. But not all of the premises are obvious to me, and I can't tell if all the conclusions follow even if they *are* true. In any case, I don't see how any fundamental psychological problem can be resolved either by lessons in logic or by the elucidation of a philosophical principle—even one that happens to be true. If someone is unhappy or afraid, does it make sense to try to convince him that everything is really all right because there was never any *him* to be troubled in the first place? Watts is undoubtedly clever, but what I've seen of his work seems to me ultimately unconvincing. Not only is it awash in false paradoxes, fallacious arguments, and chimerical "double-binds," but I'm not sure he realized that if, as he often insists, no abstract categories actually fit reality, very few sentences in any of his books can have the simple virtue of being true. In his many attacks on any attempt to grasp or "pigeonhole" the real world, he somewhere loses the fact that almost every assertion one can make—including his own—ascribes some abstract property or other to some part or aspect of reality. And, with respect to his comments about guru trickery, I have no wish to deny the power of the placebo effect, but surely that's not the *only* manner in which people can be made healthier by doctors, therapists, gurus, or whatever. Cases must certainly abound in which surgeons have greatly improved the lives of even those patients who have doubted their skills. In the area of psychotherapy, this sort of help is no doubt more difficult, but is it really true that an untrusted therapist can *never* lead a patient to an important, life-changing insight? And, more importantly, what is the basis for Watts' belief that the psychotherapist or guru can do no more than pretend to some non-existent wisdom while the patient gets better on his or her own? Does he base this conclusion on some sort of carefully controlled study, or is it simply a function of the fact that he's been unable to identify a single troubled individual who's been cured by *his* sort of logic lessons? I, for one, don't believe that psychotherapy has value only as a distraction from one's problems while one heals naturally, and I don't see that Watts' unsupported assertions to the contrary prove anything whatever. I do think, however, that if the one and only cure for neurosis were for the neurotic to grow slowly into the realization of the truth of the non-existence of ego, then psychotherapists might just as well take up juggling or storytelling as devote their efforts to affecting a sage appearance. It would help pass the time more quickly while their patients are growing on their own....(Laughing) Ah, I see I've turned your simple question about whether or not the ego is an inferred entity into an opportunity for a general diatribe against poor Mr. Watts. I apologize for that: I must have been stung by some the remarks of his you quoted.

Paul. Aha, a nerve has been stuck. Better make a note of that: (he feigns writing on a pad) never mention Alan Watts again unless it's to say something uncomplimentary about his juggling skills....But let me get this straight. Did you say you aren't sure whether or not the Buddhist denial of the ego is correct?

Rabi. To tell the truth, I'm not even entirely sure what it means.

Paul. And you're the one who claims to know "what it is that you're part of and what it is that you are"? It doesn't seem like all this success on the mysticism front has given you much to hang your hat on.

Rabi. When I perceptually take in what's around me, there's a sense in which I know what there is "out there." In another sense, however, I learn very little, since I don't have a deep understanding of the physics of macroscopic objects. That's my predicament with respect to my mystical experiences. What it is that I have learned is hard to put into words. Harder even than describing the simplest fruit of our perceptual acts. The Buddha insists over and over again that we are not any particular physical form or forms, that we are not any sensation or group of sensations, that we are not any perception or group of perceptions, and so on. He also denies both that we are some kind of collection of these different items and that we are somehow separate from all such items and combinations. He concludes from this that there is really no such thing as ego at all. He seems to be saying that each use of the word "me" or the word "I" is just a useful shorthand, analogous to the use of "America" in such locutions as "America believes in liberty for all." So, we might say he's a nominalist with respect to minds in the way that many other philosophers have been nominalists with respect to properties like *redness* or *beauty*. Now, I believe I know what I am, but I'm not at all certain whether or not this *I* is distinct from or composed of a number of fleeting mental processes. Like my understanding of most things, my grasp of what I am is very far from providing me with knowledge of every single truth about myself. Furthermore, I don't have a sense of whether there's any important difference between these two views. I mean, we could utterly deny the existence of ego as Buddha does, or instead claim that a mind is really analyzable into some kind of complex of ideas, sensations and other mental events—that it *is* nothing more or less than this bundle. What important difference is there here? And even if there *is* a difference between these two positions—let us call them "The Buddhist Theory" and "The Humean Theory"—I don't understand how it can have any significance for *sadhana* or spiritual realization. Perhaps the argument is that if I am in reality a bundle of ideas, I can still, in some sense, age or die as this bundle grows older or ceases to include any more experiences, while if there is no *I* at all, it might be held that there's no danger of the occurrence of either of these evils. This is a sort of abstract philosophy at which I'm not particularly adept. What I do believe deeply is that reaching final conclusions to questions of this complex nature has no importance whatever to religious fulfillment or enlightenment. As I've said, I'm in agreement with the Zen tradition on that point, if not on many others. We are likely to run aground where there's too much argument and not enough learning how to live.

G. So, they're all confused, eh? Watts, Suzuki, Koestler, Buddha. Not to mention Jesus, Spinoza, Lewis, Fechner, Chesterton and the rest. They've all missed something important that you've managed to grasp.

Rabi. You ask me my opinions on the views of these thinkers, and I give them to you. Maybe one or more of them is completely right, and I'm thoroughly deluded. But what can I do but provide my own views and my reasons for them and let you decide for yourself? If classifying my belief system is important to you, I suppose you could call me a Buddhist, but I'm certainly an unorthodox one: so many non-Buddhist schools and individual thinkers have influenced my thinking about religion that I'm not sure any Buddhist monk would care to have me for one of his flock. This is not a matter of importance to me. I've always been partial to Shaw's admonition that one's time is better spent finding one's own newer and better religion than it is in chafing under the tenets of any existing dogma.[62]

G. Well, let me ask you something else.

Rabi. Of course.

G. Just what is it that makes you think that what you call your "mystical experiences" are so special? Do you think they are somehow more immediate than other experiences you or other people have? Do you think they are unmediated by your background, education and prejudices? Do you really believe that if your upbringing had been radically different you'd have still taken the exact same things from these experiences that you do now?

Paul. And I'd add that G's question is just as valid for our everyday perceptions of physical objects. If not for our language and other tools of thought, our ordinary experience of the world would probably be a lot different too.

Rabi. I make no claims as to immediacy, unmediatedness, or anything of the kind for any of my experiences, mystical or otherwise. Furthermore, I have no idea to what extent they depend on the particular languages I know or the ways of thinking that I have been taught since childhood. I just find that there's something I can't doubt about them. That's all.

G. Well, my relatively direct understanding of the outside world doesn't seem to prevent *me* from saying any number of comprehensible things about it. And I find it difficult to doubt some of these things too. For example, physical objects are outside of me. They take up space. They persist whether I'm around to see them or not.

Paul. They can be red or green, but they can't be both red and green all over at the same time.

G. Right. So why isn't there a single thing you can tell us about what you claim to be your analogous knowledge of your inner self?

Paul. Even Plato's cave dwellers might have come to understand something more of the world if their unchained friend had taken the time to provide them with some instruction in geometry and optics. Maybe you could start by telling us how "what it is we are part of" interacts with what we non-seers *can* apprehend.

Rabi. I believe that anything I can say would misrepresent the true nature of my experience.

G. But that so-called ineffability just comes from the fact that it's nothing more than a feeling you're reporting on, doesn't it? The philosopher G. Dawes Hicks talks about this in one of the books here. He says,

> Mystical states are more like states of feeling than like states of intellect....[S]uch states seem to those who have them to be states of insight, of illumination, into depths of truth beyond the reach of the discursive reason....It is true doubtless that they cannot be gained by mere effort, yet it is no less true that without effort they cannot be gained at all. Ideas may illumine suddenly the minds of men of genius, but they have been prepared for by strenuous intellectual labour; they sum up in themselves, so to speak, in concentrated form the results of long and toilsome critical analysis and reflective reconstruction. They do not drop from the skies; they come to minds of wide range and profound depth, minds that are saturated with thoughts making for the new ideas and pointing the way towards them. And, even then, their claim to be experiences of what is true is entitled to recognition only in so far as they can stand the test of critical scrutiny and rational interpretation. Otherwise, they may be

legitimately regarded as open to suspicion and distrust.[63]

Rabi. All right, all right, it's enough. Let me see if I can summarize your concerns, G. You believe that any claims I make to knowledge based on my religious experiences are bogus because all experience must be mediated and informed by the prior knowledge and conceptual system of the experiencer. You also think that these experiences must be disregarded because they lack any content that can be clearly expressed in words. You believe I am arrogant because I don't completely agree with the teachings of Buddha, Jesus or any of the other sages you have listed. And you find me to be patronizing because of overconfidence in my judgments regarding the matching or mismatching of visitors' goals with their proposed solutions. And Paul, besides these, I take it you might add that I am either a conscious charlatan or an unwitting one, because that's all any guru can be, that the solutions I propose are either popular psychology or utter rubbish, that I ought to know whether or not I am an ego or that there is no ego, that I should be able to explain the causal interactions between that of which I claim to have mystical knowledge and our everyday world, that the entire Zen tradition is nothing more than a reaction to the social constraints imposed by Confucianism, that if there were anything at all to Zen, archers trained in that tradition would always sweep the Olympic medals, and, finally, that I inappropriately use poetry and even popular song lyrics to express thoughts which ought to be expressed in more sober, inaccessible and arcane language. Have I left anything out?

Paul. Not that I can think of....It does seem like a pretty harsh series of indictments, doesn't it? But keep in mind that at least we haven't stooped to criticizing your taste in clothes.

G. I...I'm...I didn't mean to be so...carping. But I still think that...

Rabi. Surely you two don't think that criticisms of this kind have never crossed my path before. I have long considered such objections, as well as many others, at least as ferocious. For example, I have a book here in which the author, Anna Robeson Burr, closely analyzes the religious confessions of scores of mystics before calmly inferring that their mental instability was so great that what we take as religious conversion is nothing more than the return of a primitive animism overtaking the sanity of each writer. She says,

> Our conclusion that [mystical religious experiences] are due to animistic revival, acting counter to the later-developed intellectual and social elements of Personality, with a result temporarily or permanently disintegrating, is a conclusion very far from the flattering theories of the mystical compromiser, at present so much in vogue. This conclusion contradicts such theories through the confessant's own testimony, by showing that the peace, the joy the reunion, are but the evanescent effects of psychological suggestion. The evidence proves that a conversion-crisis rarely establishes Personality on any higher level than before, and that it is never without a reaction, during which the subject has to suffer further crises of doubt and gloom. The records show that whenever the conversion appears to be the means of opening new channels to the energy of the subject, it does so through his impulse toward work of some kind, or by bringing him into contact with some sectarian activity...but such elevation cannot be called the effect of the conversion; it is rather the effect of the subsequent work....If the subject's emotional experience does not lead him in the direction of new work (and there are many cases where it does not), then the last state of this man is infinitely worse than his first.[64]

You must not suppose I'm unaware of attacks that have long been leveled at those who think there's anything valuable about their apparently mystical intuitions.

Paul. Well, at least we've never accused you of being a lunatic. And, now that I think of it, neither of us has ever called you a werewolf either—if that's what this woman means by being an animist. We ought to get some credit for that!

Rabi. Look, it's getting late, and I have to prepare for my next session. Let's continue this this afternoon. (He stands up and they both leave.)

Monday, 3:00 PM—The Library
(Rabi is pacing and looking through a book when Paul and G arrive. He motions them to sit down.)

G. Rabi. Paul and I had a long talk, and we both feel pretty bad about the session this morning. Obviously, we haven't been giving you a fair chance. Even if we don't agree with everything you tell us, that was no excuse for our joint attack. We were fearful and defensive, unwilling to consider any changes to our outlooks that seemed threatening to us. In fact, you could say we were like the demons in Cardinal Newman's *Dream of Gerontius*: "It is the restless panting of their being; like beasts of prey, who, caged within their bars, in a deep hideous purring have their life, and an incessant pacing to and fro." Let me just say that I'm truly embarrassed about our behavior.

Paul. Well, I'm not sure I'd go as far as analogizing us to the demons of hell, but I'm sorry for the tag team act too. In retrospect, it does seem pretty childish.

Rabi. Oh, you two are certainly not evil spirits, but I

do think that you are hounded by them. You remind me of
the fabled ascetic during the time of Siddhartha's search
for enlightenment who would wander from town to town
asking "What is the Ganges? Is it the sand? The banks? The
water?" and so on. After this troubled soul left the village
where Siddhartha was staying, the future Buddha mused,

> What he sees he does not wish for,
> But something that he does not see;
> Methinks that he will wander long,
> And what he wishes, not obtain.
> He is not pleased with what he gets;
> No sooner gained, it meets his scorn.
> Insatiate are wishes all!
> The wish-free therefore, we adore![65]

Paul (laughing). Sheesh. Is there anyone around here
besides me who can't quote any poetry? And another
thing: I'm not sure this Newman for Buddha trade was
such a good thing. Is it better to be demon from hell or a
psychotic homeless guy?

Rabi. Neither is very desirable. But the fault is not all of
your own making. I've also had a chance to think about the
concerns you expressed to me this morning: I've realized
some of the errors I've made in my sessions with both of
you, and I have some suggestions for future avoidance
of them. Most of your complaints seem to center on the
authority I have claimed for certain of my experiences. I
can't remember exactly how I came to be discussing with
you the mystical events in my own life. Perhaps it was in
response to Paul's charge that all I offer here is a kind of
psychotherapy. However that may be, I have certainly
said repeatedly that the effects of Right Aspiration,
Right Conduct and Right Reflection contain more than
simple psychological contentment, that they yield a kind

of religious insight. But you have responded to this that what I now promise is no more than a combination of contentment and ineffable mumbo-jumbo. Your point is well taken. If I can't communicate this additional element, why mention it at all? When I allude to "What it is I am part of" you quite rightly ask, "So, Rabi, just what *is it* that you are part of?" You have thus taught me that further discussion of this subject is like questions regarding whether the world is eternal, whether dogs have Buddha nature and whether more than a finite number of angels can dance on a pin. I have learned from you that, as the Buddha would say, the elucidation of this matter tends not to edification: it profits not. Tagore has a poem about this problem:

> I boasted among men that I had known you. They see your pictures in all works of mine. They come and ask me, 'Who is he?' I know not how to answer them. I say, 'Indeed, I cannot tell.' They blame me and they go away in scorn. And you sit there smiling.
>
> I put my tales of you into lasting songs. The secret gushes out from my heart. They come and ask me, 'Tell me all your meanings.' I know not how to answer them. I say, 'Ah, who knows what they mean?' They smile and go away in utter scorn. And you sit there smiling.[66]

Paul. This kind of reminds me of the trouble Kant had to face with his "thing-in-itself." He claimed we could know of the existence of a reality outside of all human conceptual schemes, but that left him in the position of not being able to say much about this realm that anyone could fathom.

Rabi. Yes, perhaps there are similarities. In the Vedantic literature there are repeated admonitions to remember that *Brahman* is "Not this. Not that." Obviously, only those who have in some sense already *seen* will understand. I therefore propose that we leave such talk alone for a time and concentrate more closely on what you need to do to achieve the goals with which you came to this Center. Let us try to avoid the taint of metaphysical questions. I will do my part by trying never to make any claims of having reached a kind of enlightenment through the means of meditation. Instead, I will simply suggest that my practices have led to a cessation of suffering and the flowering of a deep faith and leave it at that.

Paul. Well, that sounds enough like a capitulation on your part for G and me to declare total victory and begin the pillage of your lands and chattels. What do you say, G? Should we discuss our terms of surrender and split the spoils?

Rabi. I'm afraid it's not so simple as that. I will change my tack, but I expect a *quid pro quo* from you two. I have learned from you and you must now try a little harder to learn from me.

G. What do you expect of us?

Rabi. You must endeavor to join me in eschewing metaphysical questions and in concentrating on what you can do to achieve the goals you've stated in your applications. While you remain here, you must commit to giving a fair trial to the recommendations I make regarding the means of achieving those goals.

Paul. You mean we're stuck with every jot and tittle of what we wrote down when we applied? We can't make a single amendment?

Rabi. Not at all. You can revise them if you wish, and if your goals remain something I think I can help with, you'll stay and work with me along the lines I've discussed. Obviously, if you switch to a goal involving something about your golf swing or the toning of your abdominal muscles, this isn't the place for you. Some objectives can be easily rejected out of hand. As the Buddhist scripture says,

> There are five things which no Samana, and no Brahman, and no god, neither Mara nor Brahma, nor any being in the universe, can bring about. What five things are those? That what is subject to old age should not grow old, that what is subject to sickness should not be sick, that what is subject to death should not die, that what is subject to decay should not decay, that what is liable to pass away should not pass away. This no Samana can bring about, nor any god, neither Mara, nor Brahma, nor any being in the universe.[67]

Paul. I take it you're not contemplating returning any of our fees if we can't reach an agreement on what reasonable goals are, or if we find that what we really want isn't the sort of thing you can provide.

Rabi. That's correct. I made you no guarantee that your visits here would be successful. I promised only to try my best to help you reach the objectives you set forth. I'll continue to do that if you decide to stay.

G. Oh, c'mon, Paul. This isn't about the money. I'm not interested in any refund.

Paul. I guess I'm not really either. But, you know, there's no harm in asking: there might have been a double-your-money-back clause or a frequent flier offer that I didn't notice....But seriously, I think there are bound to be continuing problems. Remember, I haven't just now stopped being resistant to solutions that seem like nothing more than pop psychology or self-hypnosis.

Rabi. I believe your application simply expresses a sincere desire to grow beyond your persistent death anxieties. If your questions seem to me likely to further that objective, then I welcome them. But persistent questioning can also be a sign of resistance, of littering one's path with obstacles that are intended to be insurmountable.

Paul. Well, yes, I suppose I do want to grow, but of course the key here is what is meant by "grow." I don't want to move beyond my fears by, say, losing consciousness. And I don't want to give up all right to asking questions. What would be the point of that? It's questions that have brought us here in the first place.

Rabi. Let us not quibble about this. As I said this morning and as you must know by now, I like questioning minds, and I encourage a healthy sense of skepticism. But we must all try to remember that this isn't intended to be a summer seminar in epistemology or metaphysics. If a swimming student spends all her time asking questions about the nature of buoyancy, she may never learn a single stroke. The same is true with respect to living well. It's often the nature rather than the quantity of the questioning that is telling. Will a particular line of questioning push you closer to or farther away from your goals? Is the answer you seek something that is likely to make them appear unreachable? You must remember, *I* don't consider these objectives beyond your reach or I wouldn't have invited you here. In any case, as I have said, you may revise your applications as you wish, but I reserve the right to determine whether I think they exhibit "Right Aspirations" — that is, whether they reflect the sorts of objectives that I believe I can assist you in reaching. I think I am a better judge of that than it is possible for you to be. So, look carefully at your original applications and think about what changes you might like to make to them. And, while you undertake your reviews, perhaps you won't mind if I read to you some relevant passages from the writings of Erich Fromm that may help you in determining what if any revisions you'd like to make to your list of goals. Let's see....here is Fromm on the relationship of psychotherapy and religion, a topic that has worried Paul since his first day here:

> There are...factors in Freud's concept of psychoanalysis which transcend the conventional notion of illness and cure. Those familiar with Eastern thought, and especially with Zen Buddhism, will notice that the factors which I am going to mention are not without relation to concepts and thoughts of the Eastern mind. The principle to be mentioned here first is Freud's concept that *knowledge leads to transformation,* that theory and practice must not be separated, that in the very act of *knowing* oneself, one *transforms* oneself. It is hardly necessary to emphasize how different this idea is from the concepts of scientific psychology in Freud's...time, where knowledge in itself remains theoretical knowledge, and has not a transforming function in the knower.
>
> In still another aspect Freud's method has a close connection with Eastern thought, and especially with Zen Buddhism. Freud did not share the high evaluation of our conscious thought system, so characteristic of modern Western man. On the contrary, he believed that our conscious thought was only a small part of the whole of the psychic process going on in us and, in fact, an insignificant one in comparison with the tremendous power of those sources within ourselves which are dark and irrational and at the same time unconscious. Freud, in his wish to arrive at insight into the real nature of a person wanted to break through the conscious thought system, by his method of *free association.*[68]

And, in the same volume, Suzuki also says something on the topic of flushing out the unconscious:

> The unconscious in its Zen sense is, no doubt, the mysterious, the unknown, and for that reason unscientific or ante-scientific. But this does not mean that it is beyond the reach of our consciousness and something we have nothing to do with. In fact it is, on the contrary, the most intimate thing to us, and it is just because of this intimacy that it is difficult

to take hold of, in the same way as the eye cannot see itself. To become, therefore, conscious of the unconscious requires a special training on the part of consciousness.[69]

Getting back to Fromm, here are some of his thoughts on the relationship between the seeker and the spiritual guide. I thought of this when Paul mentioned Watts' trickery theory.

> If the patient wants to get well and to change, that is fine, and the analyst is willing to help him. If his resistance to change is too great, this is not the analyst's responsibility. All his responsibility lies in lending the best of his knowledge and effort, of giving himself to the patient in search of the aim the patient seeks him out for.[70]
>
> The master does not call the student; he wants nothing from him, not even that he becomes enlightened; the student comes of his own free will, and he goes of his own free will. But inasmuch as he wants to learn from the master, the fact has to be recognized that the master is a master, that is, that the master knows what the student wants to know, and does not yet know.[71]

Now, here are a couple of passages from Fromm on the Zen perspective with respect to seeing the world with new eyes:

> The essence of Zen is the acquisition of enlightenment (*satori*). *Satori* is *not* an abnormal state of mind; it is *not* a trance in which reality disappears. It is not a narcissistic state of mind, as it can be seen in some religious manifestations. 'If anything, it is a perfectly normal state of mind...it all depends on the adjustment of the hinge, whether the door opens in or opens out...All your mental activities will now be working in a different key, which will be more satisfying, more peaceful, more full of joy than anything you ever experienced before. The tone of life will be altered. There is something rejuvenating in the possession of Zen. The spring flower will look prettier, and

the mountain stream runs cooler and more transparent.'[72]

It is very important to understand that the state of enlightenment is not a state of dissociation or of a trance in which one *believes* oneself to be awakened, when one is actually deeply asleep. The Western psychologist, of course, will be prone to believe that *satori* is just a subjective state, an auto-induced sort of trance....On the contrary, it is of crucial importance...to differentiate between genuine *satori* experience, in which the acquisition of a new viewpoint is real, and hence true, and pseudo-experience which can be of a hysterical or psychotic nature, in which the Zen student is convinced of having obtained *satori*, while the Zen master has to make it clear that he has not. It is precisely one of the functions of the Zen master to be on guard against his student's confusion of real and imaginary enlightenment.[73]

I suppose I should stop. I see that you both seem to have completed your reviews of your applications. Are there any changes you'd like to make?

G. You know, I'd almost forgotten how long I worked on this thing before I came here. And I think I still want basically the same things. So I guess I'm not ready to give up on this place yet. No changes for me....though I promise to try not to be such a disruptive student.

Paul. I can't really think of anything important to change in my application either. I mean there are a couple of commas I don't like, but it still does pretty much express how I'd like my life to change. I still want to overcome my fear of final separation from my loved ones and my memories. I'm afraid I don't have a much better sense today than when I applied of exactly what I want from you. If you can't show me that I'm immortal, I guess I want to be OK with the idea of my death. I don't know, since I can't figure out how to make this any better, I suppose I might as well just leave it the way it is....(Laughing) Jeez, G, it seems like the only spoils of war have been that we got a nice power rush for a couple of minutes this morning. Big shots before lunch, midgets beginning with dessert.

G. Or worse. Evil demons, maybe. You know, I still feel horrible, like we've lost something important that can't be regained. Rabi, I'm not sure I really want you never to tell us about your religious experiences. Maybe it's worse this way. This is like you're giving up on us.

Paul. I guess our hard-fought victory has turned out to be pretty hollow.

Rabi. Oh, no, not hollow. Not at all. I think we've all learned something important from our conversations today. And I'll never give up on either of you, G. I'm sorry if it seems patronizing, but I hope you won't mind thinking of me as being in a role akin to that of a well-intentioned parent who must sometimes try new approaches when the old ones fail. How could I ever give up on two such bright and vital individuals as you are? It's not that parents know everything: they often know much less than their children. But good parents always want what's best for their sons and daughters, even if they are often confused regarding what that best may be. In any case, I think we should now return to our one-on-one sessions for a while. I'll see each of you, separately, on Wednesday. Before you go, though, I want to tell you something that has been said about the composer Giaccomo Rossini. It seems that when he was working on one of the scores to his operas, if a page fell off the table at which he worked, he couldn't bring himself to get off his chair, kneel down and pick the page up from the floor. Instead, he would take a blank sheet from his table and write the entire page of orchestral score over from scratch. It is said that he would do all this time-consuming and repetitive work even if the page was all but completed, just to avoid having to get out of his chair.

Paul. Funny kind of laziness, that. Reminds me of Descartes, who didn't have the energy to get out of bed and get dressed, but somehow managed to write his *Meditations* from a recumbent position.

Rabi. Yes? Well this aspect of Rossini reminds *me* of certain visitors here who can't bring themselves to sit quietly and meditate for even an hour a day, but who seem to have abundant time and vitality for so many other activities that would seem to require a great deal more time and energy.

Paul. Hmmmm.

G. Actually, I find meditating to be a lot harder than just *talking* about meditating. And when I'm trying to do it, it's so much easier to let my mind wander than to keep it focussed on particular things.

Rabi. I promise you, it gets easier with practice—much like picking up sheet music from the floor would for a sedentary composer who, for the first time in his life, began the practice of taking daily walks. (He stands up.) Well, goodbye for now, my friends.

G & Paul. Goodbye, Rabi. (They leave.)

VI.
Week Ten

Monday, 11:45 AM—The Garden

G (sees Paul sitting at a table and comes over). Paul! I haven't seen you in ages. Where've you been, stranger?

Paul. Hey, G. How you doing? I spent the weekend in Burlington. Caught a couple of movies and went to a jazz club.

G. You know anybody in Burlington?

Paul. No, but I've been there before. I just stayed in a hotel and wandered around aimlessly. Nice town.

G. When I didn't see your car around I thought you might have re-reconsidered your decision to stay here and headed back to New York.

Paul. Nah, I'm actually starting to enjoy this place. In fact, I think I'll miss it some when I leave. I just felt the need for a little less...I don't know...quietude for a couple of days.

G. It seems like I didn't see you last week either. Did you play hooky?

Paul. No, I've just been doing a bunch of hiking. It really is beautiful country around here. What about you? I haven't seen you around much either.

G. Well, I thought I'd give this meditation thing a real chance before I have to go back to the office grind. You wouldn't believe how much time I've spent sitting in my room or here in the garden.

Paul. And?

G. I don't know. I fall asleep a lot. I've had some cool

dreams, but I haven't seen any mysterious lights or anything like that. But it's very luxurious. People who spend a lot of time meditating must have an awful lot of time and money. Most of us have to go to work or school or change diapers or something. But, I *am* taking this summer off, so I figure, what the heck.

Paul. I've gotten a bit more comfortable with meditating too. At least I don't get anxious every time I try it anymore. I like doing it when I walk, though I find it makes me more likely to trip over tree roots. What have you been talking about with Rabi?

G. Well, this morning we got into some Emerson, which is nice for me since I've always loved him.

Paul. I'm embarrassed to say that I'm one of the many supposedly educated Americans who has never read a single word of Emerson. Does it count if I've been meaning to? What would you recommend if I ever get out from under all the stuff I'm in the middle of right now?

G. Well, we've been discussing his essay "Compensation," which I find very thought-provoking. He also has beautiful pieces on Love, on Nature, on Friendship and, of course, the famous one on Self-Reliance. One of the things that confuses me about "Compensation" is that Rabi seems to like the position being put forth, but to me it doesn't seem that different from something by C.S. Lewis that Rabi clearly hated.

Paul. What's the position?

G. It's that there's a moral force at work in the world that evens everything out. He says that people who violate ethical principles can't help but suffer for it right here on earth, and that people who do good works automatically get some kind of psychic benefit. You know, "Virtue is its own reward." "What goes around comes around." All that sort of stuff. But Rabi scoffed at similar things when Lewis said them. He said something like that Lewis was trying to manufacture an entire theology out of feelings of guilt.

Paul. Well, I don't know anything about either Emerson or Lewis, but it's got to be extremely hard to prove that people who act morally tend to be happier because of some sort of metaphysical principle. Why couldn't this happiness just have resulted from parental and societal influences? I mean, would a girl raised by wolves or ducks or something be just as guilt-ridden as we would be if she stole someone's dinner? And even if she would be, couldn't that just be some kind of natural disposition of human beings—like our predisposition to use language—instead of the reflection of some kind of transcendent principle of justice?

G. Exactly. That's just the kind of stuff we were talking about. It seems like there are so many reasonable alternatives to Emerson's theory. First, maybe nasty people aren't really less happy than decent people on average.

Paul. It's always been an observation of mine that assholes get the gravy.

G. Well, Emerson would say that this gravy must disagree with their digestion.

Paul. One can only hope.

G. But even if we suppose that bad guys do get their just desserts in this life, why doesn't something like Freud's super-ego explain this? Our parents, our books, our laws, our TV shows, and all the rest drum into us from the time we're babies that people who steal or lie are creeps. That's bound to have an effect. Nobody should be surprised that people who give in to their so-called "baser instincts" have misgivings about it. It's weird when they don't. Like in that movie where inner city teenage kids kill somebody and then go out to McDonalds for burgers. We find *that* shocking.

Paul. Doesn't Emerson have anything to say about the alternatives to his conception of compensation?

G. To tell you the truth, it's hard to be sure. He's such a poetic writer; he doesn't put his essays into premises and conclusions that are easy to find. They're beautiful, and I usually get the feeling that he's on to something important, but I have the hardest time trying to figure out exactly what it is.

Paul. Oh no. This sounds a lot like Rabi's "that which we're a part of."

G. Yeah, it probably is. Emerson wrote so many beautiful things that I just can't quite seem to grasp. I mean, there are a couple of passages where he seems to be suggesting that there are two kinds of compensation, and maybe one is supposed to be the Freudian, guilt-type thing while the other is some deeper transcendental retribution. But I have to admit that I'm not at all sure. What do you make of this:

> All things are moral. That soul which within us is a sentiment, outside of us is a law. We feel its inspiration; but there in history we can see its fatal strength....
>
> Every act rewards itself, or in other words integrates itself, in a twofold manner; first in the thing, or in real nature; and secondly in the circumstance, or in apparent nature. Men call the circumstance the retribution. The causal retribution is in the thing and is seen by the soul. The retribution in the circumstance is seen by the understanding; it is inseparable from the thing, but is often spread over a long time and so does not become distinct until after many years. The specific stripes may follow late after the offence, but they follow because they accompany it. Crime and punishment grow out of one stem. Punishment is a fruit that unsuspected ripens within the flower of the pleasure which concealed it. Cause and effect, means and

ends, seed and fruit, cannot be severed; for the effect already blooms in the cause, the end pre-exists in the means, the fruit in the seed.[74]

He seems to be saying that one type of compensation is instantaneous while another can take place over a long period of years. But I don't really know whether I've got him right.

Paul. Anyway, is it clear if guilt caused by the operation of some kind of Freudian super-ego is instantaneous or gradual? Both, probably. I mean maybe it kicks in right away on some level, but can also gnaw away at you for years. So, it's hard to see if either or both of Emerson's two kinds of compensation are inconsistent with psychological or sociological causes.

G. That's my sense, too. But there's some beautiful stuff in here. And a few passages that seem ahead of their time. Like warning about the objectification of women and treating individuals as means to some end.

> Treat men as pawns and ninepins and you shall suffer as well as they. If you leave out their heart, you shall lose your own. The senses would make things of all persons; of women, of children, of the poor....
> All infractions of love and equity in our social relations are speedily punished. They are punished by fear. Whilst I stand in simple relations to my fellow-man, I have no displeasure in meeting him. We meet as water meets water, or as two currents of air mix, with perfect diffusion and interpenetration of nature. But as soon as there is any departure from simplicity and attempt at halfness, or good for me that is not good for him, my neighbor feels the wrong; he shrinks from me as far as I have shrunk from him; his eyes no longer seek mine: there is war between us; there is hate in him and fear in me.[75]

Paul. I don't know. It seems an awful lot like so much of

the stuff I've read and heard since I came here. It's pretty, and there's a kernel of empirical truth in there somewhere, but the interpretations are too...I don't know...*lofty* to be taken seriously. I mean, I've been a pretty bad boy over the last few years. I've treated my family shabbily, and I'm paying for it now—both in forced separation and in huge quantities of guilt. But I can't see why we need any metaphysical explanations for my situation. Like you said, it would be weird if I *weren't* paying. It's just common sense.

G. I wonder if there's any way to test Emerson's hypothesis against Freud's. I mean, are there any actions you can think of that are generally followed by Freudian guilt but not by Emersonian compensation, or vice-versa?

P. Well, isn't the super-ego supposed to go out of whack sometimes? I mean doesn't Freud think that a certain portion of crazy people are that way because of over-active super-egos? I get the sense that Emerson thinks that compensation is always perfect.

G. Yeah, he says this:

> The dice of God are always loaded. The world looks like a multiplication-table, or a mathematical equation, which, turn it how you will balances itself. Take what figure you will, its exact value, nor more nor less, still returns to you. Every secret is told, every crime is punished, every virtue rewarded, every wrong redressed, in silence and certainty. What we call retribution is the universal necessity by which the whole appears wherever a part appears.[76]

He thinks there's an iron law or something. But I guess most people would agree there are a whole lot of people with too much guilt and another huge group who really ought to be burdened with way more.

Paul. I used to have this fantasy that people like Hitler or Stalin couldn't possibly have been happy, that they must have suffered terribly for their evil deeds. But obviously even if they did have the occasional twinge, it's absurd to suggest that compensation has been perfect.

G. And, of course, there are so many perfectly wonderful people who suffer terribly through most of their lives. The more you think about this, the more far-fetched Emerson's position seems.

Paul. I guess that's why most compensation theories involve some kind of life after death—either a visit to heaven or hell, or reincarnation, where karma can do its thing during the person's next life, as a billy-goat or turnip or something. On the other hand, as much as this poetic, almost-but-not-quite-true stuff bothers me, I have to admit that I've been very taken by Rabi's namesake on this issue.

G. Tagore?

Paul. Yeah. He has a chapter on the Problem of Evil in his book *Sadhana* that Rabi's always quoting from. I read it last week and it's very beautiful. Tagore is like Emerson in being hard to turn into syllogisms: he's a poet first. But, almost despite myself, I find the book comforting. Agghhh! I can't believe I'm saying this. If I don't come to my senses in a day or two, promise you'll have me committed somewhere.

G. Comforting?! You really *have* changed!

Paul. Don't get me wrong. I'm not saying I believe a word of it. But it's undeniably beautiful. Just listen to this:

> If we kept the search-light of our observation turned upon the fact of death, the world would appear to us like a huge charnel-house; but in the world of life the thought of death has, we find, the least possible hold upon our minds. Not because it

is the least apparent, but because it is the negative aspect of life; just as, in spite of the fact that we shut our eyelids every second, it is the openings of the eyes that count. Life as a whole never takes death seriously. It laughs, dances and plays, it builds, hoards and loves in death's face. Only when we detach one individual fact of death do we see its blankness and become dismayed. We lose sight of the wholeness of a life of which death is part. It is like looking at a piece of cloth through a microscope. It appears like a net: we gaze at the big holes and shiver in imagination. But the truth is, death is not the ultimate reality. It looks black, as the sky looks blue; but it does not blacken existence, just as the sky does not leave its stain upon the wings of the bird.

When we watch a child trying to walk we see its countless failures; its successes are but few. If we had to limit our observation within a narrow space of time, the sight would be cruel. But we find that in spite of its repeated failures there is an impetus of joy in the child which sustains it in its seemingly impossible task. We see it does not think of its falls so much as of its power to keep its balance though for only a moment.

Like these accidents in a child's attempts to walk, we meet with sufferings in various forms in our life every day, showing the imperfections in our knowledge and our available power, and in the application of our will. But if these revealed our weakness to us only, we should die of utter depression. When we select for observation a limited area of our activities, our individual failures and miseries loom large in our minds; but our life leads us instinctively to take a wider view. It gives us an ideal of perfection which ever carries us beyond our present limitations.[77]

Isn't that just gorgeous?

G. It is, and I'd love to talk to you more about it, and about the new pious Paul in general, but I've really got to hightail it, or I'm gonna be late for a hair appointment. Can we talk later?

Paul (Stands and nods, smiling beatifically with his hands clasped in prayer). Bless you, my child. You may take your leave of my most holy presence now.

G. *Ciao.*

❧

Monday, 3:00 PM—The Library

G (enters, finds Rabi in his usual place making some notes, and sits down across from him). Hi. Am I interrupting anything?

Rabi (puts down his pen and closes his notebook). Not at all, G. Good to see you. What's going on? Have you been thinking any more about the case of Freud v. Emerson?

G. I have. Quite a lot, in fact. You know, as much as I hate to admit it, it seems like an easy victory for Freud. A knock-out really. I'm hoping you have some responses, that you can rehabilitate *some* kind of religious thought after Freud's assault.

Rabi. Yes, Freud is very thorough, and he seems to close off every possible avenue of escape for the religious individual. But let's see what we two can do to discover an unobstructed passage. Would you care to summarize his criticism of religion?

G. Well, I've underlined a few passages from *Future of an Illusion.* Can I just read some of them?

Rabi. That would be perfect.

G. I guess I could start with some stuff on why human beings are religious in the first place:

> [R]eligious ideas have arisen from the same need as have all the other achievements of civilization: from the necessity of defending oneself against the crushingly superior force of nature. To this a second motive was added—the urge to rectify the shortcomings of civilization which made themselves painfully felt.
>
> [A] store of ideas is created, born from man's need to make his helplessness tolerable and built up from the material of memories of the helplessness of his own childhood and the

childhood of the human race. It can clearly be seen that the possession of these ideas protects him in two directions—against the dangers of nature and Fate, and against the injuries that threaten him from human society itself.

It is in keeping with the course of human development that external coersion gradually becomes internalized; for a special mental agency, man's super-ego, takes it over and includes it among its commandments. Every child presents this process of transformation to us; only by that means does it become a moral and social being.

[R]eligious ideas...are not precipitates of experience or end-results of thinking: they are illusions, fulfilments of the oldest, strongest and most urgent wishes of mankind. The secret of their strength lies in the strength of those wishes. As we already know, the terrifying impression of helplessness in childhood aroused the need for protection—for protection through love—which was provided by the father; and the recognition that this helplessness lasts throughout life made it necessary to cling to the existence of a father, but this time a more powerful one. Thus the benevolent rule of a divine Providence allays our fear of the dangers of life; the establishment of a moral world-order ensures the fulfilment of the demands of justice, which have so often remained unfulfilled in human civilization; and the prolongation of earthly existence in a future life provides the local and temporal framework in which these wish-fulfilments shall take place. Answers to the riddles that tempt the curiosity of man, such as how the universe began or what the relation is between body and mind, are developed in conformity with the underlying assumptions of this system. It is an enormous relief to the individual psyche if the conflicts of its childhood arising from the father-complex—conflicts which it has never wholly overcome—are removed from it and brought to a solution which is universally accepted.[78]

Rabi. It's hard to deny that religious beliefs are comforting, but his use of the term "illusion" is bothersome. As most people understand the term, to be an illusion, a belief must be false. But when it comes to the truth or falsity of a particular belief, its comfort-giving properties are neither here nor there. Surely the incorrectness of a religious view doesn't follow from the fact that many people have a strong urge to believe in it.

G. He talks about that. He even describes how something can be an illusion without being false. He gives the example of a middle-class girl harboring the illusion that some day a prince will come and marry her. He says that that belief is an illusion even in the rare case where a prince really shows up with a ring.

Rabi. So his historical/empirical explanations of how religious sentiments arise—however interesting or informative—can't be a refutation of any particular religious opinion.

G. Maybe not, but he claims that since religious beliefs are impossible to prove or refute, all they have going for them is this capacity to comfort. There's nothing else that keeps them around after they're pounded into children at an early age. I mean, lots of different things are taught to kids before they can understand the bases for these beliefs. He mentions multiplication tables, geometry, and geography as examples of other things that are absorbed by children without any real proofs being provided early on. But unlike religious opinions, all of these are susceptible of some kind of scientific or logical proof. On the other hand, that we have immortal souls, that there is a God watching over us, that there is some kind of Emersonian compensation that's always at work—he says none of that kind of stuff can ever be proved. I guess he's saying that when we repeatedly cling to a bunch of beliefs for which there can never be any decent support, there must be what he calls an illusion present.

Rabi. So you don't think he makes what philosophers term "the genetic fallacy"—confusing reasons with causes by turning psychological explanations of beliefs into refutations of them? I think I've always suspected that the thrust of his argument was that once we saw how, let us say, "childish" were the *causes* for religious beliefs, we could no longer give them any credence. And, of course, that kind of attack is just wrong. For example, the cause of my belief that the earth is round could have been that a childhood friend of mine told me that story in order to play a trick on me. But the earth is round anyway. The actual *causes* of our beliefs—whether you think of these in terms of brain chemistry or passages in books we've read—are, in some sense, irrelevant to the truth or falsity of these beliefs.

G. I think Freud would grant your point that religious beliefs *could be* true, but still deny that the need for comfort is completely irrelevant, since he says that religion has absolutely nothing going for it *other* than the need for a stronger, wiser—not to say kinder and gentler—father. When that boy tried to trick you about the shape of the earth, there were plenty of ways you could find out whether he was telling the truth, so it doesn't matter what his motives were. With lots of subjects, we can just go and see for ourselves. Freud says that lots of things we are taught

> ...demand belief in their contents, but not without producing grounds for their claim. They are put forward as the epitomized result of a longer process of thought based on observation and certainly also on inferences. If anyone wants to go through this process himself instead of accepting its result they show him how to set about it.[79]

But he says there's no way to get any kind of confirmation for things like a benevolent Providence or an after-life, and he thinks we should be suspicious both when we are told that the world is just as we would want it to be, and when it's suggested that "our wretched, ignorant and downtrodden ancestors [have] succeeded in solving all these difficult riddles of the universe."[80]

Rabi. I see his point, but couldn't it be that people from so many cultures have held these views for thousands of years not because—or not only because—they have wanted these things to be true, but also because they have managed to gain some sort of insight into these matters? Freud insists that there is no court higher than the court of reason, but we don't live in a world of pure logic. Every science must have its empirical inputs. So why can't the basic materials of religion be particular experiences of devout individuals? Freud's demeaning of appeals to "inner" experience seems improper to me. He even goes so far as to say that it is "merely an illusion to expect anything from intuition and introspection; they can give us nothing but particulars about our own mental life..."[81] But does that claim really jibe with his huge body of psychological work? Can there be any doubt of the substantial influence of Freud's inner autobiography on the content of his theoretical writings? And won't these writings be tested, at least in part, by readers who try to determine if Freud's opinions regarding jokes or dreams or neurosis comport with their own personal experiences? In my view, the important point here isn't whether what Freud calls "intuitions" play a role in the creation of a religious philosophy: in what sort of philosophy could they *not* play a role? The essential point is that they be in some sense repeatable by others. As you know, I don't care much for what might be called "textbook religion." I think I can agree with the point Freud is trying to make when he asks

> If the truth of religious doctrines is dependent on an inner experience which bears witness to that truth, what is one to do about the many people who do not have this rare experience? One may require every man to use the gift of reason which he possesses, but one cannot erect, on the basis of a motive that exists only for a very few, an obligation that shall apply to everyone. If one man has gained an unshakable conviction of the true reality of religious doctrines from a state of ecstasy which has deeply moved him, of what significance is that to others?[82]

G. I'm reminded of a similar argument brought by a couple of your own students on a beautiful summer day not so very long ago.

Rabi. I am as well. But it seems to me that what Freud misses here is that almost since the dawn of religious thought, the Perennial Solution has been provided right alongside the various theological tenets being propounded. That is, an attempt has almost always been made to show just how one may gain these conviction-providing experiences for oneself.

G. You mean prayer?

Rabi. Exactly. Prayer, contemplation, meditation: whatever you want to call it. Without the methodology and its resulting experiences, religion does seem a lot like a bundle of wishful thoughts passed down through the generations. The Perennial Philosophy needs its instruction manual before it can provide any real comfort.

G. So there's direct contact or nothing much at all.

Rabi. Yes, that's my view. And I find it interesting that Freud's explanation of what are typically called religious experiences seems far more convoluted and incomprehensible than anything in Emerson. It's true that his conception doesn't explicitly contain any supernatural elements, but as he fleshes it out, it becomes harder and harder to tell if there aren't really a few magic herbs growing down among all the erotic impulses and object-cathexes. Listen to this:

> [T]he origin of the super-ego...is the outcome of two highly important factors, one of a biological and the other of a historical nature: namely, the lengthy duration in man of his childhood helplessness and dependence, and the fact of his Oedipus complex....[T]he differentiation of the super-ego from the ego is no matter of chance; it represents the most important characteristics of the development both of the individual and of the species; indeed, by giving permanent expression to the influence of the parents it perpetuates the existence of the factors to which it owes its origin....It is easy to show that the ego ideal answers to everything that is expected of the higher nature of man. As a substitute for a longing for the father, it contains the germ from which all religions have evolved. The self-judgement which declares that the ego falls short of its idea produces the religious sense of humility to which the believer appeals in his longing.[83]

I take it he's saying here that somehow—I want to say "as if by magic"—religious intimations are created out of projections of the desire for protection. God turns out to be just a rather puffed-up facsimile of one's father.

G. Very puffed up. Beyond recognition even.

Rabi. No doubt. Obviously, not every moral person has had a father who could reasonably be used as a conscience-model—even with the aid of copious modification. What then? At that point Freud engages in Lamarckian legerdemain.

> The experiences of the ego seem at first to be lost for inheritance; but, when they have been repeated often enough and with sufficient strength in many individuals in successive generations, they transform themselves, so to say, into experiences of the id, the impressions of which are preserved

by heredity. Thus in the id, which is capable of being inherited, are harboured residues of the existences of countless egos; and, when the ego forms its super-ego out of the id, it may perhaps only be reviving shapes of former egos and be bringing them to resurrection.[84]

So, we have these buried ego offshoots called "super-ego" that, unlike the remainder of the ego, have contents that can be passed along from one generation to the next. Perhaps the super-ego is said to resemble the id in being thus transmissible because it somehow "receives its energy from the id" or because it "represents nothing but the id," and is said to tell us nothing about the external world.

G. This is getting complicated.

Rabi. Extremely. The epicycles of Tycho Brahe are multiplying and Occam's Razor is now completely gummed up with ethereal entities. But perhaps that isn't fatal. I daresay Freud's theory is still simpler than many found in cancer research or rocket science.

G. It's harder to test, though, isn't it?

Rabi. It seems so: I'm not certain. But even if every element of the super-ego theory were to be conclusively demonstrated, the religion provided by the Perennial Solution would be untouched.

G. Why is that?

Rabi. Because it can never be reduced to such items as a moral code or a longing for a divine father—however these might be derived. Perhaps Freud's theory can explain the Mosaic Code or the ethically based religion of C.S. Lewis: I really couldn't say. But it says nothing at all about what the Vedantists call *Sat-Chit-Ananda*.

G. That's Existence-Knowledge-Bliss, right?

Rabi. Exactly.

G. Well, maybe that's more a mother than a father

thing. I think I've heard it suggested that the God in which we live and move and have our being is some kind of a flashback to life in the womb—or at least to suckling at our mother's breast.

Rabi. To me, that seems quite as far-fetched as the Father-Conscience theory. Have we received the reliable testimony of infants on this matter or is the suggestion based on the similarity someone has noted between paintings of certain saints and the ultrasound photographs of the unborn with respect to their facial expressions? I admit that, as I have no recollection of these embryonic or infant experiences, I can't deny with certainty the possibility of some kind of connection. But of course *anything* is possible. As I'm sure you know, neither of us could prove to the other's satisfaction that this whole conversation isn't just one of our dreams.

G. Or the baseless hallucinations of a brain in a vat.

Rabi. Right. The point is that there's no more reason to believe the womb-remembrance theory of religious ecstasy than there is to believe that we're all being deceived by....What's that Keanu Reeves movie about alternative reality?

G. *The Matrix?*

Rabi. Right. Obviously, an infinite number of possible explanations are consistent with my experience at any moment.

G. But your own explanation also seems so...so....I mean, what are we supposed to believe? Can't we believe anything?

Rabi. Well, I take the position that it would be highly imprudent to be giving equal credence to every possibility, especially since we don't even know what the vast majority of them are. I think there's a natural tendency to, in some sense, accept the objects of our experiences in the way in which they confront us. I know that's not very clear, but I'm not sure I can do much better. Once we're adults and have been engulfed in our culture's prevailing conceptual scheme, when we have experiences in which we seem to see chairs, we immediately believe we're in the presence of chairs. That's what I do, anyway. Perhaps naively, I usually just float along with this impulse to accept what seems apparent, so long as it doesn't produce incoherencies. It's only in the rare, more complicated situation, when I think I'm only *seeming* to see chairs and not actually succeeding that I begin to think about it. Another way to put this is that I generally believe whatever seems obvious unless I'm given a good reason to doubt it. I don't think this makes me unusually gullible. I think it's the natural way for human beings to take in their world, and I don't abandon that approach when I turn to religion. Along with most of mankind, I tend not to believe that objections like "But there's a chance you're wrong!" are good reasons to doubt anything that I find myself naturally believing. I remain ready to abandon most of my beliefs when I'm *shown* that they are erroneous, but I don't think that the fact some of my views about the world are comforting is any more injurious to their probability of being true than the fact that other beliefs of mine are discomforting is harmful to *their* chance of being correct. In fact, Freud's entire critique of religion seems to me a sort of scholastic quilt that includes a number of threads involving either historical speculation or righteous indignation that, put together, can't prove or disprove much of anything.

G. You're saying he's a pedantic scold?

Rabi. In his critique of religion, yes, although I think much of his work was both brilliant and fruitful. I'm not sure Emerson would agree with me about that, however. He has some interesting things to say about the kind of scholarship I think he might have accused Freud of engaging in:

> Among the multitude of scholars and authors, we feel no hallowing presence; we are sensible of a knack and skill rather than of inspiration; they have a light, and know not whence it comes, and call it their own; their talent is some exaggerated faculty, some overgrown member, so that their strength is a disease. In these instances the intellectual gifts do not make the impression of virtue, but almost of vice; and we feel that a man's talents stand in the way of his advancement in truth.[85]

When it comes to investigations of the spirit, I think Emerson was more comfortable with comprehensive insight than he was with the trying to put together a picture dot by dot.

> After its own law and not by arithmetic is the rate of its progress to be computed. The soul's advances are not made by gradation, such as can be represented by motion in a straight line; but rather by ascension of state, such as can be represented by metamorphosis—from the egg to the worm, from the worm to the fly.[86]

When we try to reach that which is most essential to our innermost consciousness, he warns us that

> Of this pure nature every man is at some time sensible. Language cannot paint it with his colors. It is too subtle. It is undefinable, unmeasurable, but we know that it pervades and contains us.[87]

And he reverses Freud's direction of causes as between guilt and God:

Nature has delegated himself to a million deputies. From these low external penalties the scale ascends. Next come the resentments, the fears, which injustice calls out; then the false relations in which the offender is put to other men; and the reaction of his fault on himself, in the solitude and devastation of his mind.[88]

G. I can see why you admire him. He's definitely as mysterious as you are.

Rabi. I do feel a kinship. I only wish I had his poetic ability. Listen to this:

Of that ineffable essence which we call Spirit, he that thinks most, will say least. We can foresee God in the coarse, and, as it were, distant phenomena of matter; but when we try to define and describe himself, both language and thought desert us, and we are as helpless as fools and savages. That essence refuses to be recorded in propositions, but when man has worshipped him intellectually, the noblest ministry of nature is to stand as the apparition of God. It is the organ through which the universal spirit speaks to the individual, and strives to lead back the individual to it.[89]

He expresses my inchoate views so beautifully.

G. I hope you'll forgive me for saying this, but isn't part of this kinship you feel a function of the fact that where people like Freud try to be precise and specific, Emerson resorts to poetry? I mean poetic writings of that kind will keep you safe from refutation, won't they?

Rabi. That is well said, G, and there is undeniable truth to it. There is certainly a danger of senselessness here. We could, for example, be even safer than Emerson and just content ourselves with assertions like "What is, is." Of course we wouldn't have said anything whatever, but there'd be no danger of us being wrong.

G. Exactly. I know I've said this before, but I sometimes wonder whether the "Perennial Religion" I'm getting here isn't a bit *too* safe. Christianity makes assertions that may be true or false, but are certainly not both or neither. I mean, if Jesus was resurrected on the third day and later ascended into heaven where He took his seat beside God, his Father, Christianity is true. If not, not. I guess I really don't have a sense *what* would make your religion true *or* false.

Rabi. I can understand that objection. I agree that there must be some kind of falsifiable content. Without this we might be left wandering about like some unintelligible pundit, nattering on about "the it of whatness."

G (after a pause). Well?

Rabi. Forgive me. I'm trying to formulate something that won't violate my agreement with you not to rely on any of the alleged fruits of my own mystical experiences. Let me see...Hmmm....Well, at the risk of confirming your suspicion that the whole Perennial Solution approach was designed to be immune from any possible refutation, let me begin from the other side of this question. Let me concede from the outset that this religion must be consistent with the ultimate findings of science.

G. You mean rendering unto Russell?

Rabi. Yes, and to Darwin and Einstein. The world is stubbornly, rigorously coherent. Our religion should never deny this coherence or it will be stymied again and again. I suppose this is something I learned from my father.

G. Was he a scientist?

Rabi. Yes, and a physician. Interestingly, he grew up just north of Calcutta, quite near Dakshineswar, where the famous mystic Sri Ramakrishna held court for so long.

G. But your father wasn't an adherent?

Rabi. Oh, no! He thought those people were completely

crazy! He would laugh out loud when reading about Ramakrishna and would say things like "If this man hadn't spent so much of his life in a swoon and had taken the time to study something other than ancient mythology, maybe he would have learned something about the world."

G. But you rebelled against his rationalism?

Rabi. I think *he* thought so anyway. I've always tried to avoid inconsistencies with the scientific worldview, but my father would still smile sadly at my writings. Sometimes, when he became particularly agitated, he'd compare me to one or another characters from his beloved Beckett. I can still almost hear him quoting passages from *Endgame*.

G. Really? Can you give me an example?

Rabi. Of course. (He retrieves a book.) Here:

> CLOV: Why this farce, day after day?
> HAMM: Routine. One never knows. (Pause.) Last night I saw inside my breast. There was a big sore.
> CLOV: Pah! You saw your heart.
> HAMM: No, it was living. (Pause. Anguished.) Clov!
> CLOV: Yes.
> HAMM: What's happening?
> CLOV: Something is taking its course. (Pause.)
> HAMM: Clov!
> CLOV (impatiently): What is it?
> HAMM: We're not beginning to...to...mean something?
> CLOV: Mean something! You and I, mean something! (Brief laugh.) Ah that's a good one!

And then, a few pages later Hamm shouts,

> Use your head, can't you, use your head, you're on earth, there's no cure for that! (Pause.) Get out of here and love one another! Lick your neighbor as yourself![90]

My father loved that line. It sent him into hysterics.

G. Didn't that bother you?

Rabi. At first it did, yes. But then I came to feel that I *am* a bit like a Beckett character: we *all* are. That's what makes Beckett's work so wonderful. My father's pride in his scientific accomplishments, his avid interest in politics and in his various hobbies: they could also be compared with, say Molloy's fondness for sucking on smooth pebbles. To be absorbed in one's interests while one is incurably on earth—whether these interests involve Brahman or biology or baseball—that is a great gift. It is all right to be a Beckett character. Beckett may have been very sad man, but his writing is never derisive.

G. Did your father ever soften toward you?

Rabi. Oh, you mustn't think he was ever harsh to me: he was always quite kind. We just never saw eye to eye on religion. For him there was nothing to the world but that which will ultimately be explained by physics.

G. And for you there's more?

Rabi. Yes. That's the second tenet of the Perennial Solution. The *ought* that cannot be reduced *is*; the *beautiful* that is somehow undefinable in terms either of *being well-crafted* or of *capacity to generate enjoyment in millions of observers*; the *sublime bliss* that can never be correctly depicted as anything like *a high degree of bodily pleasure in conjunction with the absence of any desire*. These are philosophical rather than empirical claims, but I think they are falsifiable nonetheless. All it would take to refute them is the production of a plausible, unobjectionable reduction of these high-sounding concepts into items that are all found within the domain of empirical science.

G. And is that it? Is there nothing to your religion but a couple of unambitious philosophical claims and a promise not to offend any scientists?...I mean is there anything else to it that you can talk about without bringing in items that you say you can't describe.

Rabi. I suppose that most of the rest consists of a bundle of instructions. But, I think, not so big a bundle as we find in Islam, Judaism, Catholicism, or Buddhism. And the rules are nothing new. They are, if I may say so, Perennial. You've heard them all many, many times, and not just since coming here: *Know thyself. Love thy neighbor.* And, of course, *Say your prayers*, because, as Spinoza pointed out, all loves but the love of God are of things to which we can't hang on forever. Our parents, our spouses, our children, our careers, our hobbies: even if any of these will outlive us, our ability to interact with them begins to fail as we grow old. But whether or not there is an eternal, changeless God who hears our prayers, we can continue to engage in our little, admittedly temporal, meditations as long as we remain conscious. This is another way in which the meditation solution is "perennial." We may be terminally ill—blind, alone and in pain—but we usually retain the ability to pray, especially if we have practiced diligently when we were younger. To many, it will doubtless seem crazy to pray to some entity without being certain of its existence, but St. Augustine gives this encouragement: "All who look for him shall find him and when they find him they will praise him. I shall look for you, Lord, by praying to you and as I pray shall believe in you."[91] In any case, even if Augustine is overly optimistic here, a special kind of solace is nearly always derived from correctly practiced meditation—whether by the most pious priest or the most ferocious non-believer.

G. Well, I can't imagine anyone's father being too disappointed with a son who rebelled in your way!

Rabi. I think he was more bemused than disappointed...
But tell me, what does your father make of *your* quest?

G. Oh, he's been dead for quite some time...and we
weren't very close when he was alive.

Rabi. And your mother?

G. I guess she's fine with it, though she'd probably
prefer it if I were on a singles cruise or something like that.
Anyhow, she kicked in something for the tuition here, so
she couldn't be completely outraged.

Rabi. That was generous of her. I take it your
relationship with her is closer than the one you had with
your father?

G. I guess so, yeah. (She glances at her watch.) Wow, it's
getting really late! I should probably get going. Any reading
suggestions for me today?

Rabi. Well, since they've both come up today, what
do you think about looking at a couple of saints—one
Eastern, one Western? I'm thinking of Sri Ramakrishna
and St. Augustine.

G. Sounds good to me.

Rabi (He retrieves a couple of books and hands them to
her). Until next time, then.

G. 'Bye.

Friday, 10:00 AM—The Library

Rabi (pacing as Paul walks in). Ah, Paul, come in. Good
to see you.

Paul (sits down at a table). Hi.

Rabi. Is everything OK? You look like something's
wrong.

Paul. Oh, it's nothing. I'm just a little apprehensive

about our plan for today—you know, the role-play thing. For some reason, I always treat sessions like school assignments. And this one...it's like I'm being tested, and I want to do well...you know, impress you.

Rabi. It was just meant as a casual thing, and was mostly intended as a way to help me understand. You seemed to have a much better sense of Jung than I do and I thought I might learn more about his views this way. We can skip it, if you like.

Paul. Oh, I don't want to do that: I've spent so much time preparing. But...it's not like a trap or anything, is it?

Rabi. A trap? What do you mean?

Paul. Well, you know, first you say you don't know Jung very well, then it turns out that...you know, at the age of eighteen you wrote a book on his theories of religion or something. I don't want to get sucked into the position of pretending to be some kind of Jung expert just because I had one graduate course on him.

Rabi (laughing). Don't worry, there's no trap. I really know very little Jung. I've had trouble getting through his writings: I find him very difficult. Anyway, this is supposed to be informal. You seemed sympathetic to his work at our last session, and I was just trying to come up with a way that we might investigate it together.

Paul (laughing). Uh-oh. The trap's already closing. Remember, I didn't say *I* liked his stuff, I just said I thought *you* might like it. I mean, it seemed to me like Jung might provide you another way of defending some of the stuff I think I hear you saying.

Rabi. I'm sorry. I didn't mean to mischaracterize your position. Let's put it this way: if you think Jung might be another ally of the Perennial Solution, I want to hear more about him. But you can just summarize his position and we can forgo the role play: it doesn't matter.

Paul. No, I'm willing to give it a try: it might be fun. I'm just not sure how capable I am. I re-looked at some of his stuff yesterday, and I think have a sense of where he fits into the Freud/Emerson dispute, but I wouldn't want to bet any real money on my interpretation. He can get pretty obtuse.

Rabi. Well, let's just see how it goes. Anyway, *I'm* the one who should be worrying: I have to play *two* roles.

Paul. Somehow, I'm not too worried about you. But how do you do that? You're not planning to use some kind of Austrian accent for Freud to keep your two characters straight, are you?

Rabi (laughing). You mean go back and forth between voices like Peter Sellars does in *Doctor Strangelove*? No I don't think I'm up to that. Suppose I say either "Emerson" or "Freud" before each comment I think they might make. And I'll assume you're being Jung unless you indicate that you're coming out of role.

Paul. OK. So, how do we start?....I mean, how do *you* start, because *I'm* certainly not starting.

Rabi. All right Let's see....Emerson: There is an over-soul in—or perhaps above—the world that somehow rigorously ensures that justice is always done....Freud: I'm afraid that there is nothing like this in the world, but within each of us is a super-ego which flares up at times, producing just those feelings of guilt that you often confuse with your concept of an over-soul.

Paul. Gentlemen, beasts of the psyche are just as real as things in the physical world, so it's wrong to say that Emerson's over-soul isn't real. It simply exists in a different realm from trees and chairs—the realm of the psyche.

Furthermore, since this "justice-making God" seems to affect all of us, it also seems wrong to say that its locus is limited to a particular individual, that it's an unconscious idea in Emerson's mind. This "God" has individual effects on each one of us just like the air we breathe, even though that too becomes part of us when it's in our lungs. Clearly, what Emerson calls "over-soul" is not only real, it's part of a *collective* psyche, rather than anyone's particular collection of unconscious thoughts.

Rabi. Freud: This is utter nonsense. I have no idea how a mental process or entity can be unconnected to the activities of a particular, individual brain.

Paul. I'm so sorry to disagree with my esteemed teacher on this matter, but I say that anything that is not physical, but which can have effects on the mental lives of numerous individuals is an element of the *collective* unconscious. Otherwise, how could we explain all the common elements among these individual mental activities occurring in different people?

Rabi. Freud: But this is all wordplay. You make tendencies into things. For example, you make a disposition toward certain common taboos into a god. No one denies that there are numerous behaviors and thought structures that are common to many societies and epochs. What of it? We're all human, so we have similar brains, and, to some extent, similar environments to deal with. Why wouldn't we think and act in similar fashions? The task of the science of the mental is to classify and describe the function of all these tendencies, not to name them "Thor" or "Siva." These tendencies may be partial *causes* of the beliefs in these fictitious gods, but it's just silly to refer to the tendencies as themselves being gods....Emerson: I don't know about this, Dr. Freud. It seems to me that you also are calling many new beings into existence with your ids and your egos, your dream censors and your preconscious thoughts. I account for my recurring certitude that justice is always done by maintaining that, in actual fact, justice *is* always done. I tell you to look and see for yourself whether or not that is true. And if you agree with me that it is, we must explain why this should be so. My explanation for this amazing phenomena is what I've called "the over-soul." On the other hand, you both deny the existence of this perfect compensation, and you attempt to explain my conviction by recourse to a large number of ghostly entities. But I have more faith in my daily observations confirming the world's moral balance than you can possibly have in your super-egos, which are wispy and hard to pin down....Freud: That is wrong, my friend. I'm not creating any new entities at all. I'm just cutting up human experience in a novel way. Even if I grant your objection that my theory is unwieldy—as many complicated scientific theories are—psychoanalysis remains immune to the charge of using supernatural entities to solve problems. Your over-soul obviously goes far beyond anything that science could ever uncover. In a way, its worse than Jung's word games, since he, at some level, recognizes that he's just reifying certain empirical elements of human life. In the end, I think even Jung would admit that all of his ghosts are reducible to thoughts and feelings. You, on the other hand, happily create a deity out of whole cloth. Your mythologizing is on a par with that of the ancient Egyptians who sincerely prayed to Osiris.

Paul. I don't see what's so terrible about believing in Osiris. The prayers of those believers for relief of their suffering were probably answered to at least as great an extent as the hopes of your patients. The poor souls who come to you with severe problems and are instructed to hunt for repressed desires might do themselves a favor by forgetting about psychotherapy and sacrificing goats to an appropriate deity instead. In my view, it's been the loss of such gods as Osiris that has accounted for most of the neurosis of our time.

Rabi. Emerson: To tell you two psychologists the truth, I don't really know what either of you is talking about. Either justice is meted out in this world or it isn't. I believe it is, and I call "God" or "over-soul" the agent responsible for this compensation....Freud: I can't speak for Jung, but what *I* have tried to do explain, is not any hypothetical divine justice, but *your feelings* that this compensation exists. This can, and ought to be done without any resource to the supernatural.

Paul. If, by "the supernatural" you mean the entire psychical world that exists outside individual subjects, neurotic or otherwise, I don't believe you will be successful in your attempt at a complete explanation. There's so much more to the psyche than can be circumscribed by id, ego, and super-ego.

Rabi. Emerson: I would add to Dr. Jung's critique that I have searched in vain in your work for an explanation of joy. While forgoing the demands of the flesh can perhaps be explained by childhood instruction or the operation of super-egos, the enduring rapture of renunciation is not so easily explained. If the super-ego can provide us with the pain of guilt, can it also explain the contentment of the decent man?....Freud: Perhaps you haven't looked hard enough in my writings. The illusion of the stern but loving father, together with the feelings of superiority engendered by the super-ego as a reward for resisting the promptings of the id seem to me perfectly competent to explain the pleasures of what the religious are pleased to call "mortification." Such an explanation not only makes no reference to magic, but will also be deemed completely plausible by anyone who takes the time to understand the concepts I utilize.

Paul. I frankly can't understand this irrational prejudice you have against what you call "magic." It seems to me plainly unscientific to give in to this anti-alchemy bias of yours. No phenomenon should be ignored that has the power to affect the human condition. These gods you are so quick to derogate have altered the world as much as any physical phenomena. Surely the power of Christianity has rivaled that of Newtonianism in its ability to re-shape the world.

Rabi. Emerson: I'm not sure if you're an ally or an enemy. You say you believe in the reality of my over-soul, but you don't seem to distinguish it from griffins or leprechauns.

Paul. I'm an ally, I assure you.

Rabi. Freud: Heaven help me: I'm surrounded by a credulous child and a sophist!

Paul. Aha! In unguarded moments even the *uber*-skeptic Sigmund Freud doesn't disdain from calling on heaven for assistance!

Rabi (laughing). Wonderful! Wonderful!

Paul. That was fun. Only next time I want to do two characters too. Maybe I could throw in Joan Crawford or somebody.

Rabi. How about Martin Luther?

Paul. Um....Nah. But I might be willing to take on Luther Vandross...or Martina Navratilova.

Rabi. I don't think Ms. Navratilova would have much more patience with Freud than Emerson does.

Paul. He certainly better not try to tell her that she developed her forehand as a result of penis envy.

Rabi (laughing). Perhaps not. But let us get back to Jung. The little of his work that I've read suggests to me that he was deeply religious, but that he was embarrassed about it. He seems intent on disguising his search by sometimes—but not always—writing as if he were talking about some sort of purely psychological phenomena only. He says he isn't making any metaphysical claims about the actual "objectivity" of his archetypes, but if he thinks God actually *is* nothing more than some sort of mental entity of the collective unconscious, why not just say that he's proved that God exists and be done with it. On the other hand, if by "God" we mean an entity that—to use his odd language—may have *imprinted* these archetypes on the psyche, then I think his confidence in the truth of his overtly religious pronouncements is frequently misleading.

Paul. I don't disagree with that at all. When he says that there can be no religion without psychology, or at least without psychological activity, he seems to be confusing means with ends.

Rabi. Or, as I'd put it, ideas with their objects. *Ratio cognoscendi* with *Ratio Essendi*.

Paul. Right. He gives the example of some patient of his being cured of a clearly physical problem by his psychotherapy and he says that experiences like that

> ...make it exceedingly difficult to believe that the psyche is nothing, or that an imaginary fact is unreal. Only, it is not there where a near-sighted mind seeks it. It exists, but not in physical form. It is an almost absurd prejudice to suppose that existence can only be physical. As a matter of fact, the only form of existence of which we have immediate knowledge is psychic. We might well say, on the contrary, the physical existence is a mere inference, since we know of matter only in so far as we perceive psychic images mediated by the senses.[92]

That whole passage is kind of a mess, isn't it?
Rabi. Well, the last part, certainly. Claiming that

what we actually perceive are psychic images rather than physical objects in the world is the confusion between ideas and their objects that we've been talking about. It's a mistake that has made all manner of mischief throughout the history of philosophy.

Paul. You mean because it's caused philosophers to say that if someone has an idea of redness and hardness then—since ideas are all be in somebody's mind—at least one mind must be composed of hard red things.

Rabi. Right, the failure to understand intentionality—the fact that thoughts are *of* things, and need not *be* or *be like* their objects in any way—can produce total absurdity. In the passage you read, Jung says that the only things of which we have immediate knowledge are psychic entities and that everything else must be inferred. But, although it's no doubt true that no one could have any knowledge at all without there being psychological activity of some kind, it doesn't follow that what we're directly experiencing are mental entities.

Paul. Although it's not exactly the same thing, this equivocation on the word "idea" reminds me of F.H. Bradley's building up his entire Absolute by using the word "is" in two ways. You know, sometimes he used it to mean "identical with" and sometimes he used it to mean "has the property of". Since he agreed with the principle *if A=B and A=C, then it must be true that B=C,* Bradley's confusion about the word "is" enabled him to prove that everything is in some sense everything else. He built a huge philosophical edifice, based entirely on a pun.

Rabi. Let me see if I follow this. Can we take a particular example? Suppose my car is both blue and hard in the sense of having both of those characteristics. Is it that

Bradley infers from this that blueness must be identical to hardness?

Paul. Right, because he doesn't see that when we say "this is blue" and "this is hard" we don't have to mean *this is identical to blueness, and it's also identical to hardness.* But once he fell into that confusion he started to think he could prove the identity of just about everything....Well, actually he *did* think he'd proved the identity of *exactly* everything. His view that there is only one thing in the world, The Absolute, is an artifact of what might seem to be a little mistake—a pun.

Rabi. Yes, it's extremely important to be careful about such things. I see these sorts of confusions in so much religious literature. And are we agreed that Jung makes a similar error?

Paul. Well, he's coy. He recognizes that much of what he says is paradoxical, but he prefers embracing the paradox to altering his opinions. But I still have the sense that, if you can get past his love of paradox, you might agree with a lot of what Jung wrote. You just have to be willing to ignore a lot of the other, possibly inconsistent stuff you'll find in other passages. For example, he's perfectly comfortable saying in one breath that the Catholic sacrament "owes its undoubted efficacy to the fact that it is directly instituted by Christ himself"[93] while insisting in the next breath that he makes no claims whatever about the ultimate truth of any religious statement.

Rabi. Doesn't he call God an archetype? I don't have any clear sense what to make of that.

Paul. Well, he tries to explain it in various places, but I'm not sure whether he actually succeeds. Like in one place he says,

...when I say as a psychologist that God is an archetype, I mean by that the "type in the psyche." The word "type" is, as we know, derived from..."blow" or "imprint"; thus an archetype presupposes an imprinter. Psychology as the science of the soul has to confine itself to its subject and guard against overstepping its proper boundaries by metaphysical assertions or other professions of faith. Should it set up a God, even as a hypothetical cause, it would have implicitly claimed the possibility of proving God, thus exceeding its competence in an absolutely illegitimate way. Science can only be science; there are no "scientific" professions of faith and similar *contradictiones in adiecto.* We simply do not know the ultimate derivation of the archetype any more than we know the origin of the psyche. The competence of psychology as an empirical science only goes so far as to establish, on the basis of comparative research, whether for instance the imprint found in the psyche can or cannot reasonably be termed a "God-image." Nothing positive or negative has thereby been asserted about the possible existence of God, any more than the archetype of the "hero" posits the actual existence of a hero.[94]

On the other hand, he says over and over again that the archetypes are "the equivalents" of real religious entities, without explaining exactly *how* they are equivalent. He does say that like a religious deity, the archetype of God is not part of anybody's consciousness, and it's not a part of any individual unconscious mind either. He thinks it's a component of the collective unconsciousness.

Rabi. I must say, it all still seems very mysterious to me. Even if he could show that archetypes some sense "presuppose" imprinters, I don't know whether that means that each particular archetype must also presuppose a separate outside cause, and, if it does, what this is supposed to show about these murky, non-archetypal equivalents. Must the imprinter really resemble the archetype in any important respect? Surely he's not suggesting that the imprinter of Thor on the collective unconscious has to wield an actual hammer? Most of this is completely beyond me. But I can't deny that I'm attracted to some of what he seems to be saying. At the very least, Jung agrees that when the religious person talks about God, he's not simply referring to some part of his conscious mind. At one point he says—let me see if I can find it—that his main point about the unconscious is that it is clearly outside the control of any individual thinker....There's this passage about a godlike voice in a dream....Ah, here it is:

> As a matter of fact, the concept of the unconscious is an assumption for the sake of convenience. In reality I am totally unconscious of—or, in other words, I do not know at all—where the voice comes from. Not only am I incapable of producing the phenomenon at will, I am unable to anticipate what the voice will say. Under such conditions it would be presumptuous to refer to the factor that produces the voice as *my* unconscious or *my* mind. This would not be accurate, to say the least. The fact that you perceive the voice in your dream proves nothing at all, for you can also hear the noises in the street, which you would never think of calling your own.[95]

James makes a similar point when discussing interpretations of apparently mystical occurrences in *Varieties of Religious Experience*. Correct me if I'm wrong, but Jung seems to feel that he has shown that the mysterious "not-I" is a mental entity. It's some kind of god-equivalent resident of a collective, rather than individual, unconscious. Is that accurate?

Paul. I think so, but I'm not sure he's completely consistent on that score. At any rate, he does find reasons to call his archetypal equivalent of the totality of different God concepts by the name of "self". That's kind of like the Hindu *Atman* isn't it?

Rabi. It's similar, but for the Hindu *Atman* is *Brahman;* there's no need for any concepts like Jung's *equivalence* or *imprinting.* As we've discussed, the parts of his work that are strained mostly seem to have arisen from his mistaken view that whatever can affect human personality must be mental. But if he really wanted to be as agnostic and scientific as he keeps insisting, why did he bother with the notion of archetypal "equivalence" at all? Why didn't he simply point out that many people have these various ideas of God and so forth and—if we don't or can't know whether they comport with reality—just admit it?

Paul. That makes perfect sense to me. Give me a healthy agnosticism rather than a re-translation of what the word "God" means any day.

Rabi. But I don't think it's a simple matter of just denying the relevance to religion of unconscious mental activity.

Paul (laughing). Naturally. That would be too simple.

Rabi. Well, it seems to me that the defender of traditional religion must believe that the apparent independence of the objects of religious ideas from anyone individual's conscious thoughts—their similarity to, in Jung's words, "noises on the street"—isn't just a matter of that individual's unconscious psychic processes. There must be something he's reaching out to that is really outside him.

Paul. The imprinter?

Rabi. Let's say an object of these thoughts that really exists, that not only *seems* not to be but really *isn't* a figment of his own mind. And one way of exploring this is to ask how we come to believe about a dream that we must have been thinking of this or that when we had it. That's one of the ways we learn that these dreams weren't sent to us by, say, the sprites or the clouds. Then we can see if the same type of reasoning might apply to our religious notions.

Paul. I don't know. I guess we believe that a dream about a snake has some sexual component at its core because that explanation somehow rings true when we hear it.

Rabi. Right. And sometimes this realization is accompanied by relief from various symptoms that also seem intimately connected with the dream images. After noticing these effects repeatedly we come to believe that there are almost always mental processes going on in us of which we aren't conscious. And we also come to realize that the manner in which these processes affect one another or other kinds of events doesn't quite comport with, say, the way causality seems to work on a billiards table or in the realm of organic chemistry.

Paul. Doesn't Jung wants to go beyond this when he says that these unconscious events can't just be elements of either conscious minds or physical processes? He argues that since a number of these unconscious mental events are entities that lots of different human beings can become aware of, they must be archetypal. His conclusion is that they're unconscious parts of the universal psyche.

Rabi. I guess I'm not sure what that means. When I discover that when I had a particular dream that I was thinking about my mother, it's because there are sufficient analogues in the dream to my conscious thoughts of my mother that I'm able to make this connection. But common dream symbols, which Jung makes so much of, could be nothing more than dispositions of human beings to dream in certain ways when they have certain types of unconscious thoughts. Freud recognized the existence of such dispositions, but he didn't deify any of them. And, as we've said, propensities to symbolize in certain ways can *affect* mental activities, without *being* mental entities themselves. Anyhow, to me it seems like obfuscation to call them either "God" or "God equivalents." If you'll indulge me for a moment, we can discuss a concrete example—a dream of my own, and one which I believe to have played a significant role in the development of my religious thinking.

Paul. I'd love to hear it.

Rabi. I was at a cricket match and there in the stands was a famous musician. I was unsure whether it was Frederick Delius or Yehudi Menuhin. His eyes were closed and he seemed very peaceful. I think I've seen pictures of both Delius and Menuhin in blissful, closed-eye poses. Anyway, I went over to this man and he handed me a card. It had the letters *A-L-D-I-D-I-A-D-E-S* on it. I knew this word rhymed with "Alcibiades"—the name of the character in Plato's dialogues. The musician told me that Aldidiades was an organization that was dedicated to the principle that we shouldn't worry because, as he put it, "Our desire for life is very brief." I was very anxious when I awoke from this dream. I thought, "Of course our desire for life is brief, but that's only because our lives are brief, not because, while living, we lose our fear of death." But as I lay in bed, a calm fell over me. I seemed to understand that one *can*—while alive—lose one's fear of death, of final separation from our loved ones. Paradoxical as it may sound, our lives can become so full that we even cease to care very much whether we continue or not. Our cups runneth over. We have enough.

Paul. And your interpretation?

Rabi. Well, I suppose getting "All die" from "Aldidiadies" is pretty obvious. And the musician was not just asleep or dead, but reassuring, blissful. He was a wise, calming, fatherly figure.

Paul. Funny, I had a more Freudian interpretation.

Rabi. Really? What?

Paul. Well, wasn't Alcibiades supposed to be this randy hunk who was always pestering Socrates?

Rabi. Yes. That's right.

Paul (laughing). This will probably just show what an I adolescent I am, but I was thinking about that fact in connection with the similarity between the word "Aldidiadies" and the word for a certain kind of sexual device.

Rabi (laughing). Ah! I see what you mean.

Paul. And, of course, we'd have to associate some sort of necrophilia with the either sleeping or dead Delius.

Rabi. You know what's worse?....Delius was a syphilitic!

Paul. And, I suppose, Menuhin was gay...he'd pretty much *have* to be with the name "Yehudi," wouldn't he? Doesn't that just mean "wishing to be Judy" in some Slavic language?

Rabi (laughing). It's an interesting theory, but I'm afraid I must say that it doesn't quite ring true for me.

Paul. Resistance, no doubt.

Rabi. Perhaps. But I can tell you that whatever the ultimate meaning, my fear of dying never returned. It would seem a shame to toss out an interpretation in which the latent meanings are so intimately connected with both the manifest dream content and the ensuing change in my way of handling the world. But note that I can say that I may have been led to God through this dream without it being the case that any collection of dream symbols actually *is* God. Or, perhaps, I was just led to tranquillity.

Paul. Are you saying that, like cigars, sometimes a name on a business card is really just a death symbol?

Rabi. And sometimes a Greek youth is just a person with a sonorous, suggestive name. The important question for the religious person is what significance dreams of this kind have. Can we get from our intimations of immortality to something outside us in the same way we can move from dream symbols to *their* causes, latent or otherwise?

Paul. To be honest, I have a similar story, one that also involves names, though it's not really about a dream, and I don't know if you'll think it has any religious significance.

Rabi. I'd like to hear it.

Paul. About a year after my mother died, I had a bout of insomnia that I couldn't seem to shake. I tried and tried to figure out the cause, but I just couldn't get it. One clue I focused on for awhile was that, a couple of days before the insomnia had set in, I saw the movie *Ordinary People*, which I found upsetting. But I went over and over the plot in my head—you know, the boy who died in a boating accident and the brother who blamed himself and suffered from suicidal urges—without any relief of my symptoms. Though there was a lot about death and anxiety in that movie, I knew from prior experiences that my insomnia must be somehow connected to my mother's death, and, the Mary Tyler Moore character notwithstanding, nothing made sense. So I eventually gave up on that movie and went on to other theories. I tried to remember every conversation I had or overheard, every TV show I watched in the day or two before my insomnia kicked in, but, again, no light bulbs went off. As more days went by, my memory of pre-insomnia activities was getting fainter, and I was getting more and more anxious from sleeplessness. But I just couldn't figure out what the hell was bothering me.

Finally, when I had reached the point of total desperation, it came to me, all at once. The relief was palpable, like an electric shock down my spine. It really *was* the movie, but it wasn't any specific scene or the overall plot line either. It was the main character's name, "Conrad." You see, the night my mother died, my wife and I were staying at my in-laws' house, a couple of hundred miles from my parents' home. A phone call came at about five in the morning that she had passed away, and later, at breakfast, I felt compelled to read my wife and in-laws the final passage from the book I had finished reading the night before. The book was Joseph Conrad's *Youth*, and the passage seemed relevant, even extremely important to read at the time. Do you have it?

Rabi. I think so, yes. Let me get it for you.

Paul. It was this summation from the storyteller:

> "By all that's wonderful it is the sea, I believe, the sea itself—or is it youth alone? Who can tell? But you here—you all had something out of life: money, love—whatever one gets on shore—and, tell me, wasn't that the best time, that time when we were young at sea; young and had nothing, on the sea that gives nothing, except hard knocks—and sometimes a chance to feel your strength—that only—what you all regret?"
>
> And we all nodded at him: the man of finance, the man of accounts, the man of law, we all nodded at him over the polished table that like a still sheet of brown water reflected our faces, lined, wrinkled; our faces marked by toil, by deceptions, by success, by love; our weary eyes looking still, looking always, looking anxiously for something out of life, that while it is expected is already gone—has passed unseen, in a sigh, in a flash—together with the youth, with the strength, with the romance of illusions.[96]

Rabi. I've never read that. It's very moving.

Paul. Yeah. I guess you could say that it was easier to

read a passage from Conrad than to talk about my feelings at the time, and I don't really know what any of this has to do with what we were talking about before, but my insomnia disappeared and, after all these years, I still love that book. But I don't see any proof of God lurking around here.

Rabi. I want you to know, Paul, that I don't want you to settle for anything less than a lightning bolt of the same magnitude with respect to your doubts about religion and your anxiety about dying. I want you to insist on the same certainty that any religious interpretation is correct. Each connecting link from your experience of bliss to your knowledge of what you are part of must be seen with complete clarity so no irresolution can sneak in and fester. This, rather than your ability to construct a proof or to explain it to others should be your test. And you must also insist that your journey through life is unmistakably easier in spite of your clearly increased vigor.

Paul. Obviously, that would be lovely, but I have to admit that it still seems like a pretty pipe dream to me.

Rabi. As Shankara said,

> The Knowledge produced by the realization of the true nature of Reality destroys immediately the ignorance characterized by the notions of "I" and "mine," as the sun [destroys mistakes that one may make in the dark regarding one's direction or position]....
>
> Relinquishing attachment to illusory external happiness, the Self-abiding [liberated yogi], satisfied with the Bliss derived from *Atman*, shines inwardly, like a lamp placed inside a jar.[97]

Paul. And, of course, you think meditating is the road to this light-filled land of bliss.

Rabi. I do. But we must nourish our desire for this type of enlightenment until it grows to the point where it can take the place of the other sorts of desire that usually control our lives. Emerson wrote,

> The one thing which we seek with insatiable desire is to forget ourselves, to be surprised out of our propriety, to lose our sempiternal memory, and to do something without knowing how or why; in short, to draw a new circle. Nothing great was ever achieved without enthusiasm. The way of life is wonderful: it is by abandonment.[98]

If we attempt to gain this state of abandonment by, say, drugs or sexual conquest, nothing will be gained. In fact, ground will be lost. But through meditation we can forget ourselves in such a way that a new circle will be drawn around us, one that is too large, too all-enveloping to be susceptible to fears or doubts.

Paul. Well, I can't deny that that sounds extremely nice. And I get the picture now that you think that these kinds of life improvements aren't just psychological, but are also *religious* in an important sense, since they intimately involve feelings about things like death, God, and acceptance. But I still haven't seen how we're supposed to tell whether the cause of some emotion of mine, like bliss, is really outside me, or whether it's just something in my unconscious mind that's kicking in, like the mental equivalent of endorphins.

Rabi. Yes, this question, *Is it me or not me?* is among the most difficult the religious person must answer. However, it's quite late now. Shall we call it day and take this up again another time?

Paul. Sure....and, uh, there'll be no charge for my creative dream interpretations: those were gratis.

Rabi. I'm honored. (He rises and bows a *namaste* as Paul departs.)

VII.
Week Eleven

Monday, 10:05 AM. The Library

Rabi (entering hurriedly to find Paul already there). Paul. I'm so sorry to be late.

Paul. It's fine: I just got here. I mean, "I and whatever else" just got here.

Rabi. What?

Paul. Well, *is it all* just me?

Rabi. I don't know what you mean.

Paul. You know, *everything*. The world. You. Is it all *Atman* — the divine innermost part of my Self?

Rabi (laughing). Well...no. It's all *me*.

Paul. Ah. I was afraid of that. I knew it must be one or the other of us...but how come it always has to be you?

Rabi. OK. Next time it can be you.

Paul. Next time?

Rabi. After the next Big Bang.

Paul. That seems like an awful long time to wait. How about the world starts being all me this Thursday?

Rabi. Maybe we could share it?

Paul. That sounds fair. But...just me and you, right? Nobody else?

Rabi. Oh, I'm afraid if I let you share with me, I'm going to have to let everyone else in on the deal too.

Paul. At that point, when you get in touch with your *Atman*, and I get in touch with mine, and everybody else gets in touch with theirs, will we all be in contact with the same thing?

Rabi. I think that's the theory, yes. And since, to the Vedantist, *Atman* is *Brahman*, what each of us will be touch with is the *Absolute*, the *One.*

Paul. So many transitivity of identity problems, so little time.

Rabi. Are you talking about the F.H. Bradley issue you mentioned the other day? The point that if A = B and B = C, then A must be identical with C?

Paul. That's about the size of it. Nothing can be clearer to me than that I am not you. But if each of us is somehow identical to Brahman, we must actually be identical with each other, be the same person. If that isn't nonsense, I guess I don't know what is.

Rabi. Well, as you know, I generally prefer to talk about "what it is I am *part* of." Hegelian "identity-in-difference" doesn't do much for me either.

Paul. But you usually add the lyric "What it is that we are," don't you?

Rabi. Does that suggest that each of us must be something more than a part—or as Spinoza would have said, a "mode" of what we're part of? I certainly didn't mean to suggest that.

Paul. Well then, you don't seem a very traditional mystic to me. Almost all the stuff I've been reading lately involves some sort of realization by the mystic that he *is* God.

Rabi. I'm not surprised. There's a passage in James that confirms how widespread that conviction is:

> This overcoming of all the usual barriers between the individual and the Absolute is the great mystic achievement. In mystic states we both become one with the Absolute and we become aware of our oneness. This is the everlasting and triumphant mystical tradition, hardly altered by differences of clime or creed. In Hinduism, in Neoplatonism, in Sufis,

in Christian mysticism, in Whitmanism, we find the same recurring note, so that there is about mystical utterances an eternal unanimity which ought to make a critic stop and think, and which brings it about the mystical classics have, as has been said, neither birthday nor native land. Perpetually telling of the unity of man with God, their speech antedates languages, and they do not grow old.

'That art Thou!' say the Upanishads, and the Vedantists add; 'Not a part, not a mode of That, but identically That, that absolute Spirit of the World.' 'As pure water poured into pure water remains the same, thus, O gautama, is the Self of a thinker who knows. Water in water, fire in fire, ether in ether, no one can distinguish them; likewise a man whose mind has entered into the Self.' 'Every man,' says the Sufi Gulshan-Raz, 'whose heart is no longer shaken by any doubt, knows with certainty that there is no being save only One...In his divine majesty the *me*, the *we*, the *thou*, are not found, for in the One there can be no distinction. Every being who is annulled and entirely separated from himself, hears resound outside of him this voice and this echo: *I am God*: he has an eternal way of existing, and is no longer subject to death.'[99]

And, as you point out, there have been quite a few non-mystical monists who have said similar things.

Paul. Yeah, and if you don't mind me saying so, it's just wrong.

Rabi. I think I agree with that. I think Russell and Moore were pretty convincing on that point back at the beginning of the 20th Century. But so many peculiar things have been written on this topic that I often feel it is hard to be sure exactly where *I* end and *not-I* begins. I don't know if you're familiar with Butler's extremely odd twists on personal identity.

Paul. No.

Rabi. Well, he thought that all knowledge was remembrance, and that we must, therefore, each be identical with our parents from whom we must have received all these pre-existing ideas.

Paul. And, if I'm identical with both my mother and my father, by the transitivity of identity, my parents would have to be identical with each other. Amazing...they didn't even get along so good.

Rabi. Butler also made a great deal out of what he took to be the fuzziness of the boundaries between self and non-self. His take was that if my bones and fingernails are alive and part of me, then an equally good case could be made that a hammer in my hand is also alive and part of me. And he tried to square this with the protoplasm theory of life that was popular at the time he was writing.

Paul. I suppose the whole genome thing has made it easier to distinguish the me from the not-me, at least as far as my body goes.

Rabi. Poor Butler. Darwinism's explanatory power haunts him still.

Paul. That's right: he was a Lamarckian, wasn't he?

Rabi. Dyed in the wool. Like so many modern-day anti-Darwinians, he didn't see how random variation, even when supported by natural selection, was sufficient to have produced so much complexity and apparent progress. But unlike the modern variety, he had a legitimate gripe against Darwin, who treated him badly. And he also had a better sense of Lamarckianism than some modern-day Darwinians.

Paul. Really? Why do you say that?

Rabi. Well, if you don't mind a little tangent, I was thinking of some remarks by Stephen Jay Gould, in which he says that, for all its faults, Lamarckism is *simpler* than Darwinism....I think I can find it...Here:

Darwin's theory of natural selection is more complex than Lamarckism because it requires *two* separate processes, rather than a single force. Both theories are rooted in the concept of *adaptation*—the idea that organisms respond to changing environments by evolving a form, function, or behavior better suited to these new circumstances. Thus, in both theories, information from the environment must be transmitted to organisms. In Lamarckism, the transfer is direct. An organisms perceives the environmental change, responds in the "right" way, and passes its appropriate reaction directly to its offspring.

Darwinism, on the other hand, is a two-step process, with different forces responsible for variation and direction. Darwinians speak of genetic variation, the first step, as "random." This is an unfortunate term because we do not mean random in the mathematical sense of equally likely in all directions. We simply mean that variation occurs with no preferred orientation in adaptive directions. If temperatures are dropping and a hairier coat would aid survival, genetic variation for greater hairiness does not begin to arise with increased frequency. Selection, the second step, works upon *unoriented* variation and changes a population by conferring greater reproductive success upon advantageous variants.[100]

But, as Butler pointed out about one hundred years earlier, Gould's position is really backwards. The Lamarckians were just as wedded to, indeed, just as dependent on natural selection as the Darwinians were: without it, the new, improved variations that the Lamarckians believed could be produced by the "struggle to survive and improve" wouldn't prosper and continue. The important characteristic of Lamarckians was that they didn't believe that the mechanism of random variation was sufficient to produce the observed complexity of contemporary life forms. They thought something more was necessary, some sort of modification of the genetic materials resulting from the stuggle of living things to thrive in their environments. So, whatever its ultimate value as a scientific theory, Lamarckism certainly can't be said to be simpler or more elegant than Darwinism. Both theories need natural selection, but Darwinists believe the "dumb luck" shuffling of genetic material provided by random variation, along with the culling provided by natural selection, to be sufficient to have produced the creator of the "Mona Lisa." Anti-Darwinians doubt this. Of course, both Lamarckians and so-called "intelligent design" theorists have to explain just *how* certain types of mutations come to be more likely than others. Butler, who was a pantheist, believed that God is in some sense immanent in each species, so there is no important difference for him between a species "wanting to" improve or "improving itself" and its being improved by the hand of the deity. But, as far as I know, whether this mysterious mechanism is internal or external, no one's ever even claimed to be able to explain it satisfactorily....This, of course, is related to Butler's interest in what he took to be the fuzzy boundaries between the *me* and the *other.* There's a nice passage here in *Luck or Cunning?*:

> It may be said that the life of clothes in wear and implements in use is no true life, insasmuch as it differs from flesh and blood life in too many and important respects; that we have made up our minds about not letting life outside the body too decisively to allow the question to be reopened; that if this be tolerated we shall have societies for the prevention of cruelty to chairs and tables, or cutting clothes amiss, or wearing them to tatters, or whatever other absurdity may occur to idle and unkind people; the whole discussion, therefore, should be ordered out of court at once....People who take this line must know how to put their foot down firmly in the matter of closing a discussion....if they let the innocent interlocutor say so much as that a piece of well nourished healthy brain is more living than the end of a finger-nail that wants cutting, or than the calcareous parts of a bone, the solvent will have been applied which will soon make an end of common sense ways of looking at the matter. Once even

admit the use of the participle "dying," which involves degrees of death, and hence an entry of death in part into a living body, and common sense must either close the discussion at once, or ere long surrender at discretion....

That which we handle most unglovedly is our food, which we handle with our stomachs rather than with our hands. Our hands are so thickly encased with skin that protoplasm can hold but small conversation with what they contain, unless it be held for a long time in the closed fist, and even so the converse is impeded as in a strange language; the inside of our mouths is more naked, and our stomachs are more naked still; it is here that protoplasm brings its fullest powers of suasion to bear on those whom it would proselytise and receive as it were into its own communion—whom it would convert and bring into a condition of mind in which they shall see things as it sees them itself, and, as we commonly say, "agree with" it, instead of standing out stiffly for their own opinion. We call this digesting our food; more properly we should call it being digested by our food, which reads, marks, learns, and inwardly digests us, till it comes to understand us and encourage us by assuring us that we were perfectly right all the time, no matter what any one might have said, or say, to the contrary.[101]

Paul. Cute. But as I said, modern biology has probably solved some of Butler's problems. We can look at my genetic structure and compare it to what may or may not be another thing to find out if it is properly called *me* or is just an external tool or a tasty visitor.

Rabi. You may be right, although as I understand it, our cells have constituents that contain their own, genetic codes that are different from that of the cells they inhabit.

Paul. If that's true, maybe it *does* re-complicate things. But, anyway, I'm more interested in the *non*-physical me—or part of me. I guess what I want to know is how I can tell whether something that I have no consciousness of—and no control over—is really outside of me or just seems to be. You know, I was looking at the *Alcoholics Anonymous* "Big Book" the other day. The writers seem so sure that just because all these drinkers tried to stop and failed, and were only able to succeed after asking for help from an "outside power," that this assistance must really have emanated from outside. That's what we were talking about the other day, isn't it? Why couldn't it have been something in their subconscious that enabled them to change? I mean, if somebody hypnotizes me and makes me act like a chicken every time I hear the word "perennial," I might be completely at a loss to explain what's making me act this way. But it would still be just some command inside me that I happen to be unconscious of. And even if this hypnotist was originally an outside agent, he's not doing anything to me anymore: it's my own subconscious command that's operative: *it's* doing the controlling now.

Rabi. You're right, a mysterious behavioral change doesn't seem sufficient to prove the existence of anything actually *other*. If it were, we would be able to prove the existence of the devil from all the reports of the alcoholics regarding the mysterious, apparently independent force that, even after a dozen years of sobriety, pushes them to have a drink.

Paul. Yeah, there's all this talk in the book about the incomprehensibility of the urge to drink—especially after long periods on the wagon. But the authors are happy to attribute this to some combination of the power of strong drink and the alcoholic's personality traits. It seems to me that the incomprehensibility of the cures could just as easily be ascribed to the power of some kind of subconscious super-ego to take over when an alcoholic sincerely asks for help from what he thinks is an external, "higher order."

Rabi. Right. If the "Leave it!" emanates from God, why isn't something like the Devil given credit for the "Take it!"? The Devil certainly received more of his due from earlier Christian mystics.

Paul. Exactly. It's no fair to put a shoulder angel on one side and nothing more than a bottle of hooch on the other. They ought to be on the same footing if they're equally incomprehensible.

Rabi. I basically agree, though I think a sufficiently big and permanent behavioral conversion may provide *some* evidence of outside intervention. But certainly more is necessary before anyone should be convinced. Even The Alcoholics Anonymous *Big Book* sometimes seems to recognize that unexplained behavioral improvements often won't be enough to convince skeptics. I assume that's why they also include passages like this one:

> [One] man recounts that he tumbled out of bed to his knees. In a few seconds he was overwhelmed by a conviction of the Presence of God. It poured over and through him with the certainty and majesty of a great tide at flood. The barriers he had built through the years were swept away. He stood in the Presence of Infinite Power and Love. He had stepped from bridge to shore. For the first time, he lived in conscious companionship with his Creator.[102]

Paul. Interesting. That could be from any one of a hundred mysticism books in this room. I know that by now you're fully aware of what I think about that sort of proof.

Rabi. Yes, there's no doubt that this is a difficult issue. James spent a good deal of time on it. He says,

> When...we take religious mysticism into the account, when we recall the striking and sudden unifications of a discordant

self which we saw in conversion, and when we review the extravagant obsessions of tenderness, purity, and self-severity met with in saintliness, we cannot, I think, avoid the conclusion that in religion we have a department of human nature with unusually close relations to the trans-marginal or subliminal region....[This] B-region...is obviously the larger part of each of us, for it is the abode of everything that is latent and the reservoir of everything that passes unrecorded or unobserved. It contains, for example, such things as all our momentarily inactive memories, and it harbors the springs of all our obscurely motived passions, impulses, likes dislikes, and prejudices. Our intuitions, hypotheses, fancies, superstitions, persuasions, convictions, and in general all our non-rational operations, come from it. It is the source of our dreams, and apparently they may return to it. In it arise whatever mystical experiences we may have, and our automatisms, sensory or motor; our life in hypnotic and 'hypnoid' conditions, if we are subjects to such conditions; our delusions, fixed ideas, and hysterical accidents, if we are hysteric subjects; our supra-normal cognitions, if such there be, and if we are telepathic subjects. It is also the fountainhead of much that feeds our religion. In persons deep in the religious life, as we have now abundantly seen...the door into this region seems unusually wide open; at any rate, experiences making their entrance though that door have had emphatic influence in shaping religious history....

Let me then propose, as an hypothesis, that whatever it may be on its *farther* side, the 'more' with which in religious experience we feel ourselves connected is on its *hither* side the subconscious continuation of our conscious life....[T]he theologian's contention that the religious man is moved by an external power is vindicated, for it is one of the peculiarities of invasions from the subconscious region to take on objective appearances, and to suggest to the Subject an external control. In the religious life the control is felt as 'higher'; but since on our hypothesis it is primarily the higher faculties of our own hidden mind which are controlling the sense of union with the power beyond us is a sense of something, not merely apparently, but literally true....[W]e have in *the fact that the conscious person is continuous with a wider self through which saving experiences come,* a positive content of religious experience which, it seems to me, *is literally and objectively true as far as it goes.*[103]

Paul. That seems very Jungian to me. God is "not just me" in the sense that these religious phenomena can't all be nothing more than that which I have conscious control over. Because...well...I *can't* control a lot of this stuff.

Rabi. Yes. And, like Jung, James was open-minded about theories according to which there is something more literally non-you that is taking a part in the affair—something not just apparently, but *actually* external.

Paul. Where does this leave us on my original question of whether there really isn't *anything* that's non-me?

Rabi. Well, if you're asking for my own view, I guess I'd say "No, the world is not all you." But I'm very sympathetic to the view that you're all *it.*

Paul. Excuse me?

Rabi. I'm thinking of the pantheistic position that you are, we *all are* parts of something analogous to a 'tree of life' with, in Butler's words, an invisible woody fiber that stretches throughout the entire universe as well as indefinitely forward and backward in time.[104] So, your thoughts, far from being rogue or independent, are somehow absorbed into the thinking of that in which you live and breathe and have your being. To Butler, each of us is a

> consensus and full-flowing stream of countless sensations and impulses on the part of our tributary souls or 'selves,' who probably no more know that we exist, and that they exist as a part of us, than a microscopic insect knows the results of spectrum analysis, or than an agricultural laborer knows the working of the British Constitution; and of whom we know no more than we do of the habits and feelings of some class widely separated from our own.[105]

Butler thought that organisms are generally composed of non-contiguous constituents that think along the same lines. A parasite living in their midst is only outside the family because it thinks differently. And if it can be convinced by their 'arguments'—say by digestion—then, *voila!*—it is made into an organic component.

Paul. So, your answer is that I'm just a kind of wart on the bum of the tree of life.

Rabi (laughing). I think of you as more of a strand of hair. And depending on the nature of the part-whole relationships within organisms, we may get different answers to the question of what this thing is that made me give up my fear of dying and the pietistic alcoholic his daily bottle. But, as we saw earlier, Butler's theory, however strange, is less radical than the Vedantist "*I am that*". On that view, you're all in all.

Paul. Where do you think the Eastern mystics came up with such an odd view, anyway?

Rabi. Well, it's not so different from a number of versions of idealist monism that have been popular in the West at various times. One way to get there is to require first that what is real must be changeless and then try to "discriminate away" everything in our consciousness that is changeable so as to grasp what is actually Real. Another way to look at it is to think of reality as being what there is before any sort of categorial thinking starts parsing it one way or another. That's a key component of Alan Watts' exposition of Zen.[106]

Paul. That sort of view just seems to sanctify the experiences of the newborn and the aphasic. Unfortunately the masters always speak so cryptically.

Rabi (laughing). Well, whether you look at it as discrimination or as brain dysfunction, what's left after all the "not this, not that"—is sometimes thought to be a contentless "consciousness of".

Paul. And from that they get to *Brahman*? That's similar to the crazy Stace argument we talked about weeks ago, isn't it? Your empty consciousness can't be discerned from my empty consciousness, so they must be identical and somehow lie behind everything else.

Rabi. I think there is a similarity, yes. Shankara wrote,

> The yogi endowed with complete enlightenment sees, through the eye of Knowledge, the entire universe in his own Self and regards everything as the Self and nothing else.
>
> The tangible universe is verily *Atman*; nothing whatsoever exists that is other than *Atman*. As pots and jars are verily clay and cannot be anything but clay, so, to the enlightened, all that is perceived is the Self....
>
> Realize that to be Brahman by the light of which luminous orbs like the sun and moon are illumined, but which cannot be illumined by their light, and by which everything is illumined.
>
> The Supreme Brahman pervades the entire universe outwardly and inwardly and shines of Itself, like the fire that permeates a red-hot iron ball both inwardly and outwardly and shines of itself.[107]

I think the idea is that you try to abstract from every individual content of consciousness and what remains is that which in some sense illuminates everything else. This power of illumination, that which, on this view, creates the physical world out of nothing, is both Self and The Absolute—*Atman* and *Brahman*. Furthermore, the process of achieving this state of pure consciousness was so often accompanied by intense bliss that *Sat-Chit-Ananda* was born.

Paul. I suppose it's a beautiful picture.

Rabi. Yes, if one wants to be God. But it's enough for me to be the tiniest part.

Paul. I'd be more than satisfied with that.

Rabi. I hope you won't give up, my friend. Please don't give up. Let us finish for now....But remind me to ask you next time why you happened to be looking into the Alcoholics Anonymous book.

Paul. Uh-oh. I'm in trouble now. I guess I can't just chalk it up to picking up the wrong book by mistake?

Rabi (laughing). You could try. (He rises.)

Paul. Well...maybe I'll think of something more plausible by next time. See you. (He leaves.)

᧞

Tuesday, 2:30 PM. The Garden

(G is sitting at a table reading when she hears a car door slam. Soon she sees Paul approaching with a grocery bag.)

G. Got anything good in there?

Paul. Snacks mostly. I still don't eat in much. Care for some Jax?

G. Sure.

Paul (opening the bag). What're you reading?

G. Oh, the usual P.C. smorgasbord.

Paul. "P.C."?

G. Perennial Center.

Paul. Ah. I guess we needed a new acronym there. Politically Correct and Personal Computer were both getting so old and yesterday.

G. Completely 90's.

Paul (looking through her books). Hmmm. Let's see what you've got here. Buddha...Suzuki...*The Cloud of Unknowing*...*Vedanta for the Western World*...and what's this little guy?...*The Wonders of the Holy Name*. Looks like a pretty typical summer reading list. But why no Stephen King or Elmore Leonard?

G. Knowing Rabi, he's probably got some of their stuff around here too. But I have a more important question. What are you doing eating stuff like cheese curls? I thought you were some kind of ascetic now, drinking green tea and working on your applications to divinity schools. You aren't allowed junk food any more, are you?

Paul. I think it depends on how many creatures were tortured in the processing of the particular food item. I have it on good authority that the Jax people are extremely gentle not only with their free-range cows, but with their corn, which is husked only by young women with soft hands. Actually, I think you're making a little too much of my...I don't know...capitulation. When you get down to it, that was as much *machismo* as anything else.

G. *Macho?* You've got to be joking.

Paul. Believe it or not, it's kind of true. Rabi compared me with some prissy Trollope character who resisted any replacement of the object of her affections because of some vow she had once made to herself. Even when it was completely clear that the guy she originally fell in love with was a jerk and that there was this other, perfect guy who was not only available, but madly in love with her.

G. It sounds like Lily Dale.

Paul. Yeah, that was her name. You know the book?

G. Uh-huh. Actually, she's involved in a couple of them. I liked her. I didn't think she was prissy at all. She made a promise and wanted to keep it. There must be *something* to be said for that. What's the point of promises if you can just break them whenever it's convenient?

Paul. You're right, of course, but, you know, I just

couldn't let Rabi think I was like some Trollope character named "Lily". It's a guy thing.

G. No doubt. But how were you supposed to be acting like the too-girlish Miss Dale, anyway?

Paul. Rabi thought my scruples about meditation – you know, my squeamishness about using any kind of psychological technique to feel better about world – were tantamount to Lily Daleism. He thought that, far from exemplifying the courage needed to see the world as it is, I was just too chicken to change anything about myself. But I'm interested in what you said about this Dale woman. I've never read a word of Trollope, so I want to know whether I've just been hoodwinked by Rabi on this. Are you saying that you think he mischaracterized her, that she wasn't really afraid of change, just faithful?

G. I don't know. I suppose Rabi's interpretation of Lily isn't completely crazy. But I think it's just as reasonable to say that that she was fearlessly true to her principles.

Paul. Hmmm. There's probably a fine line there somewhere. You ever heard of Newcomb's Paradox?

G. No.

Paul. It's about this hypothetical game. Rabi reminded me of it the other day. There are two boxes. One of them always has $1,000 inside and the other sometimes has a million dollars in it and sometimes has nothing. Each player has two choices. He can either take both boxes or he can take the million dollar box only. That's the whole game. The question is: What's the most sensible choice for a player to make?

G. So far, I don't get it. Why wouldn't you take both boxes?

Paul. Exactly. The boxes are supposed to be placed in such a way that there's no possibility of any tampering with their contents after the player has chosen. That there's no jiggery-pokery going on is an important premise here. So, it seems obvious that the rational thing to do would always be to take both boxes: in that way the player will be guaranteed to get all the money that's been put in a box prior to game time.

G. Right. Like I said, why not?

Paul. Well, the problem is that history is all against that choice. It turns out that every single person who's ever taken both boxes has been stuck with an empty million dollar box, and every person who's just taken one box has found a million bucks in it. Thousands of games have been played, and all the rationalists, the people who have said "I don't care what's happened in the past: the money's either already in the million dollar box or it isn't, and there's no sense not getting it all." have gone home with only a thousand dollars. On the other hand, every single pragmatist has gotten rich. So, one school says, "Why not dump the high-falutin' principles and just join the million dollar club?" And in the end, who's really being more reasonable here, the highly rational theoretician who ignores history or the empirical scientist without any explanation for what the hell's going on? That's the paradox.

G. But it's just fanciful. There couldn't really be results like that unless either there *was* cheating or the person who puts the money in the boxes has some kind of infallible foreknowledge. Your description of the game results presuppose either sophisticated trickery or advanced ESP. Magic you might say.

Paul. True, but when you move into the area of meditation—or even into things like placebo effect or just...you know...the power of positive thinking, you start having to deal with actual empirical successes. I'm sure you've heard it a hundred times from Rabi: people who drop their rationalistic scruples and simply mediate religiously—no pun intended—become happy, healthy people. You could use the word "magic" to describe these results too.

G. It's like Pascal's Wager: you get this claim that there's all payoff and no harm on the side of belief.

Paul. Yeah, but unlike with Pascal, you don't have to try to force yourself into believing anything that's unpalatable or, even worse, try to fool some omniscient deity you don't really believe in into thinking you're sincere. Here, all you have to do is repeat some vowel sound for an hour or two and all this good stuff is supposed to follow on its own—including the belief. And, you know, it *is* possible to be *too* scrupulous about all this. I mean, we don't usually think that a patient in a drug trial who's in some sense duped into thinking a sugar pill has real medicine in it, is a less worthy individual than the skeptic who refuses to be fooled and dies because of his qualms.

G. Hmmm. I thought you were going to say that when you meditate, achieving some kind of relaxed state is like getting the thousand dollars. Pretty much everybody gets that. But to get the big prize—eternal bliss or oneness with the godhead or whatever—you have to suspend your disbelief and at least be open to something.

Paul. That's an interesting way to look at it.

G. But the whole "suspension of disbelief" thing is just a hedge, isn't it? A pretty way of saying you're trying to get comfortable with a big lie? I mean, when reasonable adults leave a movie they stop believing that there are dinosaurs—or Prince Charmings—around, by the time they get to the parking lot, don't they? I don't mean to sound cutting, but

I guess I'm not completely comfortable with the idea of dumping an important principle just because I might get some kind of benefit from it. I mean, suppose people did that with respect to stealing. There are benefits to be had there, too.

Paul. You know, I looked at it exactly the same way until Rabi and I had our Lily Dale discussion. It seemed immoral to me to be acting in some way that I was told was likely to produce the result that the world would seem a better place than it really is. But I have to say that that view seems a little self-aggrandizing to me now. I mean, I see the wrong in lying, but where's the harm in me feeling good about the world? Why should my beliefs about all this probably unknowable stuff make any ethical difference to anything or anybody at all? If anything, I'm probably a nicer person...you know, easier to be around, when I have a more positive attitude about the world. Anyway, feeling halfway decent about life was my purpose for coming here in the first place, so what's the point of being so resistant to any activity that might have that result?

G. Well, to play devil's advocate here, if lying is intrinsically bad, lying to yourself must be bad too, no?

Paul. Maybe, but who really knows about any of this stuff for sure anyhow? Do people who are basically happy have to be liars?

G. I don't know. I think most people who are basically happy don't have to delude themselves about the nature of the universe. They're not all believers, and they certainly don't harbor any deep need to shift religion's burden of proof over to the skeptic. They just don't care one way or the other.

Paul. But what about those of us who can't be happy in that uncaring way? Is there no escape for us? That seems pretty unfair. Anyhow, after about my fiftieth bout of insisting to Rabi that truth is better than illusion and that I wasn't interested in any kind of escapist solution, Rabi hit me with this Lily Dale analogy. And being a typical American male, I took it as a dare. And I have to say that there *does* seem to have been a little irrational fear mixed in with my own resistance to change—whatever might have been Miss Dale's story. I mean it's not like a couple hours of meditation is going to turn me into some kind of incurable zombie. It may be a stupid waste of time, but it might be like jogging or picking the million dollar box instead of both boxes. It doesn't necessarily make me a bad person—just somebody who's willing to change one little thing about himself in an attempt to be happy. I guess I got to the point where I'm willing to be cured by a placebo. So I stopped comparing the repetition of a phrase with having a frontal lobotomy, and I really have found it relaxing.

G. I certainly don't want to deny that this stuff can be pretty effective as a tranquillizer. I've mentioned before that I've meditated for years. But to me it's never been anything more than a way to mellow out. To be frank, I don't think it's had the slightest effect on my religious views or my theories about the world—if I actually *have* any theories about the world. I guess I never realized that simple relaxation was something you had made a solemn promise to yourself never to indulge in. I probably should ask you to forgive me for trying to tempt you.

Paul. I know, I know. It's dumb. I guess the religious interpretations always annoyed me. But instead of doing what you've done—treating meditation like a nice swim or a walk in the woods—I must have subconsciously felt that it would be a defeat of some kind to derive any benefit at all. It seemed perilously close to praying, and, as you know, prayer has always seemed to me a weak thing to do. So I've managed to resist the enticements placed before me by temptresses like you

G (testily). Yeah, I suppose it's much less girlish to be macho, stubborn and unhappy.

Paul. Ouch. Well, I've mended my ways and now I'll take my stupor wherever I can get it, just like everybody else. And I intend to make you my model with respect to resisting any religious interpretations of the psychological benefits I get from making soft, senseless noises to myself.

G. Oh, God. Don't make a guru out of me! I haven't figured out a single thing for myself here yet, and I feel like the summer is over already. You know, according to this Suzuki book, this whole question of stupor versus attainment of something important has been fought about in Buddhist circles for centuries. Suzuki spends a lot of time in this book discussing whether you can get any valuable religious benefit from doing nothing but repeating a word for Buddha fifty zillion times—and whether it matters which word you choose.

Paul. One thing I'll say for Rabi is that however credulous he might be about a lot of things, he doesn't have much use for the whole magic word business. In fact, I've even seen him get pretty impatient about the *Om* cult. It makes him crazy when people can't or won't distinguish between a word and what it's supposed to signify.

G. I just got through reading this article by Swami Prabhavananda called "The Mystic Word '*Om*,'"[108] and I can see why Rabi would find it off-putting. He keeps moving back and forth between the claim that *Om* is the perfect symbol for the power of God—how it has just the right sounds, how no other word could be nearly as good, and so on—and the claim that *Om* actually *is* the thing signified. He quotes Vivekenanda as saying that this symbol can never be separated from the thing it signifies. The article even goes so far as to call *Om* "the Sound-Brahman" and says that yogins can hear the word vibrating through the universe.

Paul. That couldn't be because they've been repeating it to themselves over and over for hours, now could it? That's just the kind of stuff Rabi gets really exercised about. It's like he thinks if he could just scrape off the obviously fallacious stuff, people would see how deep the rest of it is.

G. Yeah, I remember how agitated he got when I read him a passage from a book that suggested that every person who dies of "brain death" must achieve some sort of endless nirvana since the concepts of *before* and *after* are lost to such people.[109]

Paul. I can almost see his knowing smile as he pounded that argument into mush while pacing around the library like a caged tiger. If you can't learn to tell the difference between the sentence "Jones is having an eternal bliss experience." and the sentence "Jones is eternally having a bliss experience." you probably should find another place to seek enlightenment: Rabi might just eat you.

G. But I'm not so sure there aren't a bunch of other confusions that Rabi isn't quite so meticulous about.

Paul. I know what you mean. He doesn't seem to mind these crazy analogies of Butler about how the universe is like a tree and how there isn't any real difference between my fingernails and these Jax.

G. Actually, your fingernails *are* pretty cheesy right now.

Paul (licking them). True, but the consistency isn't

quite the same. You know, when Rabi gets into that kind of stuff it reminds me of how I used to think that an alien might believe that sausages are alive because of the way they jump and hiss and apparently squeal in pain when you throw them onto a hot skillet. Plants, magnets, lots of things look like they're exhibiting sentience if you don't examine them too carefully.

G. Funny you should mention this. The other day I stared at this little section of a maple tree for about an hour because it had these three leaves that, when the wind jiggled them, looked exactly like the silhouette of Trotsky giving a speech. The beard was perfect.

Paul. Yeah, and I've got a screensaver at home that you'd swear reacts passionately to background music. But coming up with bizarre analogies isn't really the same thing as scientific investigation. That's probably the main reason that nobody except Rabi reads much Butler anymore.

G. You mean Rabi and dupes like us. I'm ashamed to admit that I spent an entire session defending a bunch of analogies between cells, people, and the earth.

Paul. Don't be embarrassed: lots of famously brilliant people have done exactly the same thing. But however gullible Rabi is about analogies, he's definitely got the difference between words and things down. And he'll never say anything like "God is an idea in my mind." In fact, he doesn't have much use for guys like Jung who, now that you mention it, sound quite a bit like Vivekenanda and Prabhavananda on the question of whether God is an idea, a word, or some kind of three-in-one combination platter.

G. The thing is, what Rabi actually *does* believe is still pretty murky to me. I managed to find out about his own use of meditation and it's all over the place. It doesn't seem like there's any rhyme or reason to it at all. A little stupor, a little psychology, a little prayer. It's a quilt.

Paul. Cool. What did you find out?

G. Well, he's got about a two-and-a-half hour program. He does that "Flow down" thing for about a half hour. Then he does the "Thousand Petalled Lotus" meditation for about 45 minutes, and he finishes off by chanting "Baruch" for about an hour and fifteen minutes.

Paul. "Baruch"?

G. Yeah, that's his mantra. He says he got into using that word when he was a student. It's Spinoza's first name, and it means "blessed" in Hebrew. It seems he also tried the Latin "Benedict" but preferred the two-syllable version.

Paul. And he does this every day?

G. Yep.

Paul. Well, I hope there's some point to it, or he's wasted a hell of a lot of his life. You know, it's interesting to me that for someone whose main teaching focus is meditation, he's spent comparatively little time on technique with me. No more than a total of about a half hour all together. And he's never once discusssed anything that bears any resemblance to his "Baruch" practice with me. I mean, you can't be at this place without *reading* an awful lot of stuff about various techniques, but I have almost no idea what Rabi does himself.

G. You just have to ask him. He told me that his last meditation is an attempt at what's called "*Tantrika Sadhana.*" There's something about it in this book:

> In Tantrika Sadhana...the aspirant, after taking his seat, tries to fix the mind at the center of his consciousness, thinks of it as luminous, thinks that this luminosity forms part of an Infinite Ocean of Luminosity, into which he merges his gross body as well as all physical forms, then his subtle body, as well

as all subtle forms and finally his causal body, as well as all causal forms. He tries to think of that One Undivided Ocean of Luminosity, that is living, being the source of all life, that is conscious, being the source of all Consciousness. Then he tries to become merged in that.[110]

And Prabhavananda says that you should "think of your body as a luminous body...make the old perish and come to have a new body, fashioning it out of this luminosity." He says you can do this while repeating your mantra thousands of times. "Hold on to the sound," he says, and think of its meaning or of "the ideal it represents...[and] our thinking and feeling will become more definite." He says this practice will take us "nearer and nearer to the Soul of our soul."

Paul. Interesting. I wonder why Rabi's never talked to me about anything like that. I can't believe he's into all that "subtle" and "causal" body stuff, though. Doesn't seem analytical enough for him. He's not the type to be multiplying bodies all over the place.

G. The thing that gets me about all this is that there doesn't seem to me to be any consistency to his plan. Like I was saying before, the Buddhists have argued for years about whether *koans* or mantras are the correct way to go. And those who were pushing mantras fought about what, if anything, you were supposed to be thinking about while chanting. But Rabi seems perfectly content to grab a little bit from column A and a little bit from column B—even if the bits are from opposing theories. Suzuki does the same sort of flitting around. Frankly, I find it annoying.

Paul. Can you give an example?

G. Oh, there are lots of them in this book. First he tells us that

Thinking of the Buddha came first and the invocation by name followed. But as in everything else, the content that first determined the form is later determined by the form; that is the order is reversed. The Buddha's name may be invoked by a devotee without necessarily his thinking of the Buddha, of his excellent virtues, of his saving vows; but as he repeats the name it calls up in him all the memories and images concerning the Buddha, and without his being conscious of it, he is ever more absorbed in the contemplation of the Adored One. The invocation that was started mechanically is now turned in a direction that was not previously so designed.[111]

Then he tells us that "*Nembutsu* or *buddhanusmriti* literally means 'to think of the Buddha', or 'to meditate on the Buddha'. So far, so good. But then he tells us that "In the beginning the Nembutsu was a purely moral practice, but as the mysterious power of a name came to claim a stronger hold on the religious imagination of the Indian Buddhists, the thinking of the Buddha as a person endowed with great virtues ceased and gave way to the uttering of his name." And he makes a point of mentioning the advantages of uttering over thinking: "[I]f a dying man cannot think of the Buddha owing to intense pain, he is told just to utter the name of the Buddha of Eternal Life." And, he goes on,

The shifting of the centre of devotional attention from thinking to utterance, from remembrance to invocation, is a natural process....[U]ttering the name contains more and functions more effectively than thinking of the various excellent spiritual virtues and physical qualities with which the Buddha is endowed. The name represents all that can be predicated of the Buddha. The thinking of him means holding up his image in mind, all kinds of hallucinations are apt to appear before the eye. In the case of the name, the mental operations tend more towards intellection, and a different psychology obtains here.[112]

And he also seems to think that it's terribly important that any thinking that goes on must be subconscious:

> Wherever there is an intelligent meaning, it suggests an endless train of ideas and feelings attached thereto; the mind then either becomes engaged in working a logical loom, or becomes inextricably involved in the meshes of imagination and association. When meaningless sounds are repeated, the mind stops there, not having chances to wander about. Images and hallucinations are less apt to invade it. To use Buddhist terminology, the external dust of discrimination covers the original bright surface of the inner mirror of enlightenment.
>
> To avoid this tragedy, it is necessary that sounds intended for the vocal Nembutsu should be devoid of intelligible meaning.

OK. But if you think you've got a handle on this, forget it, because he says exactly the opposite in a bunch of places. Stuff like, "When the name is uttered, all that it stands for is awakened in the mind of the utterer; not only that, but finally his own mind will thereby open up its deepest resources and reveal its inmost truth which is no other than the reality of the name; that is Amitabha himself." And "If moral or spiritual enhancement is to be achieved, the mere uttering of the name, even though it be the name of the Holiest One, does not seem to elevate the mind so much as meditating on him and reading his sermons." And finally,

> When a man pronounces this name he digs down deeply into the content of his religious consciousness. Mere utterance, however, will be of no consequence, being devoid of sense; the uttering must be the outcome of deep thinking, earnest seeking, and great faith; if it is not the outcome of such intense yearnings, it must be strengthened continuously by them. Lips and heart must be in full accord in its practice.

Paul. Well, maybe to be a Zen scholar you have to be paradoxical.

G. Oh, to be fair, Suzuki could be just giving the arguments of opposing schools, but I certainly can't tell from the text. And there's all this absurd stuff about which particular words and which languages are the most powerful. It seems so much sillier than that Benson book you hated so much when we first came here.

Paul. All this "magical power of the word" business reminds me of the movie *The Last Detail* where Randy Quaid stumbles into this Buddhist cult that tells him if he chants *"Nom yo ho ren gey kyo"* he'll get whatever he wishes for. First it works, then it doesn't.

G. It's kind of like eating Wheaties to become big and strong or wearing a particular perfume to become irresistible to men. No other cereal or perfume will do—even if their composition is identical. This Jesus pamphlet is more of the same. The author says,

> We could fill pages and pages with the miracles and wonders worked by the Holy Name at all times and in all places, not only by the Saints, but by all who invoke this Divine Name with reverence and faith....
>
> The name of Jesus is the shortest, the easiest, the most powerful of all prayers. Our Lord tells us that anything we ask the Father in His Name, viz., in the Name of Jesus, we shall receive. Every time we say "Jesus," we are saying a fervent prayer for all, all that we need.[113]

Say "Jesus" a thousand times and your car won't need a new battery any more.

Paul. Or you won't care any more if it starts or not. There's this really funny passage in a memoir by James Thurber that seems to me to show exactly what's silly about this whole notion that repeating a word a zillion times is the road to someplace other than the nuthouse:

> I had been trying all afternoon, in vain, to think of the name Perth Amboy. It seems now like a very simple name to recall and yet on the day in question I thought of every other town in the country, as well as such words and names and phrases as terra cota, Walla-Walla, bill of lading, vice versa, hoity-toity, Pall Mall, Bodley Head, Schumann-Heink, etc., without even coming close to Perth Amboy. I suppose terra cotta was the closest I came, although it was not very close.
>
> Long after I had gone to bed, I was struggling with the problem. I began to indulge in the wildest fancies as I lay there in the dark, such as that there was no such town, and even that there was no such state as New Jersey. I fell to repeating the word "Jersey" over and over again, until it became idiotic and meaningless. If you have ever lain awake at night and repeated one word over and over, thousands and millions and hundreds of thousands of millions of times, you know the disturbing mental state you can get into. I got to thinking that there was nobody else in the world but me, and various other wild imaginings of that nature. Eventually, lying there thinking these outlandish thoughts, I grew slightly alarmed. I began to suspect that one might lose one's mind over some such trivial mental tic as a futile search for terra firma Piggly Wiggly Gorgonzola Prester John Arc de Triomphe Holy Moses Lares and Penates. [114]

G. That's not only hilarious, it's exactly on point. It seems so childish to be claiming that my word's better than your word. I've told Rabi that I need a bit of magic with my theology, but that's not the kind I've been looking for. Thurber's "Jersey" works just as well as Salinger's "mercy" or the Vedantist's "Om." Say it enough times and your Atman becomes everybody's Brahman.

Paul. I know what you mean. But maybe it's like the placebo effect again. If a pharmacist tells someone who has some rare disease "Just take any one of the various pills in the store—it doesn't matter which one" the sick guy probably won't believe that *any* of the pills can really help him. But if the pharmacist says that the sufferer has a slight chance of being cured by *this particular*, extremely powerful, double-secret, experimental pill, not only might there be improvement, there'll probably be nasty side-effects too. And if there really *is* a placebo effect, where's the harm in tapping it? I mean, it really could be argued that two randomly chosen words won't be any more effective as a meditation tool than two stray pills I find on the floor in someone's bathroom will be for curing a particular disease of mine. Even Benson recommended words like "God" or "Love" rather than...I don't know..."cat" or "phlegm". Can I see your books for second" I think there's some stuff on this in *Cloud*.

G. Sure.

Paul. Right. Here it is:

> [A short word] pierces the ears of Almighty God more quickly than any long psalm churned out unthinkingly. That is why it is written 'Short prayer penetrates heaven.'
>
> Why does it penetrate heaven, this short little prayer of one syllable? Surely because it is prayed with a full heart, in the height and depth and length and breadth of the spirit of him that prays it....
>
> We must therefore pray in the height, depth, length, and breadth of our spirits. Not in many words, but in a little word of one syllable. What shall this word be? Surely such a word as is suited to the nature of prayer itself....
>
> In itself prayer is nothing else than a devout setting of our will in the direction of God in order to get good, and remove evil. Since all evil is summed up in sin, considered causally or essentially, when we pray with intention for the removing of evil, we should neither say, think nor mean any more than this little word 'sin'. And if we pray with intention for the acquiring of goodness, let us pray, in word or though or desire, no other

word than 'God'. For in God is all good, for he is its beginning
and its being....

[Y]ou should fill your spirit with the inner meaning of the
single word 'sin', without analysing what kind it is, venial or
mortal, or pride, anger, envy, avarice, sloth, gluttony, or lust.
What does it matter to contemplatives what sort of a sin it is, or
how great? For when they are engaged in contemplation, they
think all sins alike are great in themselves, when the smallest sin
separates them from God, and prevents spiritual peace.

Feel sin in its totality—as a lump—without specifying any
particular part, and that all of it is you. And then cry ceaselessly
in your spirit this one thing: "Sin! Sin! Sin! Help! Help! Help!"[115]

G. Good heavens! I wonder if we can just use "Yikes!
Yikes! Yikes!"

Paul. That might work for the sin portion of the
program, but I don't think it will sell for the happy part:

In the same way too you should use this little word 'God'.
Fill your spirit with its inner meaning, without considering any
one of his works in particular, for example whether it is good,
better, or best of all, or whether it is physical or spiritual, or
whether it is a virtue wrought in a man's soul by grace, and
in this last case without classifying it as humility or charity,
patience or abstinence, hope, faith, self-control, chastity or
voluntary poverty.[116]

G. What's the Joni Mitchell line Rabi likes? "Never
mind the questions there's no answers to"?

Paul. Right. And the author here sums up the whole
thing like this: "Therefore, lift your heart up with this blind
upsurge of love, and consider now 'sin' and now 'God'. God
you want to have; sin you want to lose."

G. Well, at least he's succinct. I haven't gotten around
to that book yet, but it seems promising.... You know, if you

look at it a certain way, it kind of makes Rabi's meditation program seem not so crazy.

Paul. How?

G. The Thousand Petalled Lotus could be the 'sin' part and "Baruch" could be the God part.

Paul. True. And maybe "Flow Down—Flow Out" is just some kind of preparatory relaxation technique. Of course the distressing aspect is that maybe he doesn't think we're ready for part three yet....Maybe he feels we lack sufficient luminosity to put a decent subtle body together.

G. Oh no. Something else to fret about.

Paul. You know what seems odd to me is what you said about Buddhists arguing about this stuff for such a long time....I say this, of course, as a distinguished Buddhism scholar, one with nearly an entire week of careful study on his resume.

G. Of course.

Paul. It's arrogant, I know, but it just seems clear from what Buddha himself is reported to have said that you're supposed to actually concentrate on particular things, not just put yourself to sleep by vocalizing. You must have seen this passage:

> There are forty subjects of meditation....ten kasinas, ten impurities, ten reflections, four sublime states, four formless states, one perception, and one analysis.
>
> ...the ten kasinas are the earth-kasina, the water-kasina, the fire-kasina, the wind kasina, the dark-blue kasina, the yellow kasina, the blood-red kasina, the white kasina, the light kasina, the limited-aperture kasina.

(Laughing). That one's my personal favorite.

> The ten impurities are: a bloated corpse, a purple corpse, a putrid corpse, a hacked-to-pieces corpse, a beaten-and-

scattered-in-pieces corpse, a bloody corpse, a worm-infested corpse, a skeleton-corpse.

G. Yichh.
Paul.

The ten reflections are: reflection on the Buddha, reflection on the Doctrine, reflection on the Order, reflection on conduct, reflection on liberality, reflection on the gods, the contemplation of death, the contemplation of the body, the contemplation of breathing, reflection on quiescence.

The four sublime states are: friendliness, compassion, joy, and indifference.

The four formless states are: the realm of the infinity of space, the realm of the infinity of consciousness, the realm of nothingness, and the realm of neither perception nor yet non-perception.

The one perception is the perception of the loathsomeness of nutriment.

Not including Jax, of course.

The one analysis is the analysis into the four elements.

And then he goes into the different sorts of effects on us meditations on these various subjects will produce.

With the exception of the contemplation of the body and of the contemplation of breathing, the remaining eight reflections with the perception of the loathsomeness of nutriment and the analysis into the four elements are the ten subjects of meditation which fall short of the trances; all the others attain them....

Of those that lead to attainment, the ten kasinas and the contemplation of breathing induce all the four trances; the ten impurities and the contemplation of the body, the first trance; the first three sublime states, the first three trances; while the fourth sublime state and the four formless states induce all four.

G. So it matters: different words, different results. A single meaningless syllable can't do the whole trick.

Paul. Right, although I couldn't really say from my own experience, since I can't seem to get beyond the limited-aperture kasina.

G. It probably holds some kind of erotic attraction for you.

Paul. That must be it. Assuming, of course, that in this context the ancient Pali term "kasina" refers to a particular line of lingerie. But seriously, based on this extremely bizarre list, you could argue that a *koan* about "Wu!" can't really cover all the bases.

G. Unless the "Wu!" somehow encompasses all of the things Buddha was talking about.

Paul. Hmmm. That's a point....Hey! Look at all the ice cream leaking out of this container. It's soup!

G. A further confirmation of some important principle, no doubt.

Paul. Yeah, of the fact that I'm a complete doofus. I better get this in my fridge.

G. See you, Paul. Good conversation. Sorry if I teased you too much.

Paul. Don't be silly. We zombies deserve whatever abuse we get. And thanks. I learned a lot from this, as usual. (He runs off.)

એ

Wednesday, 3:00 PM—The Library
Rabi (enters and sees G sitting at a table reading). Ah, G. Am I late?

G. No, I think I was a few minutes early.

Rabi. Looking at the Isherwood anthology I see.

G. Yes....As usual, reading and fuming.

Rabi. Why fuming?

G. Well, because I'm annoyed. I don't like being accused of some kind of moral failure if I can't make much spiritual progress. Remember back when people were always talking about Type A and Type B personalities? And there were all these reports about how people of one of these types were more likely to get heart disease or cancer or all sorts of horrible things? That kind of baloney has always made me furious: these poor sick people have enough to worry about without being told that it's their own fault they're dying, that if they'd only controlled their tempers or were more patient or whatever, they might be fine now. It's silly, thoughtless and cruel.

Rabi. And you find that philosophy espoused in the Isherwood book?

G. Something very much like it, yes. These kind of accusations are particularly galling in writings by this Swami Yatiswarananda fellow. But it pops up elsewhere, too.

Rabi. Ah, Yatiswarananda. Can you give an example?

G. Sure, there are a bunch of them in this paper called "Warnings and Hints to the Spiritual Aspirant."[117]

> Unless all the filth and foulness which has gathered in the mind is removed from it, from all nooks and corners, our problem is not really solved. If some light just enters a room through a chink in the door and the rest of the room remains shrouded in darkness and continues to be dirty, nothing is achieved. There is no real spiritual illumination if just a tiny bit of light enters our mind and all the dirt and filth lying there is pushed away for the time being into some far-off corner. In such a case the man remains just what he was before he had this kind of "glimpse." Mere theories and philosophies do not help us in

any way, however wonderful they may be. What is essential is
the practical application, the sublimation, the removal of all the
dirt lying hidden in the mind.

Rabi (laughing). Perhaps the words "dirt" and "filth"
weren't particularly well chosen, but isn't he just trying to
say something like one has to root out one's psychological
impediments to *sadhana* before one can be enlightened?
And I believe he goes on to provide what he takes to be the
right road to this end.

G. But he treats these so-called impediments as moral
failures, as sins. And I think both his ethics and his
psychology are insipid. He says,

> Concentration and meditation become spiritually effective
> to the extent to which the mind is purified of its dross, of all
> the dirt and filth and bad impressions and tendencies it has
> been allowed to accumulate through successive evil thoughts
> and actions. With the attainment of great dispassion and purity
> alone can the aspirant take up successfully the higher forms of
> concentration and meditation, ultimately leading to the highest
> Divine experience and freedom.[118]

But what are these evil thoughts he keeps talking about?
They're things like anger and disappointment. It seems
that this holy swami feels that these kinds of emotions
are not only signs of weakness, but of error and sin. Take
anger:

> ...whenever there is anger there is some attachment or
> other, some inordinate desire or affection, for, truly speaking,
> without attachment to some person or thing there can never
> rise any form of anger. It is only our thwarted will to enjoyment
> that brings anger.[119]

I think that that's not just simplistic, it's just plain

wrong. Anger isn't always a selfish thing. I mean suppose I've promised a friend of mine I'll take her to the hospital for some procedure and I can't get to her house on time because some jerk who's talking on his cell phone instead of watching where he's going slams into me on the road and now my car won't go. I don't see any selfishness in my being angry because I can't keep my promise, because I'm letting down a friend who needs me. And, frankly, I find the whole notion that disappointment or unhappiness is a function of greed very offensive. Why shouldn't a ten-year-old girl with incurable cancer be unhappy about all the things she'll miss out on in life? Why shouldn't a poor man who's done all the work that's made his stupid, lazy and obnoxious boss extremely rich feel resentment? Maybe he minds his poverty not because he wants a flashy car, but because he believes his kids will be harmed by missing out on certain advantages that his boss's children have easy access to. Or, bringing it closer to home, why shouldn't a woman who's begun to think that she'll never be in a satisfying, committed relationship, or that she'll never have children of her own be disappointed with her lot? After all, these things—love, commitment, family—are of real value, aren't they? I'm sorry, I just don't see why all desires should be made to seem unwholesome.

Rabi. I suppose Yatiswarananda believes that nothing should be desired but union with the Absolute, that everything else is too fleeting—he might say "too vulgar"—to be sought after. After all, this *is* a holy man talking, a monk of sorts. It's natural for such people to be a bit ascetic, even a bit prudish, isn't it?

G. Well, if this is Vedantism, I can see why it's been branded "escapism," and why there's so much ink devoted to denying that charge in this book. Even the reportedly pretty randy Mr. Isherwood preaches celibacy here; and he's certainly no monk. What hypocrisy! All love to the holy Self—at least when we're not busy prowling the California beaches for pretty young men.

Rabi. Isherwood was very forthright about his struggles in that area. And, far from being escapist, he claimed that service to others would naturally follow from the renunciation of one's own separate ego, even if he himself could only intermittently reach that goal:

> "[Am I] to spend the rest of my life trying to know my real nature[?] Thinking about myself, in fact[?] What about my neighbours? Am I to forget them altogether? What about social service? What about my duty to the community?"
>
> "As soon as you start thinking and acting in the way I have shown you, your life will be nothing but social service. You will be more available to your neighbours than ever before, because you will be less egotistic. You will do your duty to the community far better, because your motives will be less mixed with vanity and the desire for power and self-advertisement. You think you love some of your neighbours now. You cannot dream how you will love them all, when you begin to see the Reality within each human being, and to understand his absolute identity with yourself."[120]
>
> "Judge every thought and every action from this standpoint: 'Does it make me freer, less egotistic, more aware of the Reality; or does it attach me more tightly to the illusion of individual separateness?' You'll find, in practice, that certain thoughts and actions obstruct your progress. Give them up. Other thoughts and actions will assist your progress. Cultivate them."[121]

G. I must say, I find this whole derogation of "I, Me, Mine" the Vedantists are so fond of rather paradoxical.

Rabi. How so?

G. Well, they seem to feel there's something unseemly about taking an interest in one's own life or prospects. But when asked what it is we *should* love, we are told, with gravity and mystery, "The Self within you." It's as if we couldn't possibly love anything deeply and abidingly unless we discover it's really been *us* all along.

Rabi. Is it so different from being admonished to "Love thy neighbor as thyself?

G. At least that commandment has the benefit of not being incomprehensible. Anyhow, I have a fondness for an older doctrine, that of Ecclesiastes.

Rabi. "All is vanity and vexation of spirit."?

G. Sort of, yes. There's no question that he was as intimately aware of the universality of old age, suffering and death as Buddha was, but his prescription wasn't to sit and meditate, but to rejoice in one's own works and to eat, drink and be merry.

Rabi. "...for that shall abide with him of his labor the days of his life, which God giveth him under the sun."

G. Right. "And whatsoever thy hand findeth to do, do it with thy might; for there is no work, nor device, nor knowledge, nor wisdom, in the grave, whither thou goest." That sort of thinking may sound like Krishna's message to Arjuna, but it seems entirely antagonistic to much of what I've found in this book. Although some of Vedanta's so-called saints don't seem quite so good at acting on their principles as they are at espousing them.

Rabi. You have something in mind, I think?

G. I do. Both you and Paul—who seems very much changed, by the way: I guess you should be congratulated— recommended that I read *The Gospel of Sri Ramakrishna*. Well, I've slogged through quite a bit of it, and I can't remember a book that's annoyed me quite so much. I admit that it's hard not to love M.[122] He's so credulous and innocent, so vulnerable. But Ramakrishna! Leaving aside his many sexist remarks, which I can put down to the culture of mid-Victorian Bengal, he's so full of himself, so anxious to impress everybody with his trances and his cutesy metaphors. He's full of warnings about the dangers of "women and gold," but in his little clique what was really prized was holiness, and he never stops trying to convince anyone who will listen just how God-conscious he is. He derides every trait he doesn't have—like book-learning or the ability to reason, but he exalts everything he thiks he's good at. He obviously cherishes his little debating victories over all these pretenders to his throne that he encounters in the *Gospels*, and he makes fun of the "fools" who won't give up their worldly ways. And everyone laughs dutifully at his put-downs. And his occasional attempts at false modesty are so transparent. It's really appalling! I mean, listen to this:

> As Sri Ramakrishna walked up and down the hall with M, he said to him: "Let me ask you something. What do you think of me?"
>
> M remained silent. Again Sri Ramakrishna asked: "What do you think of me? What percentage of the Knowledge of God do I possess?"
>
> M: "I don't know exactly what you mean by percentage. But of this I am sure: Never before have I seen such knowledge, such ecstatic love, such faith in God, such renunciation, and such liberality anywhere."
>
> The Master laughed.[123]
>
> [Ramakrishna said,] "Mere pundits are like a diseased fruit that becomes hard and puckered and will not ripen at all. Such a fruit has neither the freshness of a green fruit nor the flavour of a ripe one. Vultures soar very high in the sky, but their eyes are fixed on rotten carrion on the ground. The book-learned are reputed to be wise, but they are attached to 'woman' and 'gold.' Like the vultures, they are in search of carrion. They are attached to the world of ignorance. Comapssion, love of God, and renunciation are the glories of true knowledge."
>
> [Ramakrisha said,] "Divine Incarnations without number

appear and disappear on the Tree of the Absolute Brahman.

I accept God with form when I am in the company of people who believe in that ideal, and I also agree with those who believe in the formless God."

M (smiling): "You are as infinite as He of whom we have been talking. Truly, no one can fathom your depths."

Master (smiling): "Ah! I see you have found it out."

Master: "....I see so many visions, but I never feel vain about them."

M (with a smile): "That you should speak of vanity, sir!"

Master: "Upon my word, I don't feel vanity even in the slightest degree....Now and then I say to myself, 'What is it I know that makes so many people come to me?' Vaishnavcharan was a great pundit. He used to say to me: 'I can find in the scriptures all the things you talk about. But do you know why I come to you? I come to hear them from your mouth.'"

M: "All your words tally with scriptures."

Master: "Have you found anyone else resembling me — any pundit or holy man?"

M: "God has created you with His own hands, whereas He has made others by machine. All others He has created according to law."

Master (laughing, to Ramlal and the other devotees): "Did you hear what he said?"

Sri Ramakrishna laughed for some time and said at last, "Really and truly I have no pride — no, not even the slightest bit."[124]

I mean, really. I'll admit he had a way with quaint metaphors about clarified butter and mother's love, but he doesn't seem the least like St. Francis to me.

Rabi. Well, at least he agrees with you about the paradoxicality of replacing *I, Me, Mine* with the formless *Self*:

"...there is the saying: 'I don't want to become sugar; I want to eat it.' I never feel like saying, 'I am Brahman.' I say, 'Thou art my Lord and I am Thy servant.' My desire is to sing God's name and glories. It is very good to look on God as the Master

and on oneself as His servant. Further, you see, people speak
of the waves as belonging to the Ganges; but no one says that
the Ganges belongs to the waves. The feeling 'I am He' is not
wholesome. A man who entertains such an idea, while looking
on his body as the Self, causes himself great harm. He cannot
go forward in spiritual life; he drags himself down. He deceives
himself as well as others. He cannot understand his own state
of mind.[125]

G. But he even vacillates on that, I think.

Rabi. Well, look, I don't want to try to defend
Ramakrishna to you. (Laughing) I've spent enough time at
that futile enterprise with my father. To me he seems more
unsure of himself—even sad at times—than he does vain.
To you, this insecurity rankles; to me, it endears. At any
rate perhaps we can agree that even if you are right about
his protestations of modesty, he was no Pecksniff. He was
never malicious or deceitful. By all accounts he was a sweet,
simple, innocent man. But this is not important: there's no
need for you to admire Ramakrishna or agree that he was
a saint....But you seem so angry. It reminds me a bit of how
afraid you became about Fechner's period of incapacity. It
seems you've let another 19th Century mystic upset you.

G. I told you, I don't like being criticized about my
failures at non-attachment by people who are either
completely confused about the nature of selflessness or are
really no purer than I am.

Rabi. That's all?

G. Well, to be perfectly frank, this whole non-attachment
cult strikes me as hypocritical nonsense. Didn't Isherwood
care whether his books were well-reviewed or popular? Did
he never argue with his agent about advances? When he
delivered a screenplay to a studio, didn't he care whether
they'd use it? Didn't he ever hope his countrymen would

forgive him for his disappearing act when war was about to break out in Europe? Was he completely unaffected when a boy ignored his advances? Oh, for heaven's sake, didn't he mind when his furnace exploded or he got a traffic ticket and he was short on cash? When he had a headache didn't he hope it would go away? When he got a chest pain, didn't he hope it wasn't serious?....And it's not just Isherwood, it's that whole supercilious gang: Huxley, Heard—them and their all-knowing gurus. Who would ever believe that they "got beyond" caring when their loved ones got sick? And why would anyone want reach that point? How in the world could anyone think that was a good thing? It's all just preposterous.

Rabi. Go on.

G. Oh, and maybe I'm feeling a little depressed about summer ending too. The days have gotten so short already. It gives me a feeling of desperation....But of course one mustn't be attached. Not to a season...or even to a hope of a lasting change in one's life.

Rabi. I think you've touched on a sort of impracticality connected with the doctrine of non-attachment. Whether or not it's correctly characterized as "escapist," there certainly seems cause for calling it "sedentary." Henry David Thoreau thought of it as the pinnacle of conservatism.

G. Thoreau? Was he familiar with Eastern thought?

Rabi. He was, and he didn't think it could be roused from its inertia even by Krishna's jostling of Arjuna on the battlefield. "Resolve to fight!" the charioteer chided the warrior. "Action is preferable to inaction." But Thoreau doesn't think Krishna successfully made this case.

Arjoon may be convinced, but the reader is not....He speaks

of duty, but the duty of which he speaks, is it not an arbitrary one? When was it established? The Brahman's virtue conists not in doing right, but arbitrary things. What is that which a man "hath to do"?....What is "a man's own particular calling"? What are the duties which are appointed by one's birth? It is in fact a defence of the institution of caste, of what is called the "natural duty" of the Kshetree, or soldier, "to attach himself to the discipline," "not to fly from the field," and the like.[126]

He points out that Brahman doesn't look for particular duties from us. We are not the "subjects" of the Absolute. Krishna is not urging Arjuna to fight because he cares about the results of this battle. The consequences are of no importance whatever.

> "I am the same to all mankind," says Kreeshna; "there is not one who is worthy of my love or hatred."
> This teaching is not practical in the sense in which the New Testament is. It is not always sound sense in practice. The Brahman never proposes courageously to assault evil, but patiently to starve it out. His active factulties are paralyzed by the idea of caste of impassable limits, of destiny, and the tyranny of time.[127]

G. That's excellent. I think he's put his finger on one of the problems I have with the Vedantist worldview.

Rabi. I look at this tension between right action and what might be called "resignation" as more a matter of degree, as two points on a continuum. As Thoreau said,

> There is such a thing as caste, even in the West; but it is comparatively faint. It is conservatism here. It says forsake not your calling, outrage no institution, use no violence, rend no bonds. The State is thy parent. Its virtue or manhood is wholly filial. There is a struggle between the oriental and occidental in every nation; some who would be forever contemplating the sun, and some who are hastening toward the sunset. The former

class says to the latter, When you have reached the sunset, you will be no nearer to the sun. To which the latter replies, But we so prolong the day.[128]

And I don't see why we must generalize with respect to attachments. I don't see why we can't distinguish healthy attachments from unhealthy ones, sensible activism from compulsion. And, in similar fashion, we can also attempt to demarcate healthy conservatism from stagnation—the blindness that results from too much sun-gazing.

G. But how do we do this? Without depending on either castes or divine revelations, how can we be sure?

Rabi. I think we can tell by noticing which activities or cessations make us feel freer, stronger, less anxious. It seems to me that we usually know when we are expanding and when we are contracting, when satisfying a desire is more like achieving a long sought-after goal and when it is more like succumbing to an addiction we can't master. So I agree with with you: there's no reason that anger can't sometimes be healthy. But you must admit that it can also be self-destructive.

G. I find it very hard to tell which is which sometimes.

Rabi. Yes, it is often difficult. But let's take a concrete example. When we began talking today, I felt you were angry not just at Ramakrishna, but at the whole world. Don't you find that expression of that sort of diffuse anger unavailing?

G. In what way?

Rabi. One is still just as angry afterwards.

G. Well, why shouldn't I be? Nothing has changed.

Rabi. Yes, but rage is an unpleasant state that we hope can be dissipated by its expression. It's an emotion, not a badge of honor. Righteous indignation doesn't by itself feed the hungry or clothe the poor. In fact, it's difficult to perform such acts of service when we're full of anger. I don't say that one's wrath may not be perfectly appropriate on occasion: you've already mentioned a number of sensible objects of scorn. But venting should be a relief, not a prod to further acrimony. Like crying or the so-called primal screaming we discussed weeks ago, if our fury simply makes us feel the need to make additional complaints, I believe we're missing the appropriate locus of our anger.

G. I feel like you're chastising me now, Rabi.

Rabi. That is certainly not my intention. I'm just trying to help clarify the signs of healthy and unhealthy attachments.

G. So, what are we supposed to do with these passions you think are unhealthy?

Rabi. In the case of anger, learn to forgive.

G. Turn the other cheek?

Rabi. Oh, no! If the anger is directed appropriately, it should dissipate upon expression. If something is being repressed, root it out. Dig, meditate, free-associate, concentrate, until you're sure you've got the right target. That's most of what I mean when I say we should learn to forgive. Because once you *have* figured it out: once you understand that it's not the entire universe, or the religions of the Subcontinent that have made you furious, but rather your mother or your teacher, or a rejected job application, or whatever, the forgiveness will come on its own. This sort of knowledge allows us to forgo the largely unconscious strategies we engage in to protect our flanks at all times. When we don't feel as if we're constantly being threatened with blows, there's no need to turn the other cheek. Even if someone wanted to spend his life as a purveyor of justice, what is gained by remaining furious at Hitler or Attla or

Milosevic or the Taliban? Such anger performs no part of the hard work that is generally required of those who succeed in this field. It's a waste of energy. It makes one less rather than more able reach any sort of goal.

G. All this stuff was in the Horney books I read, wasn't it?

Rabi. Yes, I've learned a great deal from those works.

G. I liked them too. Maybe I should take another look at them.

Rabi. The most important thing is that you introspect diligently. Ramakrishna is right that booklearning ought never to be an end in itself.

G. What *is* the end we seek here?

Rabi. Freedom. Enlightenment. *Sadhana*.

G. You're not trying to get us to give up all the things we've always believed to be valuable, then? Love, family, health, kindness—even the smaller things like prestige or the desire for creature comforts?

Rabi. No, G, I'm not. Except when they pull us down. But I don't see that these items must always do that. Non-attachment to all wordly objects is not one of the principles of the philosophy I endorse. Spinoza said that thinkers have often gone wrong by holding that the body is little more than a cage that prevents the mind from soaring to the heavens. He felt that we have little knowledge of the body's tremendous capabilities. He was right, I think. We don't want to put the body down, we want to raise it up. Our attachments should be worthy of us. We should seek that which will make us grow. It is as bad to give up food or exercise as to eat chocolate all day. The candy will make us sick, no doubt, but total abstinence from nutrition or bodily activity will kill us. Buddha also had this right, I think, in his doctrine of the Middle Way. It is sometimes said that his years of strict ascetism delayed his eventual enlightenment, that it was a daze that he happily snapped out of, but of course if he hadn't gone through that period, how could he have known the limited promise of non-activity? Fortunately, we can avoid many of the hardships he underwent by learning from his example—and from Spinoza's.

G. Yes, that's true, though I admit I'm hoping for a few more worldly goods than either of them seem to have been interested in accumulating—at least after Buddha gave up his wealth and family....(She stands up.) Well, thank-you, Rabi: this was interesting...even helpful, maybe? I'm not sure. Anyway, I'll see you next time.

Rabi. Good-bye, G.

VIII.
Week Twelve

Thursday, 4:45 PM — The Library

(G is sitting at a corner table, reading. Several other people, including Rabi, are chatting in the center of the room. Paul lunges into the room dripping wet, pulls off his rain gear, and exchanges a few words about cabin fever with Rabi's group before settling in at G's table.)

Paul. Can you believe this weather?

G. Ugh. When I thought about what it would be like to stay in a secluded Vermont inn all summer, it never dawned on me that it might rain for two weeks straight. It's definitely getting to me.

Paul. Well, if it's any consolation, it's supposed to end tonight.

G. Not a moment too soon. Half of the people here are suicidal.

Paul. And the other half homicidal? (He looks down at what she's reading.) Hey! I see you've got both bases covered. *Tibetan Book of the Dead*, eh? I remember that book creeping me out when I read it in college.

G. Really? To me, it's just another example of overly moralistic preaching. The Eastern version of fire and brimstone.

Paul. I think the thing that got me was the thought of all those weeks of hanging out in a netherworld between death and rebirth, with these ghoulish cognoscenti sitting at my bedside, begging my corpse to aim for the clear light. But nobody ever seems to go after that one anyways: the colored lights must be too pretty. So I'm destined to end up being shoved through the door of a new womb like everybody else. Extremely creepy.

G. Yeah, even though the dearly departed is given all these chances to avoid the rebirth cycle, he or she never manages it. It's life all over again. The *Bardo* state just seems like a microcosm of your last existence, where you seem almost bound to fail at avoiding any evil you failed to avoid on earth, so it's back to the world as a new baby for you—where the chances are you'll mess up one more time. Most people don't think of "seeing your life pass before your eyes" as a nice way of saying "having all your failures thrown in your face again," but that seems to be what this book is about. Except here it doesn't happen in a flash, it's drawn out to a torturous length....What?

Paul (laughing). Sorry. I just remembered that when I first read it, I made up this song about (imitates Bob Dylan) "knock-knock-knocking on my womb's door." Naturally, since I was a college student at the time, there were several bawdy verses.

G. Naturally.

Paul. Let me attempt to excuse my dumb-ass self by noting that I was probably making up silly songs because I found the whole concept very disturbing. Much more so than the Christian version of hell. All these freshly dead ghosts floating around in *Bardo*. Kind of like a cross between Dr. Strange and *Night of the Living Dead*.

G. But instead of being burned, the zombies here are tortured by constant exhortations to be good, to resist this tempting light in favor of that one. And of course, they aren't able to—any more than they could when they were alive. It's like Paris's story in the *Iliad*. He's tempted by power, intelligence and love. But no matter which goddess he succumbs to, there's no doubt that he's going to start a horrible war. In the *Tibetan Book* all the sirens—the colored lights—drag you back to a womb. It seems like a great way to try to control pleasure seekers among the living, doesn't it?

Paul. Yeah. Isn't there something horrible about the idea of being thrown into another womb to do it all over again? Time after time? With no recollection of any of the past lives? It seems like I read a lot of science fiction and fantasy back then that relied on similar pictures of the afterlife. I'm thinking of stuff by guys like Philip Dick and Philip Jose Farmer. It worked because it was so creepy.

G. It's the moralistic aspect that bothers me. I've never read much sci-fi, but I did see all the *Twilight Zones* a hundred times. I remember one where this guy who dies wakes up to find himself someplace where every wish of his comes true. It's hell, of course. Another cautionary tale about how whatever we want must ultimately be bad for us.

Paul. But did you ever see that Albert Brooks movie *Defending Your Life*? That's a bit different. You get to beat the wheel of life and death if you were courageous enough to have "gone for the gusto" in your last life.

G. Yeah, I saw it. Somehow that seems almost as bad. It doesn't really matter what you want, as long as you're willing to knock somebody down to get it, you win.

Paul. Right, and you never really find out what you're supposed to win either. We know Brooks and Streep don't have to "go back," that they get to stay together and that their bus is heading onward and upward to someplace where people use a bigger percentage of their brains, but that's about it.

G. Exactly. I never got the sense of whether they were just heading to a nicer hotel. If wombs are out, what's left?

Paul. I think Mark Twain wrote something where he

talks about the horrible cacophony there'd be in a Christian heaven: all these people singing and playing harp who could never carry a tune while they were down here.[129]

G. He's right: if heaven's just another place, like a gated community or something, how much better can it be than, I don't know, a free Disneyland without the lines? I find meditating for more than twenty minutes pretty boring, so I'm not sure I'd like singing God's praises for all eternity.

Paul. In the Brooks movie, during the few days while the dead people wait for their trial to end and they can find out where they're going, everything they eat tastes great and they never gain weight. That's something at least.

G. True. But I'd probably get bored with eating delicious food too after...I don't know...ten years or so.

Paul. I'm trying to think what the alternatives are to annihilation, rebirth, or, you know, *going* somewhere. I guess there's also that *Sixth Sense* thing where you just kind of hang around dripping blood and scaring sensitive children or the person who killed you.

G. It seems like there's also a pretty common *merging* story. You know, with some light, or with "God-consciousness," or with the Self—that is, if we're not *already* merged with the Self.

Paul. That's true. There's this Huxley novel, *Time Must Have a Stop*—I read it here a few weeks ago when I was in my Huxley period—where one of the characters dies and hangs around for a while, entertaining mediums, before failing to merge with the right light and spending an eternity in isolation from the godhead. Huxley tries to describe the character's brief experiences of merging with the pure light before he gets sucked back out of the ecstasy of union because of his unwillingness to give up his memories and his individuality. Like one of those Rod Serling characters, he gets exactly what he wishes for.

G. It sounds like *Bardo* again.

Paul. Yeah, I think he was trying to give a twentieth Century, dinner-party version of the Tibetan Buddhist vision. It's kind of funny really. This obnoxious hedonist has a heart attack and then misses out on heaven because what he really wants is a cigar and a brandy.

G. Most of these pictures are pretty unsatisfying. I mean the merging thing as it's usually depicted isn't really that different from annihilation.

Paul. You mean you're merging with nothingness?

G. Kind of. You've probably read Mill's *Three Essays on Religion?*

Paul. Sounds kind of familiar. I might have read it a long time ago. He was an unreconstructed atheist right?

G. Yeah, and here's his take on the Buddhist picture of heaven:

> The Buddhist creed recognises many modes of punishment in a future life, or rather lives, by the transmigration of the soul into new bodies of men or animals. But the blessing from Heaven which it proposes as a reward, to be earned by perseverance in the highest order of virtuous life, is annihilation: the cessation, at least, of all conscious or separate existence. It is impossible to mistake in this religion,the work of legislators and moralists endeavoruring to supply supernatural motives for the conduct which they were anxious to encourage; and they could find nothing more transcendant to hold out as the capital prize to be won by the mightiest efforts of labour and self-denial, than what we are so often told is the terrible idea of annihilation. Surely this is a proof that the idea is not really or naturally terrible; that not philosophers only, but the common order of mankind, can easily reconcile themselves to it, and even consider it as a good; and that it is no unnatural part of the idea of a happy life, that life itself be laid down, after the best that it can give has been

fully enjoyed through a long lapse of time; when all its pleasures, even those of benevolence are familiar, and nothing untasted and unknown is left to stimulate curiosity and keep up the desire of prolonged existence. It seems to me not only possible but probable, that in a higher, and above all, happier condition of human life, not annihilation but immortality may be the burdensome idea; and that human nature, though pleased with the present, and by no means impatient to quit it, would find comfort and not sadness in the thought that it is not chained through eternity to a conscious existence which it cannot be assured that it will always wish to preserve.[130]

Paul. I've never been able to take the slightest bit of comfort in the thought of annihilation—except when I compare it to eternal recurrance.

G. I'm not crazy about the idea either. But according to Mill, that may just be because I feel like I haven't really lived yet. He says,

It is not, naturally or generally, the happy who are the most anxious either for a prolongation of the present life, or for a life hereafter: it is those who never have been happy. They who have had their happiness can bear to part with existence: but it is hard to die without ever having lived.[131]

Paul. I hope you don't feel that way about yourself, G. If sitting in a room in Nowheresville, Vermont, discussing Mill with a damp New Yorker who has uninformed opinions about absolutely everything isn't high living, I don't know what would be. Anyhow, I don't think Mill is right. I don't think we should feel like if our lives were somehow different—fuller or whatever—we'd be willing to cash in our chips without regrets. That just seems backwards to me. I think that if you have a wonderful life, with excellent health, a big, loving family, a great country house, and a champion Irish Setter who brings you your slippers each night, it might be harder to kiss it all goodbye than if you're living alone and destitute in a cardboard box, suffering from an acute case of shingles.

G. But doesn't the happy person ever get to the point where she can say "I'm ready now. I've had enough happiness."?

Paul. I don't know. I guess it depends on what she was looking for. If she's gotten everything she's ever wanted and she feels sated for the moment, may she's all right with the idea of being rubbed out. But what if she wants the comfort of the womb again, or to be held by her mother one more time? Come to think of it, maybe that's why so many religions promise transmigrations: a lot of people really *want* to be babies again. Carl Sagan wrote this essay where he says the reason everybody with a near-death experience reports having seen a dazzling light is that they're all re-living their birth experiences. Hang on...I think Rabi's got that book here somewhere....Yeah, here it is:

> Can it really be that the Hindu mystical experience is pre-wired into us, requiring only 200 micrograms of LSD to be made manifest? If something like ketamine is released in times of mortal danger or near-death, and people returning from such an experience always provide the same account of heaven and God, then must there not be a sense in which Western as well as Eastern religions are hard-wired in the neuronal architecture of our brains?
>
> It is difficult to see why evolution should have selected brains that are predisposed to such experiences, since no one seems to die or fail to reproduce from a want of mystic fervor. Might these drug-inducible experiences as well as the near death epiphany be due merely to some evolutionarily neutral wiring defect in the brain which, by accident, occasionally brings forth altered perceptions of the world? That possibility, it seems to me, is extremely implausible, and perhaps no more than a desperate rationalist attempt to avoid a serious encounter

with the mystical.

The only alternative, so far as I can see, is that every human being, without exception, has already shared an experience like that of those travelers who return from the land of death: the sensation of flight; the emergence from darkness into light; an experience in which, at least sometimes, a heroic figure can be dimly perceived, bathed in radiance and glory. There is only one common experience that matches this description. It is called birth.[132]

G. I thought the accepted wisdom was that birth is traumatic for the newborn, that it's an extremely nasty experience to be forced out into the cold bright world. I mean, isn't there even some psychologist who claimed that every experience of anxiety is a reliving of the birth experience? And now comes Carl Sagan who says that in spite of any protestations to the contrary, it hasn't been bliss that all these thousands of mystics have experienced and all the millions of aspirants have sought: it's just been another miserable taste of being born. Something's got to be wrong with that picture.

Paul. It does seem kind of crazy: *Sat-Chit-Ananda* as the ultimate flash-back. And if the experience of coming into this world were so desirable, you'd think the idea of re-birth wouldn't be so repellent to me. You know, now that I think about, it, it seems like it's not the having-to-be-born-again part that bothers me so much about transmigration: it's the being-a-baby-again part. The helplessness, the utter incomprehension of everything. I've often felt so sorry for Kelsey because of that. Maybe it's irrational, but I don't think we'd all see our mother's embraces as quite so comforting, and their loss as quite so devastating if we weren't completely horrified of the world beyond them. That's what gets me about eternal recurrence. I'm absolutely terrified by the thought of having to re-live my first few years. I guess I hate the idea of not knowing what the hell is going on, of being entirely at the mercy of everyone and everything else. I don't like the thought of going through all the scary experiences again. The nightmares, the falling down and bumping my head, the being yelled at, the being unable to find my parents at the beach. It's not that my own childhood was particularly unpleasant or anything. To me, there's just something excruciatingly sad about the whole institution of infancy. Terrifying, too. It's not just babyhood, though: I've even had nightmares about eternally reliving my most wonderful experiences. You know, fishing on a beautiful lake on a calm day—the kind of stuff that TV movies immediately cut to so we'll know someone has died. It's supposed to be comforting, but I find it absolutely horrific. It's this not realizing that you've done it before—the helplessness of ignorance. And you'd have to be completely ignorant, or you wouldn't be calmly fishing, you'd be scared out of your mind, wondering how the hell you got there and what would happen to you next.

G. But what possible reason could there be to suppose that we'd have to go through the same lives again anyway?

Paul. I don't think it's quite as nuts as it sounds....although I admit it's probably more than half as nuts as it sounds. I think part of what you need for it to be true is something like the "no-soul" theory of Hume or Buddhism. Each of us has to be nothing more than a particularly arranged collection of atoms. If we have individual essences or souls, I don't think repetition is an option. For the recurrence theory to be true, I think we have to be concatenations of microscopic events that at least *could* recur. I mean, it has to be true that if you took all the atoms in the universe and swirled them around in exactly the same way as they are swirling around at this moment, then you and I would be here having this same talk. There can't be anything else that would need to be true, like your soul inhabiting the particular collection of atoms sitting at right angles to my chair, or anything like that. Of course, I don't know whether this no-soul idea is true, but a lot of smart people think it is, including a bunch of philosophers and neuro-physiologists who think all mental activities are reducible to the physical states of various nervous systems.

G. OK. What else has to be true?

Paul. Well, the world has to be of endless duration.

G. It couldn't have started with the Big Bang?

Paul. No, there'd have to be an infinite number of "initial" explosions and contractions before and after any one you pick.

G. And then you're at the point of Shakespeare's plays emerging from an infinite number of monkeys banging away at typewriters for an infinite amount of time?

Paul. I'm not an expert on the probablities, but I think us sitting here again chatting about Nietzsche is much more likely. Because, you know, it's definitely happened once. Given the same physical laws, the same basic matter, the same propensities, why shouldn't the same things happen again? With monkeys, maybe there's this tendency to settle endlessly on the letter "g" or something like that. Maybe a lot of Ring Lardner gets churned out and nothing else. I don't see that we have any way of knowing whether or not an infinite distribution of monkeyscripts has to include little Bonzo's exact duplicate of *Measure for Measure*.

G. Is all this in Nietzsche?

Paul. Basically. Let me see if I can find one of his statements of it....OK:

If the world may be thought of as a certain definite quantity of force and as a certain definite number of centers of force—and every other representation remains indefinite and therefore useless—it follows that, in the great dice game of existence, it must pass through a calculable number of combinations. In infinite time, every possible combination would at some time or another be realized; more: it would be realized an infinite number of times. And since between every combination and its next recurrence all other possible combinations would have to take place, and each of these combinations conditions the entire sequence of combinations in the same series, a circular movement of absolutely identical series is thus demonstrated: the world as a circular movement that has already repeated itself infinitely often and plays its game in infinitum.[133]

G. And I suppose I couldn't do anything different next time? Make better choices? Skip some of the *faux pas* or the bad hair styles?

Paul. I'm not sure. Would it still be you?

G. Oh, God, I *hope* so! You're not saying that it wouldn't have been me if I didn't have pancakes for breakfast this morning, are you?

Paul. That does sound dumb, doesn't it? But if thirty years of exactly the same events led up to it, maybe it makes sense to guess you'd want the same thing for breakfast.

G. This is one of those "Never mind the questions there's no answers to" things, isn't it?

Paul. Yeah. But that doesn't make it any less disturbing to me, especially when I realize that—since I'll be unconscious—the eons between each of my incarnations will skip by in a flash.

G. Well, since we're getting into the realm of science fiction that either appeals to us or sends us screaming to our mommies, I suppose I should confess that I've been getting more and more attracted to the "merged-but-not-*sub*merged" theory.

Paul. Details, please.

G. Well, I'm a little embarassed, since it comes by way of my room genii again.

Paul. Fechner? You've really got a thing for him, haven't you?

G. I guess I can't live in a room with a man staring at me all the time without me starting to take him seriously after a while. The other embarassing part is that it's more of the theology-by-analogy thing that you were criticizing the other day.

Paul. Yeah, but keep in mind that I'm the same guy who's been defending a whacked-out theory whose most famous spokesman was one of Adolph Hitler's biggest heroes.

G. True. Anyhow, the two theories have something in common. I think Fechner's view also depends on the premise that our minds or souls or spirits or whatever you call them are completely made up of other things. With him, it's ideas. Like with eternal recurrence, there can't be any minds *outside* or *other than* these ideas. There can't be anything else that *has* the thoughts that we think. Mental activities that combine in certain ways just *are* minds.

Paul. OK. I can buy that.

G. And bigger or more complex minds have to be able to be made up of smaller or more rudimentary ones.

Paul. That's a bit weirder.

G. I know, but the whole thing kind of rests on the notion that each of us is composed of zillions of little minds and bodies. Because if that can happen, nothing seems to prevent us from being part of a bigger mind-and-body.

Paul. The earth?

G. Right. Let me read you this. It's from an excerpt from Fechner's book *Zend-Avesta*:

1. When a man dies, his spirit will not be absorbed in the

greater and higher spirit of which it was born to an individual existence; on the contrary, his relation to that spirit will become clear and conscious, and his whole spiritual property will appear in a higher light. By that higher spirit the earth-spirit as well as the divine spirit may be understood, as it is the spirit of the earth that connects us with God.

2. Our present life and our future life may aptly be compared to a life of *perceptions* and a life of *reminiscences*. Or we may say that the higher spirit to whom we belong will transfer us in death from his lower life, of perceptions, to his higher life, of reminiscences. As now we share his perception-life, without losing our individuality and relative independence, we shall share, in a like manner, his reminiscence-life.

3. The relation between the spirits of that higher stage and those of our lower stage, which are connected into one spritual realm, finds its analogy in the connection of our own spheres of reminiscences and perceptions. As our perceptions derive a higher significance from our reminiscences, and as our reminiscences are constantly influenced by our perceptions, which come to associate themselves with them, so do the spirits of the higher stage give a higher significance to our spiritual life and are in their turn influenced by ours; though at the same time they live their own higher and freer life, in their relations to each other and to the higher spirit.

4. As our reminiscencs require a less sharply defined place in our brain than our perceptions, so are the spirits of the higher stage less closely tied to earthly substance, though they, like our reminiscences, cannot entirely do without it. Now the material foundation of our reminiscences, whatever it may be, grows from the material of our perceptions (the images of outward objects, for instance, produce effects in our brain, with which, when perception has ceased, reminiscence will be connected), so will the material existence connected with the spiritual life in the hereafter grow from our present existence.

5. Our future spheres of existence, though all incorporated in the same great body, the earth, will not disturb, confuse or efface each other. Even here our spheres of existence necessarily cross and intersect each other, as the means of our mutual intercourse, which in the hereafter will only increase in intimacy, variety and consciousness; [just as] in our brain the

material changes connected with our reminiscences cross and intersect each other, leaving them nevertheless undisturbed and uneffaced.[134]

Somewhere else he says that the Earth-Soul ties together our disparate thoughts in the same way that we tie together the data we get from our ears with the very different sort of information we get from our eyes. It's mysterious, but we can do it somehow—otherwise we couldn't tell that this chair that we see is the same thing that squeaks if you push it.

Paul. This tying-up of disparate data into unified ideas is supposed to go on both before and after we die?

G. Right, but afterwards our experiences will be more like memories than perceptions. At least I think that's the idea.

Paul. But we have *both* kinds of experiences now. Wouldn't it be kind of barren to be endlessly rehashing our old failures and fantasies? Who wants an eternity of reminiscing? I think that's what the Huxley character was comdemned to.

G. Well, somehow these individual memories are supposed to mix with perceptions that the Earth is receiving though other, living parts as well as with the reminiscences of others. Fechner thinks this compounding of ideas will produce a richer mental life than it's possible for the living to have.

Paul. Does any of that stuff really make sense to you? I mean, can this sort of merging be more likely than what we experience with dreamless sleep? After all, *that's* what fuels the annihilation view. We often wake up in the morning remembering nothing of what happened after went to bed. So when we die, maybe we just don't ever wake up—until the zillionth big bang, of course.

G. I'm not sure. Fechner's picture *is* pretty hazy, I guess. But he's just trying to come up with analogies. You know, if we think of our current memories as the residue of dead perceptions—which are themselves just little minds, remember—then there's a sense in which most of our experience while alive is already just the connecting up of our deceased forebears. So maybe the same kind of thing could work later after death too—on a much grander scale, of course.

Paul. I don't know: there are so many premises here I don't really understand—like why we should treat parts of a mind as if they were themselves minds. My perception of this table isn't a person.

G. Wow. You're starting to sound exactly like Rabi—did you know that? He's definitely *your* genii. But anyhow, little *sensei*, if there's no "mind-of-G" other than my experiences, why couldn't little batches of ideas associated with my body be just as worthy of personhood as big batches? Is it completely impossible for somebody to live only long enough to have a perception of this table? If that could happen, that single experience would *be* the person, seeing the table, wouldn't it? I mean if there's nothing else to *have* that idea?

Paul. I don't know, G; to steal another phrase from the big *sensei* around here, I'm a little out of my depth. But it seems awfully strange to me. I guess I don't get either how people can be made up of other people or how, without any brain function, we can continue to reminisce. Are we supposed to do this using the roots of trees as our neurons or what? And if it's not me doing the reminiscing, but some bigger thing like the Earth, it doesn't really seem like *I'm* there, does it? It's sort of like being immortal in the sense of being remembered by your friends. It's nice, but kind of unsatisfying. It doesn't seem like the real thing to me, anyway. But again, I may have misunderstood Fechner completely. It seems pretty complicated.

G. Oh, I can't deny that you're probably right, Paul. It's just that...I don't know, something seems very deep about it to me. Deep and true, maybe.

Paul. Well, it's certainly got the Spinoza thing going for it. You know, the theory that ideas aren't like static pictures, that they carry their own affirmations along with them: that kind of thing. Maybe it's a short step from that to calling each idea a little mind and concluding that if you take one of these events along with the physical states associated with it—changes in some human body—you've got yourself a little person.

G. Hmmm. Maybe I *am* just falling back on Leprechauns again....Anyhow, I think I should mosey: I'm starving all of a sudden. You?

Paul. There's some stuff I wanted to look at for a minute here. I'll catch you later. Stay dry, it's really nasty out there.

G. I'll try. (She leaves.)

❧

Friday, 10 AM—The Library

Paul (enters the library and sits down across from Rabi). Good morning.

Rabi. Good morning....So, this is our final session, isn't it?

Paul. Yeah.

Rabi. Is there anything in particular you'd like to discuss?

Paul. I want to talk about mortification.

Rabi. Mortification of the flesh? I'm not sure the center has any hair shirts available for visitors.

Paul. I don't see why not. It seems like half the books in here say that you have to be pure in order to receive enlightenment. A dirty mirror won't reflect the essence of the Self and all that. You know what I mean; here's an example from Ramakrishna:

> First of all, purify the mind. In the pure heart God takes His seat. One cannot bring the holy image into the temple if the droppings of bats are all around.[135]

Rabi. Yes, that is a key tenet of the mystical tradition. But I usually connect the term "mortification" with severe types of atonement, rather than the ethically more neutral desire to overcome one's earthy passions.

Paul. Is there really so big a difference between a Western monk wearing a hair shirt and an Eastern yogin sleeping on a bed of nails?

Rabi. Perhaps not, but I can't help thinking of Ramakrishna's puzzlement of all the sin-talk among Christians. Admitting we've made a mistake, asking for forgiveness, and not doing the evil act again seemed sufficient atonement for him. The whole notion of penance—the claim that God somehow longs for our suffering and appreciates it when we are in pain—struck him as strange. Maybe that's because the Vedanta tradition doesn't involve this notion of a catclysmic battle between Good and Evil, between God and Satan. Prabhavananda has written:

> If by observing certain forms of living, or by undergoing some physical discomfort, one could gain self-control, religious life would be very easy....[T]he ideal of life is neither austerity

nor renunciation nor even meditation, but to know God, to be illumined within one's own soul.[136]

Paul. Well, maybe the moral element doesn't play so big a role for the yogin, but I don't see that there's much practical difference. There's a lot on mortification in Underhill, and I don't remember her making a big deal about regional differences. Here's her definition:

> Mortification takes its name from the reiterated statement of all ascetic writers that the senses, or "body of desire," with the cravings which are excited by different aspects of the phenomenal world, most be mortified or killed....All those self-regarding instincts—so ingrained that they have become automatic—which impel the self to choose the more comfortable part, are seen by the awakened intuition of the embryo mystic as gross infringements of the law of love...The senses have grown stronger than their masters, monopolized the field of perception, dominated an organism which was made for greater activities, and built up those barriers of individuality which must be done away if true personality is to be achieved, and with it some share in the boundless life of the One.[137]

And then she has this nice metaphor:

> By false desires and false thoughts man has built up for himself a false universe: as a mollusc, by the deliberate and persistent absorption of lime and rejection of all else, can build up for itself a hard shell which shuts it from the external world, and only represents in a distorted and unrecognisable form the ocean from which it was obtained. This hard and wholly unnutritious shell, this one-sided secretion of the surface-consciousness, makes as it were a little cave of illusion for each separate soul. A literal and deliberate getting out of the cave must be for every mystic, as it was for Plato's prisoners, the first step in the individual hunt for reality.[138]

Rabi. And do you think you've built up a hard shell between yourself and reality?

Paul. Honestly, yes. I think I may have gotten as far as I can on the road to enlightenment without blasting caps. I'm carrying too much baggage in the form of uncontrollable impulses.

Rabi. Ah. I thought you might have some concerns along those lines when you mentioned you were reading the Alcoholics Anonymous book the other day.

Paul. Actually, alcohol isn't my problem. It's affairs. "Lust" or "sins of the flesh" is what it's called in most of the books in this room—not to mention "adultery." I've had so may falls, told so many lies, made and and broken so many sincere vows. I've suffered terribly from guilt pains, but this pain hasn't had much of an effect on my subsequent behavior. No sooner does the guilt start to fade—sometimes even before—then I find myself flirting with someone else....I thought maybe a hair shirt or stones in my shoes might be the answer.

Rabi. Of course, the most important thing of all is the will to change. Are you certain you have that?

Paul. I find it hard to answer that question. I mean, I *think* I want to change, but if I always fail, maybe I don't, really. Anyways, the will to change isn't enough, is it? It may be necessary, but it's definitely not sufficient. Underhill said,

> Only [a] deep and ardent passion for a perceived Object of Love can persuade the mystic to those unnatural acts of abnegation by which he kills his lesser love of the world of sense, frees himself from the "remora of desire," unifies all his energies about the new and higher centre of his life....
>
> It is not love but lust—the possessive case, the very food of selfhood—which poisons the relation between the self and

the external world and "immediately fatigues" the soul. Divide the world into "mine" and "not mine," and unreal standards are set up, claims and cravings begin to fret the mind. We are the slaves of our own property. We drag with us not a treasure, but a chain.[139]

I haven't found any ardent passion for God, at least not yet. But there's another possible road too, isnt' there? If I find I *can't* change my behaviors, isn't there some way that I can get beyond the reach of guilt? I mean, once my divorce becomes final, if all my future relationships are consensual, then who cares if they're also serial? No one's really being hurt. Why should I have to feel bad about these activities? Why can't I lose this...I don't know...sin complex?

Rabi. I tend to doubt that there's any of *that* sort of "getting beyond" that can make you feel better about yourself over the long term. Mystics have often talked of a kind of detachment in which activities that might otherwise be detrimental can be undertaken with impunity. But this is a dangerous road. Here's Huxley on the subject:

> The earliest literary reference to 'holy indifference' occurs in the *Bhagavad Gita*, where Krishna assures Arjuna that it is right for him to slaughter his enemies, provided always that he does so in spirit of non-attachment. When the same doctrine was used by the *Illumines* of Picardy to justify sexual promiscuity, all right thinking men...were properly horrified....[N]on-attachment can be practised only in regard to actions intrinsically good or ethically neutral. In spite of anything that Krishna or anyone else may say, bad actions are unannihilatable...because, as a matter of brute psychological fact, they enhance the separate, personal ego of those who perform them....[The worldly man] may try very hard to annihilate himself in God, to practise God's presence, even while he is acting. But the nature of what he is doing condemns his efforts to frustration.[140]

Paul. But if I literally *can't* control my sexual urges — what then?

Rabi. Well, let me first give you the symbolic answer, and then get down to more practical methods. Saint Catherine of Siena's God has assured us all that

> No one need fear any battle or temptation of the devil that may come, for I have made you strong and given your wills power in the blood of my Son. Neither the devil nor any other creature can change this will of yours for it is yours, given by me with the power of free choice. It is a weapon that, as soon as you put it in the devil's hands, becomes a knife with which he pursues and kills you. But if you refuse to put this weapon, your will, into the devil's hands (that is, if you refuse to consent to his tempting and troubling) you will never be hurt in any temptation by the guilt of sin.[141]

And Ramakrishna has put the same idea in a more homely way:

> When you plunge in the water of the ocean you may be attacked by alligators. But they won't touch you if your body is smeared with turmeric. There are no doubt six alligators — lust, anger, avarice, and so on—within you, in the 'soul's fathomless depths." But protect yourself with the turmeric of discrimination and renunciation, and they won't touch you...[142]

Paul. Those are cute, but I think I need the practical advice. Why make more vows when I know they'll fail? Let's face it, I'm an addict. I don't know if it's that the turmeric doesn't work for me or if it's that I'm purposely missing a couple of key spots when I rub it on. Last weekend I went to a bookstore to pick up some light reading. You, know, the kind of pot boiler that I figured I woudn't find here. So I got a Stephen King novel, *The Shining*.

Rabi. I've never read that, but I saw the movie. Kubrick, isn't it?

Paul. Right. Anyhow, the main character in the book is an alcoholic who slowly goes nuts. There isn't any booze around, but at one point he has this conversation with an imaginary bartender. It's basically a rant about why it's so tough to stay sober. I brought it.

> Few men ever return from the fabled Wagon, but those who do come with a fearful tale to tell. When you jump on, it seems like the brightest, cleanest Wagon you ever saw, with ten-foot wheels to keep the bed of it high out of the gutter where all the drunks are laying around with their brown bags and their Thunderbird and their Grandad Flash's Popskull Bourbon. You're away from all the people who throw you nasty looks and tell you to clean up your act or go put it on in another town. From the gutter, that's the finest-lookin Wagon you ever saw....All hung with bunting and a brass band in front and three majorettes to each side, twirling their batons and flashing their panties at you. Man you got to get on that Wagon and away from the juicers that are straining canned heat and smelling their own puke to get high again....
>
> Then you start to see things....Things you missed from the gutter. Like how the floor of the Wagon is nothing but straight pine boards, so fresh they're still bleeding sap, and if you took your shoes off you'd be sure to get a splinter. Like how the only furniture in the Wagon is these long benches with high backs and no cushions to sit on, and in fact they are nothing but pews with a songbook every five feet or so....And somebody slams a songbook into your hands and says, 'Sing it out, brother. If you expect to stay on this Wagon, you got to sing morning, noon, and night. Especially at night.' And that's when you realize what the Wagon really is....It's a church with bars on the windows, a church for women and a prison for you.[143]

I feel sort of like that sometimes. When I'm gripped by some carnal itch, I *want* to be thrust along like a leaf on a river. I often don't resist at all. But I think King misses something by making it seem like a conscious decision to pick the exciting street over the boring wagon. It's visceral. There are nasty, anxious feelings in the chest associated with resisting, and there's often some very positive reinforcement for going with the flow. So many excitations in my history; so many sweet memories to reflect on in times of stress. The drunk's splintered board theory seems more like a later rationalization than an explanation of why he figured it was OK to jump back onto the street. I mean, even if I sincerely wanted to give up my whole sexual side right now, and I didn't buy a single word of the splintered boards thing, my whole organism has been powerfully altered by years of positive and negative reinforcements. Don Giovanni couldn't just decide to change into Mother Teresa one day, could he? I've taken in almost every facet of young womanhood I've come across in the last 25 years in a particular, self-titillating way. I understand on some intellectual level that this approach to life has been unhealthy for me, but this knowledge can't compete with so many years of conditioning. Think of the Peter Lorre character in *M* screaming "I can't help myself!" I'm like a defective robot in desparate need of a new program, but a huge part of my existing program is to resist any sort of new programming. Almost every non-sexual instinct of mine seems like it's been completely suborned. I can't even look at a picture of an attractive woman without schemes popping into my head. Each facial expression of mine, everything I say has some kind of selfish end pulling the strings. What willpower I ever had that was independent of this tyrant is long gone....It all seems pretty hopeless to me without some kind of radical reconditiong.

Rabi. I hope you won't despair, Paul. Everyone faces

some issue or other that seems intractable. We must all have our own struggles under the Bo tree.

Paul. Including you?

Rabi. Of course. I struggle with many things. Resentment most of all—and acquistiveness—just look at all these books.

Paul. Come on, Rabi. There are issues and there are issues. Not everyone who wants something is an addict.

Rabi. Detachment is extremely difficult for everyone. The conflicts between ascetic and hedonistic impulses, between modesty and pride, between resentment and acceptance are absolutely unavoidable and almost never easy. Why would they be? There's a wonderful set of dialogues attributed to Saint Catherine of Genoa about the constant clashes between the soul and body for mastery of the human organism.

Paul. Since she was canonized I take it the soul must have won.

Rabi. Well, at first they make an agreement to share control, each giving the other alternate weeks. But the body starts encroaching on the soul's time, by convincing her that without satisfying the body, the soul is doomed to perish. But the more the body is given to feed its cravings, the more it needs. The soul laments that,

> You have, by degrees, so changed me, or I might rather say, perverted me, that I feed on the same food as yourselves; and we are so united and agree so well, that I blindly fall in with all your desires, and have, thus, from a spiritual soul become almost an earthly body....I, poor creature, am like one chained and stifled, and, as it were, dead to spiritual things. As if deprived of interior light and taste, I go on, gazing at and tasting things earthly and corporeal, and there is no good thing remaining to me, except a certain secret remorse which leaves me but little rest. Yet I continue neglecting myself, and enjoying, as I may, these earthly

things which I feed upon, and wasting my time, while daily I bring myself into greater slavery; and the farther I withdraw from God, the more dissatisfied am I with my estrangement from my natural good, which is God himself.[144]

Paul. And is the soul rescued by the Divine Mercy of the Son of Man or something like that?

Rabi. Yes, in much the same way as so many alcoholics describe being saved in *The Big Book*. As Saint Catherine puts it, with a deep and piteous sigh the soul turns to God and cries,

'O wretched creature that I am! who will deliver me from all this misery? God alone is able: *Domine, fac ut videam lumen,* that I may escape these snares.'

No sooner had she directed her thoughts to God, and implored his help, without which she saw she had no power to move, but could only go from bad to worse, than suddenly her confidence in him became firm, and she left him to do his own will in what manner, and so far as it pleased him; and she added: 'From henceforth all that befalls me I will receive as from the benign hand of God, excepting my sins, for they are all my own; committing them is always contrary to the divine will, and therefore they are our own property; nothing is ours but voluntary sin.'

This firm resolution, made by the Soul before God, was secret and in her own spirit alone, without any outward demonstration. Now, when God sees that man distrusts himself, and places his whole confidence in Providence, he immediately stretches forth his holy hand to help him. He stands ever at our side, he knocks, and, if we open to him, he enters; he drives forth our enemies one after another.

And a little later the soul turns to God and promises,

'Lord! I give myself to thee. I know not what I am fitted for but to make a hell by myself alone. O Lord! I desire to make this compact with thee: I will give this sinful being of mine into thy hands, for thou alone canst hide it in thy mercy, and so dispose of me that nothing of myself can any more be seen. Occupy me wholly with thy love, which will enlighten in me every other love and keep me wholly lost in thee, holding me so engrossed by thee that I shall find neither time nor place for self.'

Her most sweet Lord made answer that he was content, and from that moment all thought and memory of self was lost, so that it never more disturbed her peace. On the other hand, a ray of love so burning and penetrating was infused into her heart and wounded her so deeply that in an instant it bereft her of every attachment, appetite, delectation, and natural quality that ever did or ever could belong to her. She was shorn of everything, though not without her own consent, by virtue of her correspondence with the love revealed to her, and by this she was so powerfully drawn that it astonished, absorbed, and transformed her. She sighed and lamented far more than when she beheld what a sinful creature she was.[145]

Paul. Yeah. That *is* a lot like the stories in the AA book. But I take it that after the first rush of divine love faded, Saint Catherine's soul didn't keep up her resolve by regularly attending meetings in the basement of some K of C.

Rabi. No, she—like Saint Catherine herself—followed the ways of mortification and penance:

All [her] instincts were called into action by God alone, for the Soul had no wish or aim but God, who had taken the direction, and wished to regulate all her desires and inclinations, and free her from all those that were human and worldly by giving her contrary ones. She was deprived of the use of fruits for which she had a natural inclination and an especial fondness. She ate no flesh nor anything superfluous, and when she needed food, that which she might eat appeared to be always at hand. That she might lose all relish of what she ate she was taught to carry always about her some dust of aloes, and when she found herself taking pleasure in any food or preferring one kind to another she secretly sprinkled it with a little of the bitter power before eating it. Her eyes were always cast down; she never laughed, and recognized no one who passed her, for she was so occupied with what was taking place within that her sense of exterior things was, as it were, dead.

But she consoles the vanquished body when she says,

'How long, think you, will this season of purification last? You know well that it can endure but a short time. In the beginning it seems terrible to you, but as it goes on you will suffer less, because your wicked habits will be destroyed; do not fear lest you should want powerful support, for know that God, by the decree of his goodness, never allows man to suffer beyond his strength.'[146]

Paul. Well, like I said, that's the kind of treatment I think I need, too. I want to fight fire with fire, just like Saint Catherine did. There are so many years of conditioning to be undone. Why shouldn't I put stones in my shoes and eat wormwood? I don't see how anything short of those kinds of remedies can have any chance of success.

Rabi. It seems to me that putting stones in your shoes is more likely to negatively reinforce walking than to curtail your acting on your sexual impulses.

Paul (laughing). Unless I'm in a chase situation. But seriously, that was just an example. Something else then: something that will keep me constantly in pain. After all, I have these impulses almost all the time—even when I'm asleep. I think a global, unremitting remedy is in order.

Rabi. I prefer surgical responses to systemic ones.

Paul (laughing). You mean like the one applied to Abelard by Heloise's family?

Rabi. Oh, no! I was actually thinking of the preferability of focussed negative reinforcement to systemic pain when we're trying to prevent recurrences of particular unwanted behaviours. It's akin to my preference for individual cathartic illuminations over primal screams.

Paul. So, what am I supposed to do? Stick myself with a pin every time I notice a twinge of lust or feel an erotic fantasy coming on?

Rabi. That certainly seems more sensible than a hair shirt—although a strong pinch might suffice instead of a pin prick. As Thomas a Kempis says in *The Imitation of Christ*,

> [W]e must watch, especially in the beginnings of temptation; for then is the foe the more easily mastered, when he is not suffered to enter within the mind, but is met outside the door as soon as he hath knocked. Wherefore one saith, 'Check the beginnings; once thou might'st have cured, but now tis past thy skill, too long hath it endured.' For first cometh to the mind the simple suggestion, then the strong imagination, afterwards pleasure, evil affection, assent. And so little by little the enemy entereth in altogether, because he was not resisted at the beginning.[147]

Paul. Nip it in the bud, eh?

Rabi. Exactly. As Saint Augustine has written, "When I gave in to lust habit was born, and when I did not resist the habit it became a necessity."[148] We must not allow ourselves to be swayed by any of the common arguments—call them corporeal or satanic or whatever you will. I mean the one claiming that yielding this once won't result in a binge, the one concluding that a last big binge will get the demon out of our systems once and for all, and the one that insists that since no debauchment has really destroyed our life yet, further binges won't be the end of the world. All these have to be met and mastered. We have to realize that each failure to resist today makes it doubly difficult to resist tomorrow, and that debauchments only get more and more severe.

Paul. You don't think the desires can ever be dissipated by exhaustion.

Rabi. Only for the moment. I'm sure you agree that giving in to addictive desires usually has exactly the opposite effect.

Paul. Yeah, I can't deny that. So we just have to fight it continuously? Or as you might tell us, flow the tension down, then flow it out?

Rabi. I'm afraid so. But it's often the case that a thorough understanding of the dynamics of addiction combined with negative reinforcement, relaxation and sublimation are not sufficient. That's why I don't downplay the efficacy of asking for divine assistance as well, as is suggested both in Saint Catherine's *Dialogues* and in *The Big Book*.

Paul. And some compassionate God will reach down and pull me up?

Rabi. I don't look at it in the way of a miraculous intervention.

Paul. What else would you call it? I try countless times as hard as I can, and fail; I pray, and *poof!* success. That sounds pretty miraculous to me.

Rabi. We've discussed this many times before. We know that this assistance is not within us in the sense of being under our conscious control, but without enlightenment of a kind you've forbidden me to discuss with you, we can know little more about how we come to be changed. But why do we need to understand these things in times of crisis anyway? Our first business is to get better, and it seems that we can. Lewis Thomas touched on this matter in a paper he wrote on, of all things, warts. First he tells us that they are caused by a very complicated virus which we are nowhere near being able to cure. Then, he points out what he calls "one of the great mystifications of science":

> [W]arts can be ordered off the skin by hypnotic
> suggestion....I was once told by a distinguished old professor
> of medicine...that it was his practice to paint gentian violet
> over a wart and then assure the patient firmly that it would be
> gone in a week, and he never saw it fail. There have been several
> meticulous studies by good clinical investigators, with proper
> controls. In one of these, fourteen patients with seemingly
> intractable generalized warts on both sides of the body were
> hypnotized, and the suggestion was made that all the warts
> on one side of the body would begin to go away. Within several
> weeks the resluts were indisputably positive; in nine patients,
> all or nearly all of the warts on the suggested side had vanished
> precisely as they were instructed, but it is even more fascinating
> that mistakes were made....[O]ne of the subjects got mixed up
> and destroyed the warts on the wrong side.[149]

Obviously, none of these subjects could have dismissed
their warts away just by wishing hard: they would have
failed over and over again, just as you have failed in your
attempts to remain faithful to your wife. But these same
subjects *were* able to rid themselves of this infection with
the aid of something that was beyond their control.

Paul. So you're saying I should get myself hypnotized?

Rabi. Why not? But maybe you won't have to do that
either. Maybe you'll find it is enough to just emulate the
praying alcoholics. Or maybe wearing a talisman around
your neck will do the trick, or a magic spell.

Paul. Aren't you the guy who warned G off magic her
first week her? Didn't you tell her she'd eventually have
to choose between sorcery and some kind religion fit for
adults?

Rabi. Yes, but, as you well know, there are various types
of enchantment. I have no problem with the kind we
knowingly make for ourselves. Not solid representations
of idle wishes, but visible reminders of the work we have

to do or the temptations we must resist. What matters is the desire to change and the belief that we can. Suzuki has written,

> In striving to master Zen, the thing needed is to cherish a strong desire to destroy a mind subject to birth and death. When this desire is awakened, the Yogin feels as if he were enveloped in a blazing fire. He wants to escape it. He cannot just be walking about, he cannot stay quietly in it, he cannot harbour any idle thoughts, he cannot expect others to help him out. Since no moment is to be lost, all he has to do is to rush out of it to the best of his strength and without being disturbed by the thought of the consequence.[150]

Paul. Are you saying that some combination of strong desire and the placebo effect are enough to eliminate severe addictions? Sugar pills instead of methodone?

Rabi. I wouldn't belittle the power of our physical bodies and unconscious minds to combat grave ailments of all types. There is so much we don't know about how we perform our many feats of healing. In any case, to have any chance of success at all, we mustn't give up. Furthermore, we can take heart from the fact that—as they say in AA, we need take only one day at a time. If we do this, we will soon notice that our trials have become less frequent and less taxing.

Paul. Yeah, that's a recurrent theme in a lot of the stuff I've been reading. I think there's an example in Underhill:

> Each effort to stand brings first a glorious sense of growth, and and then a fall: each fall means another struggle to obtain the difficult balance which comes when infancy is past. There are many eager trials many hopes, many disappointments. At last, as it seems suddenly, the moment comes: tottering is over, the muscles have learnt their lesson, they adjust themselves automatically, and the new self suddenly finds itself—it knows

not how—standing upright and secure. That is the moment which marks the boundary between the purgative and the illuminative states.[151]

Rabi. Yes, yes. That's very good. Now, Paul, before we end this final session, you must promise me you'll do everything—meditate to give relief from the anxiety produced by resisting your proddings; scour your psyche for causes of this behavior pattern; pray for assistance, avoid dangerous environments, find new sublimations, or at least new non-sexual distractions; negatively reinforce your unwanted behaviors and thoughts—not by guilt afterward, but by administering some small concurrent pains that will discourage continuance; resort to magic; wear crystals; enter group therapy. Whatever you can bring yourself to do. Attack from all sides with persistance and strength, and you will master these cravings. If we think of it as surgery, we must be thorough enough to achieve "clean margins" around the site of the cancer. Otherwise, regrowth is inevitable. Or, to put it another way, your healing forces must relentlessly strike at every intruder, just as in the wart-ridden subjects countless antibodies are unleashed at the prodding of the hypnotist. The point is not to give up. Can you promise me that, Paul?

Paul. If I promise you, it will be just one more thing to feel guilty about if...*when*...I fail. When I was in my early teens and first discovered the wonders of self-pleasure, these activities produced nothing worse than slight feelings of uneasiness—the sense that it would be better if my parents didn't find out. Then I read this horrible essay by D.H. Lawrence. He went on at great length about how onanists were were defective individuals, half-men at best. It was at that point that my practice, which used to be predominantly fun, became a huge source of guilt for me. It metamorphosed from something like the simple enjoyment of hot fudge sundaes into something akin to addiction to heroin. But couldn't stop myself back then, and—given any sort of stress in my life—I won't be able to stop now, either. Cut back on affairs, maybe. But purge all elements of sexuality from my life—from glances and fantasies to flirtations and erotic dreams. It doesn't seem possible. And I'm not even sure it would be healthy. Human beings were given these impulses for important evolutionary reasons. weren't they? So, why make any promises that will probably just increase my stress level and make me more likely to fall.

Rabi. When you use the term "fall" it makes me sense that you do, on some level, see that these are not healthy evolutionary instincts you're acting on. These are illicit affairs we're talking about, not relations with your wife.

Paul. Yeah. I can't deny it. I can tell that most of this stuff—even the fantasizing—is no good for me. I guess calling it *natural* is like a dying drunk complaining about the splinters he might get from the boards on the Wagon. But can you see why I don't want to make you a promise?

Rabi. Of course. But remember, I ask you for no promise of success, only that you won't give up. Only that if you succumb in one test, you'll begin the fight again, with renewed ferocity.

Paul. I still don't think I can do that right now, Rabi. But I do want to thank you for your pep talk. Your confidence means a lot to me: it almost makes me think I can succeed. In fact, I want to thank you for everything. It's been a wonderful summer for me—one that I feel will turn out to have been very important in my life.

Rabi. I'm glad to hear it, Paul. Very glad. (He rises, and

Paul does the same.) It's been a very great pleasure to have met you and learned so many things from you as well. Please take care of yourself. I hope you will write to me if you get a chance. (They shake hands and Paul leaves.)

Saturday, 8:30 AM—The Edge of the Woods

(Across the road from the center, about twenty yards into the woods, Paul is hitting a maple tree with a stick a little bigger and more unwieldy than a baseball bat. At first, he does this in silence, but as he swings harder and harder, he begins to grunt more and more loudly with each blow. Soon, he's hollering loudly. G, who was sitting by herself at a table in the garden hears him and follows the strange sounds into the woods until she finds him.)

G. Paul, is that you? What are you doing?

Paul (dropping his cudgel). Nothing. Nothing.

G. Jesus, your hands are bleeding.

Paul (looking down at his hands). Shit.

G (She takes a tissue from her pants pocket and gives it to him. He wipes his eyes with it first, then squeezes it between his two hands.) What's going on? What's wrong?

Paul. Oh, it's just another ending. That's all.

G. You mean this session? This place?

Paul. Yeah....It's over: I'm the same. I go back to my shitty life now and continue waiting to die....You know, when I was a kid I used to hate to go to summer camp each year. I'd always cry and beg my parents not to make me go. But I'd be just as upset at the end of the summer when I had to go home. The counselors would carve the letters of the camp's name out of wood and, after sunset, everyone would go down to the lake and they'd set the letters on fire and float them on the water. I'd always cry as I watched them burn. I figured I'd never see some of these people, my new best friends, again. And I never did see some of them again.

G. Are you talking about me?

Paul. Sure. You, Rabi, this place, this chance, everything.

G. What do you mean "this chance"?

Paul. Look, G. You aren't any different from me. This summer was just an interlude, a pause in your regular existence. Before you know it, we'll both be in some hospital room somewhere, trying to decide whether to have another surgery or another last chance at chemo-therapy. Maybe you'll look back at this summer, or maybe you'll have completely forgotten it and be focusing completely on the additional pain you're about to undergo just to get the possibility of another few years of consciousness. You'll be weighing the likelihood of success of the treatment options. But even if whatever the doctors throw at you *is* successful, what good will that do? Another couple of years? You'll be back in that hospital room facing another final crisis before you know it. Don't you see? This reading and talking and meditating won't have stopped anything. We can't stop it. It can't be stopped. I don't know what I was thinking about when I came here. I should have known that the summer would be over in a flash, and I'd be suffering from the unhealthiness of thinking about my mortality so much for three months. The only thing that ever really helps anyone is distraction. A gripping movie, a funny TV show, an exciting basketball game, an affair. You should never break up the regular pattern of your life—especially to consider "Perennial Solutions." Each break just provides a new opportunity to notice where you are, to estimate how many more remaining breaths you have.

Kelsey used to ask me all the time how many hours, how many minutes, how many seconds she'd been alive so far. She was too young to fret about the fact that each second she expends cuts into those she has left. When I think about her finally coming to that realization I....Oh God. (He starts crying again.)

G (tentatively putting a hand on his shoulder). I know you can't see this right now, Paul, but things really aren't that bad. I've seen you a lot over the last few months and you're usually a pretty happy guy. You're just in a funk right now. It'll pass. And don't forget, Kelsey's got a lot of Laura in her too—she might turn out to be the type that thinks it's pointless or unhip or even childish for young, healthy people to be worrying about dying.

Paul. Maybe I seem content to you, but I'm not sure I've ever been happy. There's always this *thing* just below the surface, gnawing at my gizzard like Prometheus's eagle. I guess I've tried to keep up this delusion that I might change. That's probably why I came here. But I don't change. I never change. I just get older.

Rabi (approaching from the road). Excuse me, Paul, but I think you *have* changed.

Paul. Rabi! I can't believe it. Seeing you outside the library is like coming across a Panda among these maples. I've heard you like to take walks, but I never see you out here.

Rabi. Vera and I go hiking nearly every Saturday when the weather is good. But we don't often walk around here. At our age, we prefer dirt roads to mountain trails. But Vera said she heard something odd out here, so I came out to take a look. Did you know your hands were bleeding?

Paul. Yeah, it's nothing. Forget about it. I want to hear how you think I've changed.

Rabi. Well for one thing, you meditate regularly now,

where you used to be unable to do that. For another, I believe you've passed up several opportunities for romantic liaisons this summer. That's not something you would have predicted when you came here, is it?

Paul. No, I guess not. But those don't seem like changes of any real significance: the point is, I'm just as miserable, if not more so. I was just talking to G here about how much I'm looking forward to returning to my regular lifestyle. I don't worry so much about dying when I'm watching a ball game, shopping for a new car, or planning a first date. I might be fretting about the cost of adding leather seats or what shirt I'll look best in, but that definitely beats deciding between burial and cremation. Look, it's not your fault, Rabi. I don't blame you anymore, and I'm sorry I was so combative when I first came here. You can't help any of this: it was stupid of me to think you could. We're all mortal, and I'm going to die. There's nothing you can do about it. I understand this fact of nature doesn't bother you. Good for you: I congratulate you. I've had enough of arguing. Let's just say I don't feel the same way and forget about it, shall we? You can continue to hold your little sessions about Butler and Suzuki until *you* die, and I'll keep raging against the dying of the light until *I* die....But look, I don't want you to think I'm being unfair about this or giving you less credit than you're due. So, I tell you what: I'll give you one last chance to prove there's more to you than a quaint, deluded librarian. It's a perfect place for that kind of showing—out here in the beauty of rural Vermont. And when could be a better time than now, when I'm regaled with my faux stigmata? It's the ideal opportunity for you to do your guru thing. Touch my forehead or say a prayer and let me see the blinding light. Give me the peace that passeth understanding. Now. *Libera me.*

G. Oh, Christ, Paul. Do you think you can be any more

melodramatic? (Sarcastically) You poor, poor thing. You know, maybe someone would be a little bit sympathetic if you had an actual problem that anyone could relate to. Let's see. You're in perfect health. You're rich enough to never have to work again if you don't feel like it. You have a healthy, beautiful daughter who loves you. You're smart, handsome, funny, and streams of women apparently flock to you....But you're not immortal. Bummer.

Paul. Without that, none of the other stuff really matters, does it?

G. It matters to me. I have to report back to work on Monday. I'd like a child, but I don't have one, and I don't have any prospects of having one soon. I thought I might have had a chance to make some kind of connection with you this summer, but I guess I'm not thin enough or pretty enough for you to think of me that way.

Paul. Can't you see that that wasn't easy for me—not to treat you like a one night stand? I thought you deserved better.

G. Maybe that's true, and maybe not. There *are* alternatives besides friendship and abuse, you know. Look, when I get home, I'll probably have about fifteen phone messages waiting for me from my sister who feels oh-so-awful about having stolen my last boyfriend and figures the solution to this problem is for me to hurry up and forgive her. There'll be fifty bills waiting to be paid, and a huge stack of stuff that's piled up for me at work....But, somehow, this summer is just about you and the fact that, unlike Vishnu or Hercules, you're not immortal. Because, after all, what else really matters but the fact that you're going to die some day? You're in the same boat as every other human being, and you don't see why you shouldn't get to be in a bigger, nicer boat than everybody else. And it's actually pretty understandable. You've always been given a very nice boat to sail over every other annoying fact of life most people have to wade through. Why no present of immortality if you want it really badly? How amazingly unfair! I do have one other discouraging piece of news for you, though, Paul. You're way less tough than Lily Dale. She had real character: she was acting on principle. You're just giving in to your fears. You talk tough, but deep down you're a little baby—as you'd put it, a *girly* little baby, which is probably why you're bullying Rabi right now. I suppose it makes you feel more macho.

Paul. I don't deny a lot of what you're saying, G. I *am* selfish and adolescent about these things. But what am I supposed to do about it? It's the way I am. I hope you don't agree with Rabi in thinking people can change by chanting some mantra. Let's face it: there's no more to his so-called "solution" than counting sheep.

G. Let me tell you something. My father used to drink. And I used to hear the same kind of crap from him: "It's not my fault, G. I can't help it. If I get drunk, and push your mother around, there's nothing I can do about it. That's just the way I am when I drink. And anyhow, she should know by now to stay away from me when I get liquored up." But at least my father—and with a lot more obligations and a lot fewer advantages than you have—finally grew up and stopped drinking. But you just wallow in self-indulgence and expect everybody to feel bad for you.

Paul: I don't expect anything from anybody. Maybe your father was tougher than I am. He could change and I can't. That's all. Coming here is about the limit of what I'm capable of doing on the change front. I tried, I failed, and tonight I'll lie in bed just as wide awake as if I hadn't come. For a longer time probably. It was worse than a waste of time and money. It roiled me up for no reason, and I managed to piss you off in the bargain because I didn't want either of us to get hurt.

G. Thank you so much.

Rabi. Paul, you're wrong. As I said, you *have* changed, and for the better.

Paul (sarcastically). Oh really? How?

Rabi. I've told you. You've managed to resist self-destructive liaisons all summer, and you now know how to meditate to help you relax. If you devote the time and energy each day to concentration and self-analysis, things will get easier and easier for you, just as they no doubt did for G's father. You are intelligent enough to understand that it's not a matter of me touching your forehead or saying magic words. It's a matter of daily practice, like learning Spanish or working out with weights. Each individual improvement is microscopic, but each is necessary. And over time, the difference produced can be monumental. Changes of the kind you seek don't happen without effort.

Paul. You can't seem to get it, can you, Rabi? I've told you over and over that I don't want to not worry about dying. Listen carefully this one last time: I want not to die.

Rabi. And given the choice between acceptance and terror, you choose terror?

G. Of course. He wants to wallow. It's so much easier, and it gratifies his martyr complex. I think we should leave him out here blubbering and thinking of other insulting things he can say to you; it's what he says he prefers, and I think it's exactly what he deserves.

Rabi. Let me say to you again, Paul. Those who meditate correctly and learn to understand themselves not only cease to fear: they also begin to believe. The counting of sheep produces sleep and nothing more. This is an empirical truth, and one you can easily test in your own case. Your certainty that you will age and die is no barrier to belief. On the contrary, it's one of Buddha's noble truths. Without this certainty no believer could ever reach the heights you seek.

Paul. Don't you even care whether these believers are right or are just deluding themselves?

Rabi. *They* think they're right, and they don't give any indication of having become suddenly stupider or more credulous. On the contrary, they seem in every way clearer, more alert and more focused. I've seen you move in that direction too, during the weeks when you've practiced diligently. We can spend our lives wrangling about the possibility of genuine worship, or we can try it and see for ourselves. As Carlyle said,

> ...ascribe what origin and genesis thou pleasest, *has* not that Worship originated, and been generated; is it not *here*? Feel it in thy heart, and then say whether it is of God! This is Belief; all else is Opinion—for which latter whoso will let him worry and be worried.[152]

Paul. I don't know. I don't know. I don't know.

G. OK. You don't know. You don't really want to know either—not if it involves cutting into your leisure time. Blubber, freakout, wallow, watch TV, have an affair, whack a tree: those are the things you want to do. I'm all for it. Knock yourself out. Can we forget Paul for a minute, Rabi—he's happy wallowing. What about *me*? I've tried so hard this summer. Why haven't *I* gotten any benefits? I feel so much less certain of everything than when I came.

Rabi. Oh, you've changed a great deal, too, G. You

can talk openly about yourself now, even to the point of discussing your father or criticizing your sister. You're much more direct. You can tell people how you're feeling without flinching. You may be uncertain about your future and sad about your past, but I think your anxiety is lessening as you begin to understand the forces and motives that influence your travels through this world. When you're angry now, you know why. Where we used to find a combination of diffidence, anxiety and rage, there's a firmness now, a focus to your thinking and your actions, almost a serenity. You now have the tools both to relax fully and to comprehend yourself to a much greater degree than ever before. You're unafraid of facing the future without Santa Claus or a magic wand. You even pushed the merits of Freud over Emerson to me. You are a brave woman now. Your "little faith" is slowly being superseded by a deep knowledge.

G. Knowledge of what?

Rabi. Ah, what? Will you allow me to say "of yourself and your world" without accusing me of obscurantism or of plagiarizing from popular song lyrics?

G. But I'm so sad now. Sad that fall is coming. Sad to be leaving, to be losing you, to have failed—or at least not completely succeeded—either in my search for liberation or for love.

Rabi. No search of that kind can ever be completely successful while we live. The search is, if not all, so nearly all.

Paul. You don't need to convince me about the thrill of the hunt, Rabi. It always *is* better than the prize. By the way, G, I haven't done so much wallowing this summer that I haven't seen all these changes in you that Rabi is talking about. You're just as ferocious, but it doesn't seem like desperation anymore: it's healthier. Plus, you don't laugh at my jokes unless they're actually funny.

G. Maybe you just got less funny after you tried to get yourself elected Mr. Junior Guru Vermont.

Paul. Girly wallowing teacher's pet and unfunny to boot? Ouch. I guess somebody could say you've got some pretty strange taste in men, G, but maybe it would be better if we also avoided some of the *accusations* that there's no answers to. Anyhow, I hope some day you'll see that your anger for me has been misplaced. I'm just not ready to have a real relationship with a real person. You must know that as well as anybody. Even I could tell there wouldn't be any thrill in *that* hunt, just pain. And getting back to the hunt thing, Rabi, tell me, are you now saying that enlightenment is one percent inspiration and 99 percent perspiration? If so, I think you should go back to quoting from rock songs — there's better material available there.

Rabi (laughing). Yes, Paul, it's nearly all effort, but with just the slightest trace of grace. Our struggles so often seem unavailing, but each trial, each drop of sweat, becomes a jewel—a symbol of our striving, our love. And, gradually, mysteriously, this work becomes beautiful. We find we enjoy it. We don't want to abandon it, even when it seems most futile or absurd. Like the octogenarian in the weight room or Arjuna on the battlefield we don't shirk, whatever may be the result. We find our desires are now all for what is best for us. We can give in to them willingly, as to a restful sleep. And you must neither of you think that you will lose me. I can't ever be completely separated from either of you now. Whether my solution deserves its capital letters or not, it is undeniably perennial, at least for us. To quote Tagore,

This song of mine will wind its music around you, my child,

like the fond arms of love.

This song of mine will touch your forehead like a kiss of blessing.

When you are alone it will sit by your side and whisper in your ear, when you are in the crowd it will fence you about with aloofness.

My song will be like a pair of wings to your dreams, it will transport your heart to the verge of the unknown.

It will be like the faithful star overhead when dark night is over your road.

My song will sit in the pupil of your eyes, and will carry your sight into the heart of things.

And when my voice is silent in death, my song will speak in your living heart.[153]

G (crying). That's beautiful.

(Rabi opens his arms and the three embrace for a moment.)

Rabi. And now, go forth my friends, back to your work and play, to your joys and your difficulties. My prayer for you is that you will meditate, both when you feel you need to and when it seems unnecessary. Also that you will not give in when you feel impelled to do something that you know on a deeper level is unwise for you. As so many alcoholics have learned, all you must do is resist for one day, *this* day. And finally, I pray that you will learn to stop wishing for things that will do you no good. Things like money or sexual conquests or prestige or revenge against those who may have harmed you. You need not, like the hero of Isherwood's "Wishing Tree"[154] refuse to take any help from every mysterious power that makes itself available or refrain from wishing altogether, but you must discover which desires, if satisfied, will make you more free and which can do nothing but generate ever greater demands. To put it another way, you must learn how to distinguish legitimate prayers from bargains with the devil. In any case, as most of us learn in childhood, wishing is almost always insufficient to produce any result at all—good or evil—and can never be depended upon to produce serenity or fulfillment. As the Buddha said, Right Thinking, Right Speech, Right Action, and Right Contemplation are all necessary for enlightenment. The practice of Right Contemplation—*meditation*—is the most important thing you can take from here, since it is that which can teach you which temptations must be resisted and how to choose those goals that will enlarge you. Meditation can also make clear to you the methods by which your appropriate goals may be reached and help to calm you when your difficulties seem insurmountable. You must leave the Perennial Solution Center now. But do not think you leave me when you leave this place, for I am, or at least my ideas are, part of you now. True or false, reasonable or absurd, they...*I*...mix with you, making you the slightest bit different. Stronger, I hope, and yet also softer and more malleable. More accepting of the world, and more sure of yourselves in it.

Paul. Oh, Rabi, Rabi. Why do you always turn philosophy into psychology? Why do you insist on answering questions about the nature of the world with advice about how we can feel better about ourselves? I, for one, still have some interest in the truth, even if it turns out not to be entirely pleasant. Is there a single shred of what I've heard at this place over the past three months that is anything more than a pretty bedtime story for adults? Do you send us off now with nothing more than a bunch of sophisticated fairy tales and a folksy way to relax? Is that your solution: placebos and obscure, mystical explanations?

Rabi. I think there is something deeply important about such gifts, that they can indeed lead you to an understanding of the nature the world. Still, what I have given may be less than you expected—even unworthy of you. In the end, of course, one can make presents only of what one has. But I want to be as generous as I can, so allow me to give you one more thing. Let me offer you, as a further remembrance of our summer together, this bit of song: (he sings) *Oh. It's the old forgotten question. What is it that we are part of? And what is it that we are?* (They embrace again, and then, hand in hand, begin their walk back to the Center.)

Endnotes

[1] John Bayley (ed.) *Great Short Works of Leo Tolstoy,* Louise and Aylmer Maude translation, (Harper & Row, 1967).

[2] Herbert Benson with Miriam Klipper, *The Relaxation Response,* (Avon Books, 1975).

[3] "Sutta 63" in Henry Clarke Warren (ed. and trans.) *Buddhism in Translations,* (Atheneum, 1968).

[4] H.L. Mencken, "Ad Imaginem Dei Creavit Illum," in *Prejudices: Third Series,* (Alfred A. Knopf, 1922).

[5] Benson, *op. cit.*

[6] *Ibid.*

[7] *Ibid.*

[8] Bertrand Russell, "Mysticism and Logic," in *Selected Papers of Bertrand Russell* (Modern Library, 1927).

[9] *Ibid.*

[10] C.S. Lewis, *Mere Christianity* (MacMillan, 1943).

[11] Bantam, 1975.

[12] Russell, *op. cit.*

[13] Walter Lowrie (ed. and trans.) *Religion of a Scientist: Selections from Gustav Th. Fechner* (Pantheon, 1946).

[14] Lawrence LeShan, *How to Meditate* (Bantam, 1975).

[15] *You Are Not The Target* (Farar, Straus & Giroux, 1966).

[16] Sigmund Freud (Riviere, trans.) *General Introduction to Psychoanalysis* (Pocket Books, 1915-17); Karen Horney, *New Ways in Psychoanalysis* (W.W. Norton, 1939)

[17] Sigmund Freud and Josef Breuer (Strachey, ed. and trans.), *Studies on Hysteria* (Basic Books, 1893-95).

[18] L. Ron Hubbard, *Dianetics: The Modern Science of Mental Health* (Bridge, 1981).

[19] Adolf Grunbaum, *The Foundations of Psychoanalysis* (University of California Press, 1984).

[20] Karen Horney, *Our Inner Conflicts* (W. W. Norton, 1945)

[21] *Ibid.*

[22] Terry Lynn Taylor and Mary Beth Crane (Harper Collins, 1997).

[23] *Ibid.*

[24] *Ibid.*

[25] Horney, *op cit.*

[26] Aldous Huxley, *Eyeless in Gaza* (Harpers, 1936).

[27] William James, *Varieties of Religious Experience* (Longmans, Green and Co., 1904).

[28] *Ibid.*

[29] *Ibid.*

[30] *Ibid.*

[31] Aldous Huxley, *The Perennial Philosophy* (Harper & Brothers, 1944).

[32] G.K. Chesterton, "Christmas and the Aesthetes," in *Heretics* (John Lane, 1905).

[33] Meister Eckhardt, *Deutsch Werke*. Quoted in Oliver Davies, *God Within: The Mystical Tradition of Northern Europe* (Darton, Longman and Todd, 1988)

[34] *The Life of Saint Teresa of Avila by Herself* (Penguin, 1957).

[35] *Taittiriya* (Prabhavananda and Manchester, ed. and trans.), *The Upanishads* (Mentor, 1948).

[36] George Moore, *The Brook Kerith* (Macmillan, 1936).

[37] C.S. Lewis, *op. cit.*

[38] J.D. Salinger, *Franny and Zooey* (Bantam, 1961).

[39] W.T. Stace, *Mysticism and Philosophy*, (J.B. Lippincott, 1960).

[40] *Ibid.*

[41] *Ibid.*

[42] *Ibid.*

[43] *Ibid.*

[44] Jean-Paul Sartre (Lloyd Alexander, tr.), *Nausea*, (New Directions, 1959).

[45] *Ibid.*

[46] *Ibid.*

[47] In *Fechner*, *op. cit.*

[48] Lewis Thomas, *The Lives of a Cell* (Viking, 1974).

[49] *Ibid.*

[50] Rabindranth Tagore, *Sadhana* (MacMillan, 1916).

[51] Bertrand Russell, *The Problems of Philosophy* (Henry Holt, 1912).

[52] See, e.g., Roderick Chisholm, *Perceiving* (Cornell University Press, 1957).

[53] Ludwig Wittgenstein (D.F. Pears & B.F. McGuinness, tr.), *Tractatus Logico-Philosophicus* (Harcourt Brace, 1922).

[54] Norwood Russell Hanson, *Observation and Explanation* (Harper & Row, 1971).

[55] G. Dawes Hicks, *Hibbert Lectures: The Philosophical Bases of Theism* (AMS Press, 1931).

[56] *Ibid.*

[57] Alan Watts, *Psychotherapy East and West* (Vintage, 1961).

[58] "The Half-Remarkable Question" (Warner-Tamerlane—BMI), on *Wee Tam* (Elektra, 1968).

[59] Arthur Koestler, *The Lotus and the Robot* (Harper & Row, 1960).

[60] *Ku-tsun hsu Yu-lu*. Quoted in Alan Watts, *The Way of Zen* (Pantheon, 1957).

[61] Quoted in Coomaraswamy, *op cit.*

[62] See, in particular Shaw's *Major Barbara* (Penguin, 1913).

[63] G. Dawes Hicks, *op. cit.*

[64] Anna Robeson Burr, *Religious Confessions and Confessants* (Houghton Mifflin, 1914).

[65] Henry Clark Warren, *op. cit.*

[66] Rabindranath Tagore, *Gitanjali* (MacMillan, 1913), verse 102.

[67] From the Oldenberg translation, in Ananda K. Coomaraswamy, *Buddha and the Gospel of Buddhism* (George G. Harrap, 1916).

[68] Erich Fromm, "Psychoanalysis and Zen Buddhism" in Fromm, D.T. Suzuki, and Richard D. Martino, *Zen Buddhism and Psychoanalysis* (Harper & Brothers, 1960).

[69] D.T. Suzuki, "Lectures on Zen Buddhism, in *Ibid.*

[70] Fromm, *op.cit.*

[71] *Ibid.*

[72] *Ibid.* quoting D.T. Suzuki's *Introduction to Zen Buddhism* (Doubleday Anchor, 1956).

[73] *Ibid.*

[74] Ralph Waldo Emerson, "Compensation" in *Selected Essays, Lectures, and Poems* (Simon & Schuster, 1965).

[75] *Ibid.*

[76] *Ibid.*

[77] Rabindranath Tagore, *Sadhana* (MacMillan, 1916).

[78] Sigmund Freud, *The Future of an Illusion*, in Peter Gay (ed.) *The Freud Reader*, (W. W. Norton & Co., 1989).

[79] *Ibid.*

[80] *Ibid.*

[81] *Ibid.*

[82] *Ibid.*

[83] Sigmund Freud, *The Ego and the Id,* in Gay, *op. cit.*

[84] *Ibid.*

[85] Ralph Waldo Emerson, "The Over-Soul" in *The Works of Emerson,* (Walter J. Black, Inc., n.d.).

[86] *Ibid.*

[87] *Ibid.*

[88] Ralph Waldo Emerson, "Worship" in *The Works of Emerson,* (Walter J. Black, Inc., n.d.).

[89] Ralph Waldo Emerson, "Nature," *op. cit.*

[90] Samuel Beckett, *Endgame* (Grove Press, 1958).

[91] St. Augustine (R.S. Pine-Coffin, trans.), *Confessions* (Penguin, 1961).

[92] C.G. Jung, "The Autonomy of the Unconscious," from *Psychology and Religion* (1938-40). Reprinted in (Laszlo, ed.), *The Basic Writing of C.G. Jung* (Princeton University Press, 1990).

[93] *Ibid.*

[94] C.G. Jung, *Introduction to the Religious and Psychological Problems of Alchemy* (1936) in *Ibid.*

[95] C.G. Jung, "Dogma and Natural Symbols" in *Psychology and Religion, op. cit.*

[96] Joseph Conrad, *Youth and Two Other Stories* (Doubleday, Page and Co., 1923).

[97] Swami Nikhilananda (Ed. and Trans.) *Self-Knowledge* (Ramakrishna-Vivekananda Center, 1946).

[98] "Circles," in *The Works of Emerson, op. cit.*

[99] William James, *Varieties of Religious Experience* (Longmans, Green and Co., 1904). Footnotes omitted.

[100] "Shades of Lamarck" in *The Panda's Thumb* (W.W. Norton, 1980).

[101] Samuel Butler, *Luck or Cunning?* (Trubner & Co., 1887).

[102] *Alcoholics Anonymous* Third Edition (Hazeldon, 1976).

[103] James, *op. cit.*

[104] Samuel Butler, *God the Known and God the Unknown* (Jonathon Cape Ltd., 1879).

[105] *Ibid.*

[106] Alan W. Watts, *The Way of Zen* (Pantheon, 1957).

[107] Swami Nikhilananda (ed. and trans.) *Self-Knowledge* (Ramakrishna-Vivekananda Center, 1946).

[108] In Christopher Isherwood (ed.), *Vedanta for the Western World*, (Vedanta Press, 1945).

[109] See, for example, Laurence O. McKinney, *Neurotheology* (American Institute for Mindfulness, 1994).

[110] Swami Prabhavanda, "Towards Meditation" in Isherwood, *op. cit.*

[111] D. T. Suzuki, *The Zen Koan as a means of Attaining Enlightenment* (Tuttle, 1994).

[112] *Ibid.*

[113] Fr. Paul O'Sullivan, O.P., *The Wonders of the Holy Name*, (Tan Books and Publishers, undated).

[114] James Thurber, *My Life and Hard Times* (Harper Brothers, 1933).

[115] *The Cloud of Unknowing and Other Works* (Penguin, 1961).

[116] *Ibid.*

[117] In Isherwood, *op. cit.*

[118] Swami Yatiswarananda, *op. cit.*

[119] *Ibid.*

[120] Christopher Isherwood, "Introduction," in *op. cit.*

[121] *Ibid.*

[122] Pseudonym for Mahendranath Gupta, the author of *The Gospel of Sri Ramakrishna*.

[123] Swami Nikhilananda (trans.), *The Gospel of Sri Ramakrishna* (Ramakrishna-Vivekananda Center, 1942).

[124] *Ibid.*

[125] *Ibid.*

[126] Henry David Thoreau, *A Week on the Concord and Merrimack Rivers* (Parnassus Imprints, 1987).

[127] *Ibid.*

[128] *Ibid.*

[129] Bernard DeVoto (ed.), *Letters from the Earth* (Harper & Row, 1962).

[130] John Stuart Mill, "Utility of Religion," from *Three Essays on Religion*, in Marshall Cohen (ed.), *The Philosophy of John Stuart Mill* (Modern Library, 1961).

[131] *Ibid.*

[132] Carl Sagan, "The Amniotic Universe," in *Broca's Brain*, (Random House, 1979).

[133] Friedrich Nietzche, *Will to Power* trans. W. Kaufmann & R. J. Hollingdale (Random House, 1968).

[134] Reprinted in "Translator's Preface" (Hugo Wernekke, trans.) to Gustav Fechner, *Life After Death* (Open Court, 1906).

[135] *The Gospel of Sri Ramakrishna, op. cit.*

[136] Swami Prabhavanada, "Renunciation and Austerity" in Christopher Isherwood, *Vedanta for the Western World, op. cit.*

[137] Evelyn Underhill, *Mysticism* (Oneworld, 1993).

[138] *Ibid.*

[139] *Ibid.*

[140] Aldous Huxley, *Grey Eminence* (Harper & Row, 1941).

[141] Catherine of Siena, *The Dialogue*, (Paulist Press, 1980)..

[142] *The Gospel of Sri Ramakrishna, op. cit.*

[143] Stephen King, *The Shining* (Doubleday, 1977).

[144] Catherine of Genoa, *Spiritual Dialouge Between the Soul, the Body, Self-Love, the Spirit, Humanity, and the Lord God Divided Into Three Parts* (Christian Press Association, 1907).

[145] *Ibid.*

[146] *Ibid.*

[147] Thomas a Kempis, *The Imitation of Christ,* trans. by William Benham (P.F. Collier and Son, 1909).

[148] *Confessions*, Pine-Coffin, trans. (Penguin, 1961).

[149] Lewis Thomas, "On Warts" in *The Medusa and the Snail* (Viking, 1979).

[150] D.T. Suzuki, *The Zen Koan as a means of Attaining Enlightenment* (Tuttle, 1994).

[151] Evelyn Underhill, *op. cit.*

[152] Thomas Carlyle, *Sartor Resartus* (J.M. Dent, 1908). Book II.

[153] Rabindranath Tagore "My Song" in *Crescent Moon*; reprinted in *Collected Poems and Plays* (MacMillan, 1913).

[154] In *Vedanta for the Westeran World, op. cit.*

Index of Names

A

Abelard, Peter, Week 12 — Fri., 10 AM

Alcibiades, Week 12 — Fri., 10 AM

Allen, Woody, Week 1 —Tues., 9 AM;   Week 6 — Fri., 10 AM

Arjuna, Week 11 —Wed., 3 PM;   Week 12 — Fri., 10 AM;
    Week 12 — Sat., 8:30 AM

Attla ("The Hun"), Week 11 —Wed., 3 PM

Augustine, St., Week 1 —Tues., 9 AM;   Week 10 — Mon.,
    3 PM;   Week 12 — Fri., 10 AM

B

Beckett, Samuel, Week 10 — Mon., 3 PM

Benson, Herbert, Week 1 — Mon., 10 AM;   Week 1 —Tues.,
    9 AM;   Week 11 —Tues., 2:30 PM

Bradley, F. H., Week 10 — Fri., 10 AM;   Week 11 — Mon.,
    10:05 AM

Brahe, Tycho, Week 10: Mon., 3 PM

Breuer, Josef, Week 2-Mon., 3 PM

Brooks, Albert, Week 12 —Thurs., 4:45 PM

Buddha, Introduction;   Week 1 — Mon., 10 AM;   Week
    1 —Tues., 9 AM;   Week 2 — Mon., 3 PM;   Week
    3 —Tues., 8:30 PM;   Week 7 — Mon., 10 AM;   Week
    7 —Mon., 3 PM;   Week 11 —Tues., 2:30 PM;   Week
    11 —Wed., 3 PM;   Week 12 —Thurs, 4:45 PM;   Week
    12 — Sat., 8:30 AM

Burr, Anna Robeson, Week 7: Mon., 10 AM

Butler, Samuel, Week 1 —Wed., 3 PM;   Week 2 — Mon.,
    3:25 AM;   Week 6 —Wed., 3 PM;   Week 11 — Mon.,

10:05 AM;   Week 11—Tues., 2:30 PM;   Week
12 — Sat., 8:30 AM

C

Carlyle, Thomas, Week 12 — Sat., 8:30 AM
Catherine of Genoa, St., Week 12—Fri., 10 AM
Catherine of Siena, St., Week 12—Fri., 10 AM
Chesterton, G. K., Week 3—Mon., 3 PM;   Week 7—
    Mon., 10 AM
Chisholm, Roderick, Week 6: Fri., 10 AM
Chuang Tzu, Week 1—Tues., 9 AM
Close, Glenn, Week 7—Sun., 10:15 AM
Conrad, Joseph, Week 10—Fri., 10 AM

D

Darwin, Charles, Week 2—Mon., 3:25 AM;   Week 10—
    Mon., 3 PM;   Week 11—Mon., 10:05 AM
Delius, Frederick, Week 10—Fri., 10 AM
Descartes, Rene, Week 6—Fri., 10 AM;   Week 7—Mon.,
    3 PM
Dick, Philip K., Week 11—Wed., 3 PM
Dylan, Bob, Week 12—Thurs, 4:45 PM

E

Eckhardt, Johannes ("Meister"), Week 2—Mon., 3:25 AM;
    Week 3—Mon., 3 PM
Einstein, Albert, Week 2—Mon., 3:25 AM;   Week 10—
    Mon., 3 PM
Eliot, George, Introduction
Emerson, Ralph Waldo, Week 1—Wed., 3 PM   Week
    10—Mon., 11:45 AM;   Week 10—Mon., 3 PM;   Week
    10—Fri., 10 AM;   Week 12—Sat., 8:30 AM

F

Farmer, Philip Jose, Week 12—Thurs, 4:45 PM

Farrow, Mia, Week 1—Tues., 9 AM

Faulkner, William, Week 2—Tues., 1:30 PM

Fechner, Gustav, Week 1—Tues., 9 AM; Week 1—Wed., 3 PM; Week 2—Mon., 3:25 AM; Week 2—Mon., 3 PM; Week 6—Wed., 3 PM; Week 7—Sun., 10:15 AM; Week 7—Mon., 10 AM; Week 11—Wed., 3 PM; Week 12—Thurs, 4:45 PM

Fox, George, Week 3—Mon., 10 AM

Francis of Assisi, St., Week 3—Mon., 10 AM

Freud, Sigmund, Week 1—Wed., 3 PM; Week 2—Mon., 3 PM; Week 2—Tues., 1:30 PM; Week 3—Mon., 3 PM; Week 7—Mon., 3 PM; Week 10—Mon., 11:45 AM; Week 10—Mon., 3 PM; Week 10—Fri., 10 AM; Week 12—Sat., 8:30 AM

Fromm, Erich, Week 7—Mon., 3 PM

G

Gould, Stephen J., Week 11—Mon., 10:05 AM

Grunbaum, Adolf, Week 2—Mon., 3 PM

H

Hanson, N. R., Week 6—Fri., 10 AM

Harrison, George, Week 1—Tues., 9 AM; Week 7—Sun., 10:15 AM

Heard, Gerald, Week 7—Sun., 10:15 AM

Hegel, G. W. F., Week 6—Wed., 10 AM; Week 11—Mon., 10:05 AM

Hicks, G. Dawes, Week 7—Sun., 10:15 AM; Week 7—Mon., 10 AM

Hitler, Adolf, Week 10—Mon., 11:45 AM; Week 7—Sun.,

10:15 AM;   Week 12—Thurs, 4:45 PM

Horney, Karen, Week 2—Mon., 3 PM;   Week 2—Tues., 1:30 PM;   Week 3—Mon., 3 PM;   Week 7—Sun., 10:15 AM

Hubbard, L. Ron, Week 2—Mon., 3 PM

Hume, David, Week 2—Mon., 3:25 AM;   Week 7—Mon., 10 AM;   Week 12—Thurs, 4:45 PM

Hunter, Holly, Week 1—Tues., 9 AM

Huxley, Aldous, Introduction;   Week 2—Tues., 1:30 PM;   Week 3—Mon., 3 PM;   Week 6—Fri., 10 AM;   Week 7—Sun., 10:15 AM;   Week 12—Thurs, 4:45 PM;   Week 12—Fri., 10 AM

Huxley, Laura Archera, Week 2—Mon., 3:25 AM

I

Isherwood, Christopher, Week 7—Sun., 10:15 AM;   Week 12—Sat., 8:30 AM

J

James, William, Introduction;   Week 1—Tues., 9 AM;   7 Week 3—Mon., 10 AM;   Week 6—Wed., 10 AM;   Week 6—Wed., 3 PM;   Week 6—Fri., 10 AM;   Week 10—Fri., 10 AM;   Week 11—Mon., 10:05 AM

Jesus, Introduction;   Week 1—Wed., 3 PM;   Week 2—Mon., 3:25 AM;   Week 3—Mon., 3 PM;   Week 3—Tues., 8:30 PM;   Week 7—Mon., 10 AM;   Week 10—Mon., 3 PM;   Week 10—Fri., 10 AM;   Week 11—Tues., 2:30 PM;   Week 12—Sat., 8:30 AM

John of the Cross, St., Week 1—Tues., 9 AM;   Week 2—Mon., 3:25 AM

Joyce, James, Week 2—Tues., 1:30 PM

Jung, C. G., Week 10—Fri., 10 AM;   Week 11—Mon., 10:05 AM;   Week 11—Tues., 2:30 PM

K

Kant, Immanuel, Week 7 — Mon., 3 PM

Keats, John, Week 1 — Tues., 9 AM

Kennedy, John F., Week 6 — Fri., 10 AM

King, Stephen, Introduction; Week 11 — Tues., 2:30 PM;
   Week 12 — Fri., 10 AM

Koestler, Arthur, Week 7 — Sun., 10:15 AM; Week 7 —
   Mon., 10 AM

Krishna, Week 1 — Tues., 9 AM; Week 3 — Mon., 3 PM;
   Week 7 — Sun., 10:15 AM; Week 12 — Fri., 10 AM

Kubrick, Stanley, Week 12 — Fri., 10 AM

L

Lamarck, Jean-Baptiste, Week 10 — Mon., 3 PM; Week
   11 — Mon., 10:05 AM

Lardner, Ring, Week 12 — Thurs, 4:45 PM

Lawrence, D.H., Introduction; Week 12 — Fri., 10 AM

Leonard, Elmore, Week 11 — Tues., 2:30 PM

LeShan, Lawrence, Week 2 — Mon., 3:25 AM

Lewis, C. S., Week 1 — Wed., 3 PM; Week 3 — Tues., 8:30
   PM; Week 10 — Mon., 11:45 AM; Week 10 — Mon., 3 PM

Lodge, Oliver, Week 1 — Tues., 9 AM

Lorre, Peter, Week 12 — Fri., 10 AM

Luther, Martin, Week 1 — Tues., 9 AM; Week 3 — Tues.,
   8:30 PM; Week 10 — Fri., 10 AM

M

Maharishi Mahesh Yogi, Week 1 — Tues., 9 AM

Mencken, H. L., Week 1 — Tues., 9 AM; Week 1 — Wed.,
   3 PM; Week 7 — Mon., 10 AM

Menuhin, Yehudi, Week 10 — Fri., 10 AM

Mill, John Stuart, Week 12 — Thurs, 4:45 PM

Milosevic, Slobodan, Week 7 — Sun., 10:15 AM
Mitchell, Joni, Week 1 — Mon., 10 AM;   Week 1 — Tues.,
    9 AM;   Week 1 — Wed., 3 PM;   Week 7 — Sun., 10:15 AM;
    Week 7 — Mon., 10 AM;   Week 11 — Tues., 2:30 PM
Montague, Margaret Prescott, Week 6 — Wed., 10 AM
Moore, G. E., Week 11 — Mon., 10:05 AM
Moore, George, Week 1 — Wed., 3 PM;   Week 2 — Mon.,
    3:25 AM;   Week 3 — Mon., 3 PM
Moore, Mary Tyler, Week 10 — Fri., 10 AM

N

Navratilova, Martina, Week 10 — Fri., 10 AM
Newcomb, William, Week 11 — Tues., 2:30 PM
Newman, John Henry, Week 7 — Mon., 3 PM
Newton, Isaac, Week 2 — Mon., 3:25 AM
Nicholson, Jack, Week 11 — Tues., 2:30 PM
Nietzche, Friedrich, Week 12 — Thurs, 4:45 PM
Nijinsky, V. F., Week 6 — Fri., 10 AM

P

Parker, Dorothy, Week 6 — Wed., 3 PM
Pascal, Blaise, Week 11 — Tues., 2:30 PM
Paul, St., Week 2 — Mon., 3:25 AM;   Week 3 — Mon., 10 AM;
    Week 3 — Mon., 3 PM
Penn, William, Week 3 — Mon., 3 PM
Pirsig, Robert, Week 1 — Wed., 3 PM
Plato, Introduction;   Week 3 — Tues., 8:30 PM;   Week 6 —
    Fri., 10 AM;   Week 7 — Mon., 10 AM;   Week 10 — Fri.,
    10 AM;   Week 12 — Fri., 10 AM
Prabhavananda, Week 11 — Tues., 2:30 PM;   Week 12 — Fri.,
    10 AM

Q

Quaid, Randy, Week 11—Tues., 2:30 PM

R

Ramakrishna, Week 11—Tues., 2:30 PM; Week 7—Sun.,
  10:15 AM; Week 12—Fri., 10 AM
Reeves, Keanu, Week 11—Tues., 2:30 PM
Robertson, Pat, Week 6—Wed., 3 PM
Rossini, Giaccomo, Week 7—Mon., 3 PM
Russell, Bertrand, Week 1—Wed., 3 PM; Week 2—Mon.,
  3 PM; Week 6—Fri., 10 AM; Week 11—Tues., 2:30 PM;
  Week 11—Mon., 10:05 AM

S

Sagan, Carl, Week 12—Thurs, 4:45 PM
Salinger, J.D., Week 3—Tues., 8:30 PM; Week 11—Tues.,
  2:30 PM
Sartre, Jean-Paul, Week 3—Mon., 10 AM; Week 6—
  Wed., 10 AM; Week 6—Fri., 10 AM
Schwarzenegger, Arnold, Week 7—Sun., 10:15 AM
Shakespeare, William, Week 12—Thurs, 4:45 PM
Shankara, Week 10—Fri., 10 AM; Week 11—Mon., 10:05 AM
Shaw, George Bernard, Introduction; Week 1—Wed., 3
  PM; Week 7—Mon., 10 AM
Shawn, Wallace, Week 2—Tues., 1:30 PM
Socrates, Week 7—Sun., 10:15 AM; Week 10—Fri., 10 AM
Spinoza, Baruch, Introduction; Week 1—Mon., 10 AM;
  Week 2—Mon., 3 PM; Week 6—Wed., 10 AM;
  Week 6—Wed., 3 PM; Week 6—Fri., 10 AM; Week
  7—Mon., 10 AM; Week 11—Tues., 2:30 PM; Week
  11—Mon., 10:05 AM; Week 11—Tues., 2:30 PM; Week
  7—Sun., 10:15 AM; Week 12—Thurs, 4:45 PM

Stace, W. T., Week 6 —Wed., 10 AM;   Week 11 — Mon.,
    10:05 AM
Stalin, Joseph, Week 10 — Mon., 11:45 AM
Streep, Meryl, Week 12 —Thurs, 4:45 PM
Suzuki, Daisetz, Week 6 — Fri., 10 AM;   Week 7 — Mon.,
    10 AM, Week 7 — Mon., 3 PM;   Week 11 —Tues., 2:30 PM;
    Week 12 — Fri., 10 AM;   Week 12 — Sat., 8:30 AM
Swedenborg, Emanuel, Week 1 —Tues., 9 AM

T

Tagore, Rabindranath, Introduction;   Week 6 —Wed., 3 PM;
    Week 7 — Mon., 3 PM;   Week 10 — Mon., 11:45 AM;
    Week 12 — Sat., 8:30 AM
Tennyson, Alfred, Week 1 —Tues., 9 AM
Teresa, Mother, Week 1 —Tues., 9 AM
Theresa of Avila, St., Introduction;   Week 1 —Tues., 9 AM;
    Week 2 — Mon., 3:25 AM;   Week 3 — Mon., 10 AM;
    Week 3 — Mon., 3 PM;   Week 6 —Wed., 10 AM;   Week
    6 —Fri., 10 AM
Thomas a Kempis, Week 1 —Tues., 9 AM
Thomas, Lewis, Week 6 —Wed., 3 PM;   Week 1 —Tues.,
    9 AM
Thoreau, Henry David, Week 3 — Mon., 3 PM;   Week
    7 — Sun., 10:15 AM
Thurber, James, Week 11 —Tues., 2:30 PM
Tolstoy, Leo, Week 1 — Mon., 10 AM
Trollope, Anthony, Week 3 — Mon., 3 PM;   Week 11 —
    Tues., 2:30 PM
Twain, Mark, Week 12 —Thurs, 4:45 PM

U

Underhill, Evelyn, Week 12 — Fri., 10 AM

V

Vandross, Luther, Week 10 — Fri., 10 AM
Vivekenanda, Week 11 — Tues., 2:30 PM
Voltaire, Week 1 — Wed., 3 PM;   Week 7 — Mon., 10 AM

W

Watts, Alan, Week 7 — Sun., 10:15 AM;   Week 7 — Mon.,
    10 AM;   Week 7 — Mon., 3 PM;   Week 11 — Mon.,
    10:05 AM
William of Occam, Week 10 — Mon., 3 PM
Williamson, Robin, Week 7 — Sun., 10:15 AM;   Week
    7 — Mon., 10 AM
Wittgenstein, Ludwig, Week 6 — Wed., 10 AM;   Week
    6 — Fri., 10 AM
Wordsworth, William, Week 1 — Tues., 9 AM

Y

Yatiswarananda, Week 11 — Wed., 3 PM